Coercive Inducement
and the Containment of International Crises

COERCIVE

[and the Containment of
International Crises]

INDUCEMENT

Donald C. F. Daniel

and

Bradd C. Hayes

with

Chantal de Jonge Oudraat

**United States
Institute of Peace Press**

Washington, D.C.

The views expressed in this book are those of the authors alone. They do not necessarily reflect views of their employers or of the United States Institute of Peace.

United States Institute of Peace
1200 17th Street NW, Suite 200
Washington, DC 20036-3006

First published 1999

Printed in the United States of America

The paper used in this publication meets the minimum requirements of American National Standards for Information Sciences—Permanence of Paper for Printed Library Materials, ANSI Z39.48-1984.

Library of Congress Cataloging-in-Publication Data
Daniel, Donald C. (Donald Charles), 1944–
    Coercive inducement and the containment of international crises / Donald C. F. Daniel and Bradd C. Hayes with Chantal de Jonge Oudraat
      p. cm.
    Includes bibliographical references and index.
    ISBN 1-878379-85-2 (hardcover)
    ISBN 1-878379-84-4 (pbk.)
    1. United Nations—Armed Forces. 2. Intervention (International Law) 3. Security, International. I. Hayes, Bradd C. II. Jonge Oudraat, Chantal de. III. Title.
KZ6376 .D36 1998
341.5'84—dc21   98-49655
                                                      CIP

CONTENTS

FIGURES AND TABLES

Figures

Tables

FOREWORD

The 1990s has been a busy decade for peacekeeping. From 1989 through 1994, we saw an unprecedented proliferation of peacekeeping *missions,* as the Permanent Members of the UN Security Council celebrated the end of the Cold War by authorizing two dozen new operations, many of them much more ambitious than the "traditional" operations mandated during the preceding forty years of their rivalry. In the latter half of the decade, we witnessed a proliferation of peacekeeping *studies,* as scholars and practitioners have tried to figure out what exactly the international community accomplished in the early '90s, and, more particularly, what worked and what didn't.

While it is inevitable that reflection should follow action in this fashion, it is unfortunate that attempts to formulate the basic concepts and precepts of the new, more ambitious types of peacekeeping should not have preceded the operations themselves. Lacking a clear concept of how they were supposed to act, the peacekeeping troops and their commanders were often left to invent their own ground rules, set their own concrete objectives, and otherwise fend for themselves. In a number of cases, especially those where the peacekeeping forces were sponsored by the United Nations but were actually under the control of their own governments, this learn-by-doing approach worked remarkably well. But in other instances, especially those plagued by a divided chain of command, disasters occurred and the missions collapsed. After the fatal mistakes made in Somalia and Bosnia, the international community's eagerness to authorize these new forms of UN peacekeeping missions quickly faded—along with references to "muscular multilateralism."

At about this time, analysts began to increasingly review and critique what the politicians and troops had done. In truth, a good deal had already been written on peacekeeping in the early '90s; but from 1995 onward, the literature has swelled considerably. Although the torrent of essays, articles, and books has at times threatened to overwhelm even those who specialize in the subject, it has also helped to bring to the surface the key issues regarding the theory and practice of contemporary peacekeeping. For that reason, it is a most propitious time for this book to appear, since it addresses the most important of these issues—how to define and employ the new, more ambitious types of operations attempted this decade.

First, should we categorize these operations as a variant of traditional UN "Chapter 6" peacekeeping (based on consent and characterized by the minimum use of force), as a variant of peace enforcement ("Chapter 7," nonconsensual operations with a mandate imposed by force), or as a distinct category that lies between these other two categories? Second, if indeed a "middle option" does exist, what are its distinguishing features, and what guidelines should govern when and how it is employed?

To the first of these questions, the authors of this volume answer that there is indeed a middle option, which they name "coercive inducement." (Actually, this name is not their invention but that of Kofi Annan, who coined the term in 1996 while he was UN under-secretary-general for peacekeeping. However, it should be noted that Annan was responding to the broader concept of "inducement" that had earlier been introduced into the peacekeeping debate by coauthors Donald Daniel and Bradd Hayes.) "By coercive inducement," the authors explain, "we mean the judicious resort to coercive diplomacy or forceful persuasion by the international community in order to implement community norms or mandates vis-à-vis all the parties to a particular crisis."

To the second question, the authors respond by defining coercive inducement with admirable care and cogency. It would be unproductive to try and summarize those defining characteristics here, and the reader must turn to chapter 2 for a complete portrait. Perhaps, though, the following quotation will serve as a thumbnail sketch: "[Coercive inducement's] focus is on getting one's way through the employment of military forces as opposed to using force per se. It aims to persuade rather than to seize or bludgeon, and it must form part of a concerted campaign involving a variety of means—politico-diplomatic, economic, hortatory, as well as military—to influence behavior."

After laying out the principles of coercive inducement and contrasting them with the principles governing peacekeeping and enforcement missions, the authors then present four case studies of UN-controlled and UN-sanctioned operations—in Bosnia, Somalia, Rwanda, and Haiti—to show the results of following or ignoring those principles. Drawing on the case studies, chapter 7 moves from analysis to prescription, and offers operational guidelines for future coercive inducement operations.

Throughout, the authors proceed systemically and carefully, marrying analytical rigor with in-depth research and unambiguous presentation. The result is a book that stands out from the crowd of peacekeeping studies; a study that by virtue of its merits and the reputation for pioneering work enjoyed by its authors is sure to find readers within UN headquarters and a host of state departments, defense ministries, and foreign policy think tanks. This is not to say that all readers will agree with its approach and conclusions. *Coercive Inducement* itself acknowledges that "the principles and guidelines presented in this analysis are not chiseled in stone. They remain subject to refinement and are not intended to preempt judgment."

In publishing this book, produced with the support of the Institute's Grant Program, we seek not to silence but to stimulate debate. Debate spurs conceptual progress. And as I remarked above, the new-style peacekeeping of the early 1990s suffered from the fact that it was implemented before it was conceptualized. Now, at least, the process of conceptualization is well under way, and everything that can be done to facilitate its refinement is surely to be welcomed.

Coercive Inducement is by no means the first study on peacekeeping and related topics to be published by the Institute. One of this book's inspirations was the concept of "coercive diplomacy" as outlined by Alexander George in *Forceful Persuasion,* which the Institute published in 1991. Since then, we have funded and published a wide variety of studies that address the theory and practice of peacekeeping activities, including Fen Hampson's *Nurturing Peace: Why Peace Settlements Succeed or Fail,* William Zartman and Lewis Rasmussen's edited volume *Peacemaking in International Conflict,* Michael Lund's *Preventing Violent Conflict,* John Hirsch and Robert Oakley's *Somalia and Operation Restore Hope,* Mohamed Sahnoun's *Somalia: The Missed Opportunities,* Richard Synge's *Mozambique: UN Peacekeeping in Action,* Paul Hare's *Angola's Last Best Chance for Peace,* and David Yost's *NATO Transformed.* In our Peaceworks series of reports, the Institute has published Denis McLean's *Peace Operations and Common Sense,*

Roxanne Sismandis's *Police Functions in Peace Operations,* and Michael Hardesty and Jason Ellis's *Training for Peace Operations.*

In addition to these published works, the United States Institute of Peace's Grant Program and its Education and Training Program actively support creative research into peacekeeping, and our Research and Studies Program organizes seminars and workshops for military and civilian participants in ongoing and future peace operations.

It remains to be seen if peace operations will be as widely employed and discussed at the start of the twenty-first century as they have been at the end of the twentieth. Whatever turns out to be the case, we trust that analytically rigorous and pragmatically grounded studies such as *Coercive Inducement* will help prepare U.S. policymakers and practitioners, and the U.S. public, to more effectively face the challenges of managing international conflict in the 2000s.

Richard H. Solomon, President
United States Institute of Peace

ACKNOWLEDGMENTS

The authors wish to thank the United States Institute of Peace for its generous support in funding our research and for the encouragement we were given to turn it into a book.

ACRONYMS AND ABBREVIATIONS

APC	armored personnel carrier
CARICOM	Caribbean Community
CDR	Coalition pour la Défense de la République
CIA	Central Intelligence Agency
CIMIC	Civil-Military Coordination Organization
CJTF	Commander Joint Task Force
CMOC	Civil-Military Operations Center
CNN	Cable News Network
EC	European Community
EU	European Union
FAdH	Forces Armées d'Haiti
FAR	Forces Armées Rwandaises
FNDC	Front National pour le Changement et la Démocratie
FRAPH	Front pour l'Avancement et le Progrès Haitien
FRY	Federal Republic of Yugoslavia
HDZ	Croatian Democratic Union
HRS	humanitarian relief sectors
ICRC	International Committee of the Red Cross
IFOR	Implementation Force (Bosnia)
IPSF	Interim Public Security Force
IPTF	International Police Task Force
JNA	Yugoslav People's Army

MDR	Mouvement Démocratique Républicain
MICVIH	OAS-UN International Civil Mission in Haiti
MIPONUH	United Nations Civilian Police Mission in Haiti
MNF	Multinational Force (Haiti)
MRND	Mouvement Révolutionnaire National pour le Développement
NAC	North Atlantic Council
NATO	North Atlantic Treaty Organization
NGO	nongovernmental organization
OAS	Organization of American States
OAU	Organization of African Unity
OFDA	Office of Foreign Disaster Assistance
OHR	Office of the High Representative for the Implementation of the Peace Agreement on Bosnia and Herzegovina
ONUC	United Nations Operation in the Congo
ONUVEH	United Nations Observer Group for the Verification of Elections in Haiti
OSCE	Organization for Security and Cooperation in Europe
PDC	Parti Démocrate Chrétien
PDD	Presidential Decision Directive
PL	Parti Libéral
PSD	Parti Social Démocrate
QRF	Quick Reaction Force
RGA	Rwanda Government Army
ROE	rules of engagement
RPA	Rwandan Patriotic Army
RPF	Rwandan Patriotic Front
RRF	Rapid Reaction Force
RTLMC	Radio Télévision Libre des Mille Collines
SACEUR	Supreme Allied Commander Europe
SAM	surface-to-air missile
SDA	Muslim Party of Democratic Action (Bosnia)

SDA	Somali Democratic Alliance
SDM	Somali Democratic Movement
SDS	Serb Democratic Party
SFOR	Stabilization Force (Bosnia)
SNA	Somali National Alliance
SNF	Somali National Front
SNM	Somali National Movement
SPM	Somali Patriotic Movement
SRSG	Special Representative of the Secretary-General
SSDF	Somali Salvation Democratic Front
SSF	Somali Salvation Front
TNC	Transitional National Council
UNAMIR	United Nations Assistance Mission for Rwanda
UNCRO	United Nations Confidence Restoration Operation in Croatia
UNDHA	United Nations Department of Humanitarian Affairs
UNEF	United Nations Emergency Force (Suez)
UNGOMAP	United Nations Good Offices Mission in Afghanistan and Pakistan
UNHCR	United Nations High Commissioner for Refugees
UNIDIR	United Nations Institute for Disarmament Research
UNITAF	Unified Task Force (Somalia)
UNMIBH	United Nations Mission in Bosnia and Herzegovina
UNMIH	United Nations Mission in Haiti
UNOMUR	United Nations Observer Mission Uganda-Rwanda
UNOSOM	United Nations Operation in Somalia
UNPA	United Nations Protected Area
UNPROFOR	United Nations Protection Force (Bosnia)
UNSMIH	United Nations Support Mission in Haiti
UNTAES	United Nations Transitional Administration for Eastern Slavonia, Baranja, and Western Sirmium
UNTMIH	United Nations Transition Mission in Haiti
USAID	United States Agency for International Development

USC	United Somali Congress
USCENTCOM	United States Central Command
USF	United Somali Front
USLO	United States Liaison Office
USP	United Somali Party
VOPP	Vance-Owen Peace Plan
WEU	Western European Union

Coercive Inducement
and the Containment of International Crises

INTRODUCTION

A peace support operation is one endorsed by the international community in order to contain a crisis or conflict; its aim is to keep the crisis from worsening while also providing scope for indigenous peoples, peacemakers, and humanitarian workers to make things better. Military personnel nearly always constitute the most numerous participants in peace support, and our study concerns their utilization in UN-sanctioned missions, in areas racked by civil strife, where peace support elements may confront significant local resistance as they carry out assigned tasks. Suggestions that the international community should forgo or cease intervention in such cases may often constitute wise counsel, but moral imperatives reinforced by accounts of human suffering or calculations of national interests such as sparked by a massive inflow of refugees can at times make (continued) intervention the best option. The question then is how to proceed. Former Secretary-General Boutros Boutros-Ghali alluded to this when he wrote in 1995 that the United Nations' recent unhappy experiences in peace support, particularly in Bosnia, have "compelled renewed reflection on the instruments available to the international community in its efforts to maintain international peace and security."[1]

We offer this book as part of the reflection process. Although numerous reasons have been offered to explain the difficulties plaguing UN-sponsored peace support in the first half of the 1990s, our focus is on concepts, doctrinal principles, and operational guidelines. They go to the essence of what a peace support mission is about and how it ought to be undertaken. Agreement on them is the basis for resolving other well-publicized issues such as resource requirements and command-and-control arrangements.

A 1995 observation by Adam Roberts captures our perspective. He concluded that proposals to provide the United Nations with more military muscle may have the undesired effect of deflecting attention from deficiencies "which are as much conceptual as physical," and he suggested that the United Nations and its members "may need to recognize that occasionally there is a need for, and a possibility of, an approach which is conceptually distinct both from impartial peacekeeping based on consent of the parties and simple enforcement action on behalf of an attacked state" such as South Korea in 1950 or Kuwait in 1990.[2] Although there remains today resistance to recognizing a middle or third approach, we believe that such an approach constitutes a practicable alternative that should not be ignored. Indeed, we are convinced that, if left with only traditional peacekeeping and simple enforcement as options, the international community may likely reject responding to a crisis—seeing peacekeeping as ineffective and enforcement as too bloody-minded—when response might have been the best course for all concerned. In the end, one reason some may not want to recognize a middle option is that they do not want to act.

In an article published in late 1996, we offered a concept, "inducement," to fill the need to which Roberts refers.[3] Kofi Annan, then under-secretary-general for peacekeeping operations, built on it and differentiated between its positive and coercive elements, the first employing carrots and the other sticks.[4] Our focus is on the latter, and we readily accept his more specific term, "coercive inducement," to designate the central concept advocated and described herein.

In addition to clarifying the option designated by that concept, we suggest doctrinal principles and operational guidelines for its implementation.[5] Doctrine encompasses broad basic principles that may require judgment in application and are usually the province of higher-level political and military leaders. Operational guidelines constitute still broad but more specific directives for commanders in the field, and they encompass what logic and experience have shown to be generally effective ways of implementing doctrine. Developing doctrinal and operational principles within a national military establishment is usually a long and laborious cycle of drafting, argument, testing, and refinement or redrafting. The cycle is longer and more trying when the principles are being devised to govern the combined employment of different national military forces, each with its own doctrines, directives, capabilities, languages, and cultures. We hope this study will contribute to the initial drafting step.

This book has eight chapters. The first frames our focus. It provides a short historical background and identifies problems of, and reasons for, the conceptual confusion and operational discord that characterized recent, important peace support operations. Chapter 2 offers coercive inducement as a distinct and practicable option that can help avoid such problems, and also lays out doctrinal principles to guide its implementation. Chapters 3 through 6 present four case studies of UN-controlled and UN-sanctioned operations: in Bosnia, Somalia, Rwanda, and Haiti. These case studies demonstrate the consequences of abiding by or contravening the principles laid out in chapter 2. They also provide the basis for the specification in chapter 7 of operational guidelines for implementing principles. Finally, chapter 8 contains a few final thoughts about when and to what degree the international community should commit itself to undertake coercive inducement.

1

CONFUSION AND DISCORD IN RECENT UN PEACE SUPPORT OPERATIONS

During the first half of the 1990s, peace support operations dominated many agendas in the United Nations and increasingly caused frustrations. Overshadowing quiet successes were highly publicized missions plagued with confusion and discord over how far UN contingents should go to secure observance of the organization's mandates. This chapter puts that experience in its historical context, lays out accepted reasons for the conceptual and operational problems, and offers a controversial explanation focusing on UN military options when a peace support mission confronts significant resistance. A proposed solution to that controversy forms the central concern of this study.

HISTORICAL CONTEXT

The League of Nations established the precedent of employing military personnel from member states to facilitate the peaceful settlement of territorial disputes. League commissions created for that purpose often either consisted of a small number of individual military officers or were supported by formations that ranged from a few hundred to a few thousand men. Depending upon the case at hand, military personnel engaged in monitoring, reporting, or investigatory activities; supervised the separation of opposing forces or the execution of frontier agreements; established and oversaw neutral zones between parties; confirmed the implementation of mandates promulgated by the League's Council; or administered territory being transferred from one party to another. The last League operation occurred in 1934 when it authorized the deployment of an international force of 3,300 men to the Saar before and during a plebiscite to determine whether the region would fall under French or German jurisdiction. Consistent with its mandate, the force established a "visible presence throughout the region," and succeeded without having to employ violence in "deter[ring] any who were disposed to upset public order."[1] Thus UN peace operations were not created ex nihilo; like many other UN activities, their roots go back to the League.

There are three eras in the United Nations' experience with peace support. The first encompasses four cases, all of which were initiated between 1947 and 1949. Each was an observer mission where a small number of unarmed individuals engaged in much the same kinds of tasks as their predecessors in the League commissions. In two of the missions—the UN Truce Supervisory Organization in Palestine and the UN Military Observer Group in India and Pakistan—the UN Secretariat directly controlled the employment of the soldiers provided it by the contributing states. In the other two—the Consular Commission in Indonesia and the UN Special Committee on the Balkans—national authorities retained control of their own personnel while operating under UN mandate.

A jump in mission size and makeup (involving armed units) occurred in 1956 with the Suez Crisis, when the United Nations dispatched 6,000 soldiers in its Emergency Force (UNEF I) to interpose themselves between the conflicting parties. The dimensions of the operation forced the international community to self-consciously consider the instrument it had employed. Beyond how such activity should be labeled—it was then that the term "peacekeeping" came into vogue—were issues on budgetary arrangements, troop contributors, rules governing use of the force, and legitimacy vis-à-vis the UN Charter. On this last, Secretary-General Dag Hammarskjöld concluded that UNEF I was a logical extension of the powers granted the organization in Chapter VI to further the pacific settlement of disputes.[2] Although that chapter was originally envisioned as the province of diplomats, mediators, lawyers, and judges, the military peacekeepers were seen as adjunctive since their task was to assist diplomatic processes and not impose any solutions.

Another ten missions were initiated through 1978, and all except one—the 1960–64 United Nations Operation in the Congo (ONUC)—ranged in force size from only a handful of personnel to several thousand. Most involved the classical peacekeeping tasks of monitoring, interposition, or cease-fire implementation in the aftermath of interstate crises or conflicts, but a few also saw peacekeepers responsible for domestic affairs such as maintaining public order, helping provide basic services, or administering an area in anticipation of a national sovereign either taking over for the first time (such as the UN Temporary Executive Authority/Security Force in West Irian) or regaining control (such as the UN Interim Force in Lebanon). ONUC was a unique exception for this period not only because of its size (20,000 soldiers), but also because its "peacekeepers" engaged in relatively large-scale combat to help maintain the Kinshasha government's authority over the entire country. When ONUC ended, there was a general sense that the United Nations had badly overreached and that such missions should be avoided.

Largely because of U.S.-Soviet differences, the United Nations initiated no new missions in the decade after its approval of the Interim Force in Lebanon in March 1978. Thus the total number of operations in the organization's first forty-three years was fifteen. This number was enough to allow a consensus to build up on the doctrinal principles that should characterize peacekeeping:

- Peacekeepers function under the command and control of the secretary-general.
- They represent moral authority rather than force of arms.
- They reflect the universality of the United Nations in their composition.
- They deploy with the consent and cooperation of the parties involved and do not seek to impose their will on any of the parties.
- They are impartial and function without prejudice to the rights and aspirations of any side.
- They do not use or threaten force except in self-defense.
- They take few risks and accept a minimum number of casualties.[3]

These principles were well accepted at the beginning of the second or activist era—from 1988 through 1994—in the evolution of peace support, but as that era unfolded, peacekeeping as traditionally understood was stretched beyond its conceptual limits. In particular, the operational applicability of three principles—those concerning consent, impartiality, and use of force only in self-defense—was called into question in missions where UN contingents confronted recurring resistance to implementing the organization's mandates.

THE ERAS OF ACTIVISM AND RETRENCHMENT

Six features characterize the era that began in April 1988 when a positive turn in U.S.-Soviet relations allowed the Security Council to agree to the first new operation in a decade, the United Nations Good Offices Mission in Afghanistan and Pakistan (UNGOMAP). One feature is a near-explosive growth in the number and scope of missions. The United Nations looked to peace support so often that the trend almost overwhelmed the organization administratively and financially. Twenty-six UN-controlled or -endorsed operations were authorized through 1994. Whereas only 9,700 military personnel were deployed in 1988 in five missions, there were over 73,000 in 1994 in seventeen UN-controlled cases with another 21,000 in the UN-endorsed, U.S.-led Multinational Force (MNF) in Haiti. About half of the twenty-six were classical missions in that they much resembled what the United Nations had grown accustomed to regarding the size and tasks of the operational contingents. The other half, however, were generally far more ambitious, dangerous, and expensive. They involved more people— civilian specialists as well as military—being thrust in the midst of civil conflicts where, often as not, fighting continued; where at least one faction consisted of poorly disciplined armed irregulars; where governmental institutions and societal infrastructures were in paralysis or collapse; and where populations were displaced or subjected to genocide. They were usually also multifunctional in nature with UN contingents being given numerous, wide-ranging tasks. Then Secretary-General Boutros Boutros-Ghali outlined these in a 1995 report:

> The United Nations found itself asked to undertake an unprecedented variety of functions: the supervision of cease-fires, the regroupment and demobilization of forces, their reintegration into civilian life and the destruction of their weapons; the design and implementation of de-mining programmes; the return of refugees and displaced persons; the provision of humanitarian assistance; the supervision of existing administrative structures; the establishment of new police forces; the verification of respect for human rights; the design and supervision of constitutional, judicial, and electoral reforms; the observation,

supervision, and even organization and conduct of elections; and the coordination of support for economic rehabilitation and reconstruction.[4]

UN soldiers had earlier performed similar functions, but generally not to the extent, either within a mission or across the totality, that was expected of them in the first half of the 1990s.

A second feature of the era is that some peace support contingents were authorized to act under the broad authority of Chapter VII of the UN Charter if they faced local resistance implementing the terms of a mandate. Specifically, Articles 39, 41, and 42 allow the Security Council to utilize either nonmilitary (for example, economic) or military coercion "to give effect to its decisions." Among those given a Chapter VII remit were missions in Somalia (both the U.S.-led Unified Task Force and the second UN Operation in Somalia), Bosnia (the UN Protection Force), Haiti (the U.S.-led Multinational Force),[5] and southwest Rwanda/eastern Zaire (the French-led Operation Turquoise). Those authorizations occurred against the backdrop of the United Nations' endorsement, for the first time since the Korean War, of a large-scale military operation in 1990 against an identified malefactor, Iraq, in order to compel its removal from Kuwait. This was a case of simple enforcement and not of peace support,[6] but it signaled a willingness not seen for decades to endorse the threat or use of military coercion to compel observance of international norms. That willingness factored in the Security Council's endorsement of Operation Provide Comfort to administer relief to ethnic Kurds being victimized by Saddam Hussein's forces in northern Iraq. It entered as well into the Security Council's approval, against Iraq's wishes, to establish the Iraq-Kuwait Observer Mission to monitor the border between the countries.

A third feature is that the relative novelty of the above two developments triggered a confusing redefinition or proliferation of terms to describe what UN forces were now about. Up to that time "peacekeeping" was generally regarded as consisting primarily of interposition or monitoring functions conducted in accordance with traditional principles. Now some people broadly applied the word to operations assigned numerous other functions and/or possessing Chapter VII authority. In reaction, the word "peacekeeping" was now often preceded by the qualifier "traditional" to designate its original narrower definition, and new concepts arose to describe operations that were broader in function or authority. These included "peace enforcement," "inducement," "coercive inducement," "peace imposition," "peace restoration," "peace implementation," "muscular peacekeeping," "aggravated peacekeeping," "gray-area operations," "middle-ground operations," "hybrid operations," "second-generation operations," "the new peacekeeping," "wider peacekeeping," and "multifunctional peace-keeping." In addition, the terms "peace support operations" and "peace operations" came into use to encompass the traditional and the new under one rubric.

A fourth feature hearkens back to League of Nations and early UN precedents in which military personnel acted as members of national del-egations and were not placed under the direct control of either world body. The 1992–93 Unified Task Force (UNITAF) in Somalia, France's 1993 Operation Turquoise in Rwanda, and the 1994–95 Multinational Force in Haiti (Operation Uphold Democracy) were given mandates that provided the force contributors great leeway to do as they saw fit. Because the mis-sions were particularly hazardous, the Security Council felt they could be carried out more speedily and efficiently if the UN Secretariat—never intended to be a general staff—was not in the direct line of control. The secretary-general concurred while cautioning that the United Nations needed to be careful when providing states with an a priori blanket of legitimacy.[7]

A fifth, and for many the defining, feature of the era was the recurring controversy about how far to go to secure the observance of mandates by the local parties. The controversies usually revolved around the degree to which UN contingents should (continue to) abide by the traditional peacekeeping principles of consent, impartiality, and use of force only in self-defense. Some operations, especially in Cambodia, Angola, Somalia, Rwanda, and the Balkans, were so problem ridden in this regard that they dominated governmental and media discussions about the United Nations and threw a pall over its fiftieth anniversary in 1995.

In a prescient article five years earlier, Brian Urquhart had foreseen the steep increase in the Security Council's resort to peace support, and he advised that it would necessitate a reconsideration of the principles of peacekeeping. It was imperative, he went on, that any changes be systemat-ically agreed to by all concerned.[8] This did not occur, and two examples starkly illustrate the depth and near intractability of the problems that arose instead.

Resolution 814 (1993) called upon the second United Nations Operation in Somalia (UNOSOM II) to confront any faction that threatened or violated the cessation of hostilities. It was authorized to do so under Chapter VII, the first time a force under UN control was so empowered. Its passage led to controversy among the force contributors. "So distinct was the disagreement . . . that they could label themselves as a 'Chapter VI' or 'Chapter VII' nation. This shorthand was used to differentiate those contingents that had arrived in Somalia prepared to use force proactively from those that were not . . . except in self-defense."[9] These differences vitiated the unity of command necessary to deal with the volatile situation in Mogadishu and strongly influenced the decision to withdraw UN troops.

The United Nations Protection Force (UNPROFOR) in Bosnia provides the second example. Although it had been assigned Chapter VII enforcement authority in word, its resources constrained it to act like a traditional Chapter VI peacekeeping force in deed. The resulting confusion on how to characterize the mission was highlighted by Boutros-Ghali. In March and April 1995 the Security Council directed him to report on and make recommendations about UNPROFOR's future. After noting that the force by then had been in Bosnia for nearly three years, he stressed that the core issue continued to be the "basic question of whether UNPROFOR is to be a peacekeeping operation, conducting itself in accordance with the established principles and practices for such an operation, or an enforcement operation."[10] If the former, then it should be recognized, he added, that UNPROFOR should abide by the core peacekeeping principles of consent, impartiality, and noninitiation of force. If the latter, then UNPROFOR obviously had wider scope for action, but could exercise authority only to the extent that capabilities allowed. The failure of the international community to agree on UNPROFOR's role and to follow through accordingly had resulted, he concluded, in "a mission impossible" that would lead to "more United Nations casualties and more damage to the Organization's credibility."[11]

The problems illustrated above went hand in hand with a sixth feature of the second era: linked shortages in available forces and money. As the number of operations and deployed troops increased rapidly, the states that could always be counted on to provide properly outfitted and well-trained soldiers became stretched to the limit. Particularly affected were donors (for example, Canada) that were simultaneously undergoing reductions in their national forces in the aftermath of the Cold War. A $1.3 billion funding shortfall by the end of 1994 additionally limited the United Nations' ability to purchase mission equipment or deploy enough soldiers to handle adverse contingencies. It also put the organization far behind in its reimbursements to states providing forces. This led some to warn the secretary-general that lack of timely reimbursement would cause them to withdraw their units.[12] These problems undermined enthusiasm for peace support and contributed to an increasingly felt determination to extricate the United Nations from its difficulties.

That determination led to the third and current era of retrenchment and rethinking. As good an indicator as any that a new era had begun was the former secretary-general's issuance of his *Supplement to An Agenda for Peace* in January 1995. It assessed the United Nations' recent experiences in peace support and suggested "corrective measures."[13] The Security Council implemented its own corrective. From mid-1995 to mid-1996, the number of troops in UN-controlled peace support operations declined by over 40,000 (to nearly 25,000), a drop largely due to the termination of UNPROFOR in Bosnia and Herzegovina and its replacement by NATO's Implementation Force (IFOR). Also, of the seven UN-controlled operations authorized after December 1994,[14] five flowed from internationally supervised agreements that caused a restructuring or termination of earlier UN missions in the Balkans; one was a restart of UN efforts in Angola; and only one, a small observer group to Guatemala, was a first-time deployment to a crisis. More significantly, a consensus solidified among member states that any proposed UN-controlled mission must conform to traditional peacekeeping principles, especially concerning the consent and cooperation of the parties. This new consensus applies even when UN forces are assigned multidimensional responsibilities in the aftermath of a civil conflict or humanitarian disaster.[15] In addition, there may be two other elements to this new consensus. The first is that missions should not be deployed until adequately supported, and the second is that cases where coercion may be necessary are better suited for coalitions of the willing working under UN endorsement but not under its command and control.[16]

Some of this new thinking is not universally applauded. When Kofi Annan was the under-secretary-general for peacekeeping operations, he wrote, "The conventional wisdom . . . is that the Organization should do less peace-keeping, either by not getting involved at all in certain conflicts or by working only at their margins. Aside from the overriding fact that inaction in the face of massive violence is morally indefensible, non-involvement is an illusory option."[17] It is so, he says, because domestic political imperatives driven by accounts of human suffering, concern for refugee migration, and foreign policy interests will drive some states to intervene. They will do so either independently, fueling rivalries with competing nations or groups, or under a UN framework that may sometimes require, as Urquhart had foreseen, going beyond peacekeeping principles as traditionally understood.[18]

Any effort to develop a new UN framework must first diagnose the causes for the conceptual and operational problems illustrated in the UNOSOM II and UNPROFOR examples above. There is agreement on several causes and controversy about another.

AGREED-UPON FACTORS

It is generally accepted that several overlapping factors contributed to problems. One is that the United Nations' deliberative bodies, the Secretariat, and force contributors were not well prepared by experience or resources to deal expeditiously with the very urgent situations they confronted in Somalia, the former Yugoslavia, Rwanda, Haiti, and elsewhere. Traditional peacekeeping had usually been resorted to only after the local parties had agreed to cease recurring violence, but the problematic operations of the second era were mandated because killing and destruction were ongoing and the international community wanted them stopped without itself engaging in warfare. Perversely, the more urgent the situation, the less time was available to resolve issues that proved nearly overwhelming. Questions of sovereignty and intervention in internal affairs defined the outer limits of the debate among member states. A Secretariat that in 1989 had only nine people to deal with peacekeeping now grew hurriedly in number to meet its mission-by-mission responsibilities to assemble, deploy, provide for, coordinate, and supervise thousands of soldiers from tens of countries. The deployed forces found themselves in a doctrinal gray zone where neither the principles of peacekeeping developed over the previous forty years nor the principles of enforcement as recently applied in Desert Storm constituted appropriate guides for action.[19] Relatively novel ideas on what peace support forces ought to do "did not develop into operational concepts before they were attempted in the field."[20]

A second factor was that the proliferation or redefinition of terms to describe UN military missions too often confused time-sensitive policy debates while also contravening the expectations of force providers and of the peoples in areas where forces deployed. The UNOSOM II and UNPROFOR examples amply illustrate this point.[21]

A third factor is that the impact of conceptual ambiguity and confusion was magnified by tendencies among many UN member states toward wishful thinking and an overestimation of the United Nations' moral authority. E. H. Carr observed nearly sixty years ago that the wish is often father to the thought in international politics and other human endeavors.[22] Conor Cruise O'Brien echoed this theme when he described the United Nations' mandate-approval process as grounded in "the feeling that the thing feared may be averted, and the thing hoped for to be won, by the solemn and collective use of appropriate words."[23] Cases in point were the mandates on the Bosnian "safe areas":

> The Security Council resolutions . . . required the parties to treat them as "safe," imposed no obligations on their inhabitants and defenders, deployed United Nations troops in them but expected their mere presence to "deter attacks," carefully avoided asking the peacekeepers to "defend" or "protect" these areas, but authorized them to call in air power in "self-defence"—a masterpiece of diplomatic drafting, but largely unimplementable as an operational directive.[24]

It is no wonder that UNPROFOR Commander General François Briquemont of Belgium declared in frustration that he stopped reading the very resolutions that were supposed to guide his decisions.[25]

A fourth factor is that such resolutions were also the written manifestations of a policy of artful dodging driven by domestic politics. Affected by pictures of civilian suffering—and also in some cases by fears of being flooded by refugees—the publics in many countries demanded action. Sensitive to this opinion and often driven by the same concerns, national leaders arranged for peace support missions under UN control. They also realized, however, that there were sharp limits to the sacrifices—in men, money, casualties, and loss of operational independence—that their publics were willing to accept. The response of most Security Council members, caught in the middle, is not surprising. They made great shows of passing ambitious resolutions—some with explicit enforcement authority, but they also directed that implementation be on the cheap. They accepted rosy estimates, but the favorable outcomes they hoped for proved frustratingly elusive in missions with uncooperative local parties. For example, although the secretary-general had estimated that 34,000 soldiers would be required to guarantee the integrity of the Bosnian "safe areas," the Security Council called for only 7,950 on the assumption that the parties would abide by the mandate. They did not, and the term "safe areas" inspired among their inhabitants more cynicism than security.

Also caught in the middle were force contributors who were not on the Security Council and had no direct role in the mandating of missions. The problem was particularly acute for those states that for nearly four decades had been part of the United Nations' peacekeeping "fire brigade" by virtue of their consistent willingness to contribute military personnel to missions. Volunteering as well in the 1990s, but having grown used to peacekeeping principles as traditionally understood, they became quite uncomfortable for domestic political reasons with any changes that could increase the risk to their nationals.[26] Some thus placed restrictions on the use of their forces that sharply limited operational flexibility. They were not encouraged to lift those restrictions when they found that Security Council members, including the United States, were also imposing restrictions for domestic reasons.

Finally, another factor contributing to confusion and discord was a seeming conceptual blind spot or lacuna in some peoples' conceptions of the options available in peace support. There was disagreement then (and it continues today) about whether this was indeed the case, and this disagreement magnified the confusion and discord.

THE CONTROVERSY OVER A MIDDLE OPTION

In a 1991 article on how to end civil wars, Brian Urquhart offered what was at the time a relatively novel suggestion:

> A third category of international military operation is needed, somewhere between peacekeeping and large-scale enforcement. It would be intended to put an end to random violence and to provide a reasonable degree of peace and order so that humanitarian relief work could go forward and a conciliation process could commence. . . . Unlike peacekeeping forces, such troops would be required to take, initially at least, certain combat risks in bringing the violence under control.[27]

By 1993 John Gerard Ruggie was able to observe that an unprepared United Nations was already involved in such activities. The organization, he said, had "entered a domain of military activity—a vaguely defined no-man's-land lying somewhere between traditional peacekeeping and enforcement—for which it lacks any guiding operational concept."[28]

Other observers have since reiterated the call for a third option and the development of associated doctrine and guidelines, but this view probably constituted the minority position. Especially in UN corridors and among most peacekeeping practitioners, the predominant reaction seemed negative.[29] One of the most articulate and effective spokesmen against a middle option was Charles Dobbie. He was central to the development of British military doctrine on these questions, and both the doctrine and his arguments greatly influenced or reinforced the thinking of many in New York, London, and elsewhere.[30] As he put it, a middle option must be rejected because it "can lead to peacekeeping being subject to a set of common principles that impose combatant, adversary-oriented attitudes on the impartial third-party activities that constitute peacekeeping."[31] Utilizing the analogy of a game, he described a peacekeeper's role as that of a referee while an enforcer's role "demands" that he enters the fray as a player. "No middle ground . . . lies between player and referee—he can only be one or the other." Their attitudes, motivations, and intentions are so radically different that in a world of civil and international crises, "middle-ground theories" are "dangerously destabilising" and can lead only "to much confusion, and possibly bloodshed."[32]

Ironically, former Secretary-General Boutros-Ghali may himself have inadvertently contributed to confusion by helping popularize the term most often utilized to designate the middle option. In June 1992 he published *An Agenda for Peace* and in it he offered a lexicon to standardize terminology. Rather elliptically he also introduced the concept of "peace enforcement" for the maintenance of cease-fires and vaguely described the task as one that "can exceed the mission of peace-keeping forces and the expectations of peace-keeping force contributors."[33] A few months later he characterized peace enforcement as an operation "deployed without the express consent of the two parties (though its basis would be a cease-fire previously reached by them). UN troops would be authorized to use force if necessary."[34] In this way he sanctioned the term "peace enforcement" and, whatever his intentions, helped advance the view that the international community now had available a continuum of options with peace enforcement in the middle. If he ever did hold that position, he later seemed to move off it to emphasize instead that one should not mix peace-keeping and enforcement in the same mission. When he wrote in 1995 that the fundamental question about UNPROFOR was whether it should be seen as peacekeeping or enforcement, he deliberately offered only two choices and explicitly rejected an alternative between them.[35] He did not stop referring to "peace enforcement" but did begin to use the term interchangeably with the word "enforcement."[36] Official UN documents, in turn, listed Desert Storm, a quintessential large-scale enforcement operation, as an example of peace enforcement,[37] and though speaking unofficially, prominent individuals in the Secretariat referred to "peace enforcement" as "another term for war" and "practically indistinguishable from warfighting."[38]

Boutros-Ghali's role as secretary-general put him at the intersection of theory and practice, and it seems that, as with many others, the United Nations' unhappy experiences in Somalia and Bosnia greatly affected his thoughts and words. To opponents of a middle or third option, UNOSOM II and UNPROFOR constituted clear evidence of its impracticability. Proponents countered, however, that this assessment constituted a misdiagnosis of why those operations faltered badly. In an analysis of the Somalia case, for example, three coauthors adjudged:

> It was not to be a genuine test of the "third option" or of anything that could be labeled "peace enforcement." Rather, in the absence of a "peace enforcement" doctrine, operations shifted between the black and white options of no force or too much force. Yet the wrong lessons have been taken away about the middle ground on the pretext that the use of force has failed the test.[39]

We agree with this assessment.

CONCLUDING REMARKS

Ever since the League of Nations, the international community has built up a considerable body of practice in employing military personnel for peace support. The peacekeeping principles codified during the first UN era summarized the then collective wisdom. The second era raised questions about the applicability of some principles for hazardous missions where local cooperation was not always assured. The resulting confusion and discord were so problematic that they helped usher in the present period of scaling back on missions and avoiding difficult ones altogether. This is also a time of renewed reflection driven partly by a fear that the pendulum may swing too far—that is, that the United Nations as the embodiment of the international community may remain aloof from situations where a collective response is most appropriate.

Any reflection must include a diagnosis of the conceptual and operational problems of the first half of the 1990s. There is broad consensus that the causes were a complex mix of lack of time and preparation, semantic confusion, wishful thinking, overestimation of the United Nations' moral authority, and political expediency, but still open to debate is whether and under what circumstances there is indeed a discrete and practicable "middle option." As against those who view it to be "a much needed addition to the tools available to the United Nations," there are others who insist that the international community must choose between peacekeeping or enforcement and follow through accordingly.[40]

What should policymakers believe and what possibilities should they include in their consideration of alternatives? Is there a realizable middle option after all? We believe there is. The next chapter presents our concept, coercive inducement, and addresses objections made about middle-ground thinking in general. It also lays out suggested doctrinal principles to govern the practice of coercive inducement in UN peace support missions. The later case studies illustrate the practice of coercive inducement and provide concrete bases for deriving, in chapter 7, operational guidelines for implementing the suggested principles.

2

A PRACTICABLE MIDDLE OPTION AND ASSOCIATED PRINCIPLES

This chapter offers coercive inducement as a conceptually distinct and practicable middle option. Part one outlines the concept; parts two and three present and employ second-order categories to distinguish it from traditional peacekeeping and simple enforcement; part four responds to arguments made against middle-ground thinking; and part five focuses on a central feature of its implementation. The chapter ends with suggested doctrinal principles to govern resort to coercive inducement.

THE COERCIVE INDUCEMENT OPTION

Former Secretary-General Boutros-Ghali's term "peace enforcement" has probably been utilized most often to designate the middle option, but because it has not been uniformly applied—with some seeing it as discrete from and others as equivalent to large-scale enforcement—it is best to set it aside to avoid confusion. A concept centered on inducement is a most attractive alternative because the word goes to the heart of our understanding of the middle option. To induce is to influence or persuade, and the process can involve reasoned discussion, blandishments, appeals to emotions or conscience, rewards, threats, or punishments. The focus is on a party's state of mind, on getting it to do as one desires while allowing it to retain the capability for independent action.

By coercive inducement we mean the judicious resort to coercive diplomacy or forceful persuasion by the international community in order to implement community norms or mandates vis-à-vis all the parties to a particular crisis. Use of the qualifier "judicious" is deliberately redundant— done to stress the special care that the international community must exhibit when acting militarily—because coercive diplomacy is a centuries-old technique of states and empires that involves the judicious employment of military forces to influence perceptions of targeted actors to get them to behave as desired. Its focus is on getting one's way through the employment of military forces as opposed to using force per se. It aims to persuade rather than to seize or to bludgeon, and it must form part of a concerted campaign involving a variety of means—politico-diplomatic, economic, hortatory, as well as military—to influence behavior. As Thomas Schelling wrote, it "is less military, less heroic, less impersonal, and less unilateral" than force employed to overpower an opponent militarily:

> There is a difference between taking what you want and making someone give it to you, between fending off assault and making someone afraid to assault you, between holding what people are trying to take and making them afraid to take it, between losing what someone can forcibly take and giving it up to avoid risk or damage. It is the difference between . . . brute force and intimidation, . . . action and threats.[1]

The coercive side of coercive diplomacy is usually effectuated through the transmittal of latent or explicit military threats, the deployment or massing of forces, their peaceful displays of capabilities, and demonstrative resorts to violence. Their diplomatic leverage is a function of their credibility, of whether they are physically up to the task of intimidation and whether political leaders are committed to employing them violently if necessary. Demonstrative violence should be as narrowly circumscribed as possible with careful attention given to avoiding unnecessary casualties. Military efficiency would take second place to politico-diplomatic concerns, the most important of which is not military victory but change in the target state's or group's behavior. With indications of a positive change in that behavior, the use of force would immediately cease even if the recalcitrant party were capable of further mischief.

In the end coercive diplomacy may require not only preparing for the worst—that is, war—but also waging it if a recalcitrant party remains unresponsive to a limited campaign of demonstrative force. In other words, it can fail, and the price—moving toward war or humiliating retreat— could be high.

Coercive inducement is a particular variant of coercive diplomacy. Its immediate purpose is the implementation of international norms or mandates without the Security Council singling out in resolutions any particular state or group as a malefactor. When Secretary-General Boutros-Ghali originally introduced his "peace enforcement" concept, his linking it to the maintenance of cease-fires made clear that he then saw it as an activity applicable to all parties to a crisis with specific action being directed against whatever elements acted in violation of the agreement as signed up to by their leaders. In such a conception the peace support contingent is somewhat like a policeman on the beat with authority to enforce community-backed norms against all comers regardless of their affiliation. The same policeman analogy broadly applies to a coercive inducement force. Its purpose is the implementation of Security Council mandates that do not specifically single out any particular state or group as a malefactor. It too could be tasked with enforcing not only cease-fires but also more narrowly circumscribed agreements (such as to allow the transit of foods or medicines) or more comprehensive political pacts (such as the Governors Island Agreement calling for the reinstatement of President Aristide). Alternatively, without any prior formal agreement among competing parties, a coercive inducement force could also be employed as part of an international response to a man-made catastrophe such as when innocent civilians are being slaughtered in the midst of an ethnic or civil conflict (the events in Rwanda being a worst-case example in this regard). The underlying purpose of all coercive inducement, as with peacekeeping, would not be to unduly favor the victory or defeat of one or another of the competing groups (as might be a nation's purpose when engaging in coercive diplomacy in general) but rather to help contain the crisis, to keep it from getting worse so that peacekeepers and peacemakers can work with the conflicting parties to help make things better.[2] In the area of crisis this would usually involve providing a secure environment and often basic services to needy locals. Even when highly capable and endowed with Chapter VII authority to employ "all necessary means," the long-term underlying preference of an inducement force is to be more reactive than initiatory, employing when possible essentially defensive measures—*cordon sanitaire,* safe havens for civilians, and the like—and focused violence such as striking only at specific weapons causing death or injury.

Fully appreciating the middle-option nature of coercive inducement means understanding its similarities and differences with peacekeeping and enforcement. It will facilitate comparison if second-order conceptual categories are laid out first.

CONCEPTS FOR COMPARISON

Four categories provide bases for comparisons. The first centers on consent, the fulcrum around which many arguments revolve. The others are impartiality, self-defense, and offensive military operations. At first blush, each appears clear-cut, but such is not the case, and that fact contributed to the conceptual confusion that characterized the second era of the United Nations' experience with peace support.

Varieties of Consent

Consent simply means giving assent. Although it initially seems an all-or-nothing phenomenon—that is, either one consents or one does not—reality is more complicated. Consent can be *implied* or *expressed*. The former is evidenced by offering no resistance to what others are doing or by acting in a manner consistent with what is being demanded. Expressed consent usually obtains when political or military leaders sign a negotiated agreement presumably binding the entities they represent to follow its terms. Leaders possess the power of *strategic consent* because of the presumed broad impact of their decisions, while the rank and file are capable only of *local* or *tactical consent*.[3] When the leaders do in fact commit all or most of the rank and file, then the situation is one of *widespread consent*, but if they do not—if many of the rank and file resist on their own or with the covert sanction of their leaders—then consent is *ineffectual*.

The deployment of peace support contingents usually does not occur without the expressed consent of strategic and local leaders, but how the contingent will operate once on the ground then depends on *follow-on consent*, which can prove difficult to sustain. This is particularly so when agreements and mandates are vague in order to get all the parties to sign on in the first place or when the parties signed on in bad faith. It would be surprising if most consent, no matter how detailed, were not *provisional* as opposed to *firm*. At the least, each side would carefully look for cheating by its rivals and make its continued adherence to an agreement dependent on the adherence of all others. Provisional consent becomes *decaying consent* when a party pulls back from willingness to abide by an agreement because circumstances are not working out as it hoped or envisioned.[4] Its obverse is *grudging consent,* acceptance of what a mandate or prior agreement requires because that acceptance is the least bad of the alternatives available.

In short, numerous possibilities must be considered, and except where consent is expressed, firm, and widespread, there is always ambiguity on how much consent actually obtains. The degree can significantly impact what peace support forces should be expected to do.

Varieties of Impartiality

To be impartial means to act without bias, yet it is necessary to distinguish intent from effect. Concern for intent leads to an emphasis on *blind impartiality* or *impartiality toward a mandate,* including one that calls on UN forces to facilitate implementation of an agreement. It involves a good-faith effort to fulfill the provisions of the mandate or referenced agreement regardless of the negative consequences to any party that desires to act otherwise. Determining what the provisions require would be the product of a neutral process vice accepting one party's unilateral interpretation. Each party would be treated equally, but the impacts would not necessarily be equal. In other words, UN forces acting without prejudice could nevertheless prejudice the interests of one or the other party.

Conversely, UN forces could focus on not prejudicing any faction's interests in order to guarantee continued consent and cooperation. Their role in the face of resistance is to negotiate, insist, plead, or cajole, but unless they are capable of forcing cooperation, they must either cease their activities or work within the limits of what a party allows in follow-on consent as proof of the United Nations' determination not to harm the party's interests. Thus, one can speak of *impartiality toward the parties* or *symbiotic impartiality* because of the link with consent.

Blind impartiality seems to have risen in salience over the last few years, especially in humanitarian missions, when compared with symbiotic impartiality. As one study put it, "the notion of impartiality had to be reconceived as no longer pertaining to the parties, whose lack of clear consent would frustrate an operation thus reliant, but as a reference to the integrity with which a mandate would be implemented."[5]

Varieties of Self-Defense

This concept has breadth and time dimensions. The "self" in "self-defense" can consist of more than just *individuals*. It can extend to *military units, equipment, and areas of responsibility*. There is also *mandate defense,* where it is "theoretically permissible . . . for UN troops to use armed force if others were attempting to use [force] to obstruct them while they were trying to fulfill the mandate entrusted to them."[6] Thus, the range of "selves" in "self-defense" is wide.

In addition, self-defense is usually thought of as an ex post facto phenomenon with force used only in response to someone else's hostile act. Nevertheless, in some interpretations, the defending force need not wait until it is fired upon when faced with hostile intent, that is, with the prospect of an immediately impending attack that leaves the defender with no choice other than resort to force to avoid grievous harm. This *preemptive defense* contrasts with *preventive defense.* The latter refers to action taken to forestall the possibility that a party might militarily oppose the efforts of a peace support force to implement a mandate or agreement. For example, it could involve air strikes against tanks to ensure that they do not harass a humanitarian convoy a day later. Such an example highlights, however, the near impossibility of distinguishing between preemptive self-defense and offensive military operations.

Varieties of Offensive Military Operations

Offensive military operations encompass the self-initiated employment of military forces in order to induce or compel compliance from uncooperative parties. There are unlimited theoretical possibilities that differ only in degree.

At the high end is *war:* an extensive and general resort to systematic violence. At the low end is *intimidation:* the threat of the use of force to induce compliance so that a war need not be fought. Verbal or written threats, displays of military power, exemplary resort to violence—all are instruments of intimidation. Just on the other side of intimidation is a *limited coercive campaign:* a recurring but time-restricted, tightly controlled use of focused violence to compel compliance from an especially resistant party.

OPTIONS FOR THE USE OF MILITARY FORCES IN UN OPERATIONS

The concepts outlined above provide a common basis for comparing coercive inducement with the two options with which it shares some characteristics: traditional peacekeeping and enforcement.[7]

Traditional Peacekeeping

Whether traditional peacekeeping be of the classical (interposition/monitoring) or multifunctional variety, a defining feature is one that Dag Hammarskjöld adopted when he directed the activities of the United Nations Emergency Force in response to the Suez crisis. He set the standard when he insisted that a peacekeeping contingent be "para-military in nature, not a Force with military objectives," and that its military functions be restricted to those "necessary to secure peaceful conditions on the assumption that the parties to the conflict take all necessary steps for compliance" with UN resolutions.[8] In other words, traditional peacekeeping is premised on firm and widespread consent with expressed, strategic consent being evidenced in the initial cease-fire or peace agreement as well as in the follow-on agreements about when and how the UN force will arrive, where it will garrison, how it will function, and the like.[9] The consent of each belligerent or faction is presumed to be broad based and firm with any nonconsent being only sporadic and local. Peacekeepers are to keep consent from decaying or becoming ineffectual by exhibiting impartiality and avoiding the use of force except in self-defense.

Consistent with blind impartiality, Hammarskjöld directed that peacekeepers restrict themselves to implementing the organization's mandates and resolutions, and he devoted much of his time to their "interpretation in practice."[10] Consistent with symbiotic impartiality, he also directed that UN contingents not alter the political and military balances governing the voluntary resolution of a crisis. His experience reveals the tension between blind and symbiotic impartiality and how consensual peacekeeping, while aspiring to the former, is ultimately driven either to emphasizing the latter or to ceasing operations when confronting a recalcitrant party. For example, about UNEF's deployment to Egypt, he wrote:

> The fact that a United Nations operation . . . requires the consent of the Government on whose territory it takes place creates a problem, as it is normally difficult for the United Nations to engage in such an operation without the

guarantees against unilateral actions by the host Government which might put the United Nations in a questionable position.[11]

The way to resolve the problem, he said, was for both Egypt and the United Nations to engage in "good faith . . . interpretation" of the purposes of the UNEF and to enter into "an exchange of views . . . towards harmonizing the positions." If they could not agree, he concluded, then the United Nations could decide to terminate the operation, for it was imperative that both it and Egypt mutually recognize "that the operation, being based on collaboration between [both], should be carried on in forms natural to such collaboration."[12]

The historic record shows that, once committed, the United Nations has generally "soldiered on" in difficult missions as long as good could be done or disaster averted.[13] Such determination underscored the need for local cooperation and thus the salience of symbiotic impartiality both in the field and in UN Headquarters in New York. Having volunteered for a mission on the assumption of compliance by the parties and possessing only modest military capabilities, most peacekeepers in the field sought to avoid action that, while in line with a blindly impartial interpretation of a mandate, might also have harmed a party's interests and thus caused it to be less cooperative.[14] UN officials in New York, predisposed to consensual operations and wanting to retain the services of peacekeeping contributors, reasoned along the same lines. In addition, the organization's mediator role reinforced the ethos of limiting how far peacekeepers pressured recalcitrant local actors lest they see the United Nations as biased and thus unfit to mediate.[15]

In short, traditional peacekeeping's impartiality principle turned out in the face of resistance more oriented toward the parties than toward the mandate. This is not to gainsay the willingness of peacekeepers to apply their "traditional skills of patience, firmness, negotiation, and goodwill,"[16] but in the end they are hostage to the willingness of the parties to cooperate. When parties are especially obstructionist, the result can be, said one UN official in Bosnia, a "policy of impartiality to the point of appeasement" if the Security Council is not willing to take up Hammarskjöld's alternate option of pulling the force out.[17]

Well-armed peacekeepers might try to impose the United Nations' will, but it was again Hammarskjöld who originally framed the principle that peacekeepers use force only in self-defense and that they bring only limited firepower weapons.[18] Beyond defense of a soldier being subjected to attack, traditional peacekeeping rules of engagement have over time and in varying operations allowed for defense of the unit, vehicles, other equipment, areas of responsibility (such as an observation post, airfield, or voting site), UN personnel being subjected to arrest or abduction, preventive self-defense, and defense of the mandate.[19] In practice, however, peacekeeping forces have generally been very conservative, tending toward narrow interpretation of the right to self-defense and setting up strictly restrictive rules for exercising that right.[20] An experienced peacekeeper provided an example of the ethos when he wrote, "The best weapons in peace-keeping are long-range, direct-fire weapons . . . with pin-point accuracy to be sure to miss the target."[21]

There is a noteworthy gap both within theory as well as between theory and the practice on the question of mandate defense. The standard theoretical formulation is drawn from a 1973 secretary-general report written for UNEF II:

> [The Force] shall not use force except in self-defence. Self-defence would include resistance to attempts by forceful means to prevent it from discharging its duties under the mandate of the Security Council. The Force will proceed on the assumption that the parties to the conflict take all the necessary steps for compliance with the decisions of the Security Council.[22]

If the last sentence is truly an operating assumption, then it seems unnecessary, if not contradictory, to specify a separate right of mandate defense over and above the general right military forces inherently have to defend themselves. This tension within the theoretical formulation helps explain why UN force commanders have rarely invoked it in practice. Under-Secretary-General Marrack Goulding has observed that such reluctance is grounded in "sound calculations related to impartiality, to . . . reliance on the continued cooperation of the parties and to the fact that [the UN] force's level of armament was based on the assumption that the parties would comply with . . . commitments."[23] In other words, the presumption of cooperation justified a contingent's never being given the forces required to defend the mandate in the first place. Thus, the gap within theory underlaid the gap between theory and practice.

Goulding's observation underscores the claim that the "intrinsic [military] weakness" of a UN peacekeeping contingent is an "advantage" precisely because it reassures the indigenous parties that, at the end of the day, the United Nations cannot and will not function without their consent.[24] Any thought of enforcement is out of the question.

Enforcement

As the antipode to traditional peacekeeping, this option should be simple to explain; nevertheless, there is not full unanimity over its breadth. In the narrower conception (to which we subscribe), enforcement arises when a party so egregiously violates international norms and so stubbornly refuses to amend its wrongdoing that the United Nations can remain neither impartial nor inactive. Singling out the offender in mandates, the United Nations authorizes coercive measures to compel the offender's compliance at both strategic and local levels. Such measures can differ in the degree and continuity of violence employed. Classic high-end examples are the wars against North Korea in the early 1950s—widely and euphemistically referred to at the time as a "police action"—and against Iraq in 1991. A mid-range example might be the offensive campaign against the Katangese rebel forces of Moise Tshombe in the Congo in the early 1960s, and a low-end example would be Operation Provide Comfort where a U.S.-led contingent moved into northern Iraq in 1991 to protect the Kurds against retribution from the Baghdad government.[25] Another low-end example could involve the use of military forces in support of a trade embargo such as that enacted against Belgrade in 1992 and indefinitely suspended in 1995.

Many critics of middle-ground thinking offer a broader conception of enforcement that encompasses almost any military activity undertaken without a party's presumably firm, expressed, strategic consent. They thereby incorporate within their concept activities that others (the authors included) would categorize as middle option in nature, and they characterize this broad enforcement concept as the sole alternative to peacekeeping.[26] The implications of their so doing will be dealt with after fitting coercive inducement into the consent, impartiality, and use-of-force framework.

The Middle Option: Coercive Inducement

Coercive inducement explicitly aims to augment or firm up consent at the strategic and tactical levels on the premise that even grudging cooperation limits inhumane or destabilizing behavior and buys time for those working for long-term improvement. It assumes that initial strategic consent is provisional at best and that the parties will test the limits of the United Nations' willingness to insist on full adherence to its resolutions. Its mandates must be intended to apply equally to all parties as opposed to designating any malefactor, and the UN contingent must be blindly impartial in implementation. Should implementation harm a party's conception of its interests, the contingent should make clear that it is guided by the mandate and not by any predisposition to favor or harm any of the disputants.[27]

Augmenting or firming consent requires acting as much like a peacekeeper as possible by working with the parties, reasoning with them, keeping them informed, and constantly seeking their cooperation. It can also involve intimidation, robust defensive cordons, limited exemplary preemptive self-defense, or, at the extreme, a restricted coercive campaign against carefully selected military targets. Any use of force must occur only after the party had been clearly warned. At the end of the day, military credibility is to coercive inducement what intrinsic military weakness is to peacekeeping.

Working midway between traditional peacekeeping and enforcement can be extremely difficult. Unlike their counterparts in consensual peacekeeping, inducement contingents must assume some resistance that is either centrally coordinated or, even worse, sporadic—such as roadblocks manned by drunken irregulars—with no clear indication whether it is rule or exception. Unlike their counterparts in full-fledged enforcement, furthermore, they cannot assume that theirs is a combat task intended to break all resistance once and for all. Rather, the same personnel expected to demonstrate resolve and augment consent are also expected to do so with the lightest touch possible in the hope that the parties will finally assent to the United Nations' will. They have to avoid taking sides and still alleviate the suffering of innocents being subjected to unspeakable cruelties. They may have to deal with leaders whom in other circumstances they might arrest as thugs or war criminals. While acting against pockets of opposition, they must also maintain the goodwill and cooperation of local populaces.

This unity of opposites at the heart of coercive inducement is a major reason why some criticize all middle-ground thinking.

ACCOUNTING FOR OBJECTIONS TO A MIDDLE OPTION

There are at least four overlapping objections to proposals of a middle option. The first is that the distinction between enforcement and any middle option is too subtle to be practicable. The reason is the great similarities between them in respect of the capabilities that must be assembled and the commitment that must be made to employ violence when necessary to secure compliance.[28] UN officials, national political representatives, and military practitioners of peacekeeping have often gone to the heart of the matter when characterizing middle-option operations either as indistinguishable from or effectively equivalent to warfighting.[29]

In response, one cannot gainsay the similarities, but the point remains that the middle option aims to so impress a party on the capability and resolve of a UN contingent that large-scale offensive operations need not be undertaken. If middle-ground thinking is not to remain a doctrinal "void," then it is necessary, as John Gerard Ruggie has argued, that UN member states and administrators "appreciate the classic distinction between the utility of force and its actual use."[30] In 1990 John Mackinlay may have been the first to observe that many people closely involved in peacekeeping thought only in terms of "peace-keeping and general war" with "the step from 'defensive protection' to 'the use of force' [being] seen as absolute." He attributed this mindset to those with "no experience of violence or active [military] duty except in the narrow terms of peacekeeping."[31] It cannot confidently be said that the violence that plagued the third era contributed to widespread acceptance of middle-ground thinking, but the efforts of Kofi Annan, then under-secretary-general for peacekeeping operations, to offer a "new paradigm"[32] for peace support built around inducement[33] does evidence that some UN administrators do indeed appreciate such thinking.

A second objection is that the logic and dynamics of peacekeeping and enforcement do not allow for a middle ground between them. As was previewed in chapter 1, an influential spokesman used a player-and-referee analogy to argue that soldiers in UN service cannot simultaneously be peacekeepers and enforcers at the same time.[34] Any party they subject to intimidation or coercion will regard them as partial, harden its position in any ongoing UN mediation, and retaliate against UN personnel and humanitarian workers.[35] It will thereby force the United Nations toward either violence or retreat. If the United Nations resorts to violence, it will transition from neutral facilitator to being a party to the crisis. If it retreats, it will humiliate itself.

This objection has value, but there is a problem with the analogy and its underlying premise. A referee can assume he will retain his status even if he is tougher on one team than another (specifically the team that seems more prone to violate the rules) and significantly prejudices its interests (for example, by expelling a star player). He does not become a contestant by so doing. Unless the players believe him corrupt or obviously biased, they will continue to see him as the referee as long as they are willing to play the game and accept that he can hurt their interests. They will presumably play with that more caution because of his exhibited willingness to act without asking for their consent. Indeed, he strengthens his credibility by acting, for he shows that he will harm a team's prospects for victory if it continues to violate the rules.

Analogy aside, it is true that a peacekeeping contingent cannot be counted on to enforce for the same reason that mandate defense occurs so rarely: the contingent does not possess enough capability to intimidate or coerce. This point has understandably been pressed by those who argue that the United Nations restrict itself to consensual operations only. But it is also true that a contingent postured for enforcement can act like a peacekeeper, that is, it can be both peacekeeper and enforcer at the same time when tasked and appropriately equipped to implement a mandate against all comers—much like the policeman on the beat—vice an identified aggressor. As the case study in chapter 4 shows, the U.S.-led and UN-endorsed Unified Task Force (UNITAF) in Somalia possessed highly visible military credibility in view of its size, weaponry, and rules of engagement. The nature of its deployment, where it moved decisively and quickly to establish its authority, also drew the respect of the parties. It had the intent and the wherewithal to shape both strategic and local consent as it protected the delivery of humanitarian aid within specific geographic areas. It did so not only through general intimidation and the selected use of violence, but also by communicating with all the parties, keeping them informed, resisting taking them by surprise, and going back to explain when it did use force.[36] In short, though postured for enforcement, it behaved in many ways like a peacekeeping contingent, and it did so in an environment where each of the parties was ultrasensitive to any hint of bias against its interests. In contrast, UNOSOM II failed largely because it could not act like a peacekeeper after the decision to subject General Aideed to a "vendetta-disarmament war."[37]

That failure contributed to a third objection to a middle option: to wit, that its promise is false and must be resisted. The reason is that the crises that come to the attention of the United Nations are precisely those not easily amenable to quick fixes, especially of a forceful nature. Because their resolution requires patience and determination, it is necessary, some say, to resist the temptation to use military power to speed the process.[38] One must wait until conditions are "ripe," that is, until the parties are themselves ready to consent to impartial outside intervention.

This argument has much merit. History is replete with agreements that became irrelevant as soon as they were signed and with conflicts that were impervious to outside intervention until the time was ripe. Yet opportunities do occur when speedy and vigorous international action can make a difference. For example, international pressure can provide one or another belligerent leader with the excuse to resist diehards who wish to continue fighting. Robert Cooper and Mats Berdal make an argument akin to this:

> There will always be a point, even in ethnic conflicts, when two sides find they have a shared interest in a cease-fire. There may also be times when, either because some shreds of decency remain, or because they do not wish altogether to alienate outside opinion, the parties decide to let outsiders perform humanitarian tasks. They may allow this even when it is contrary to their strict military objectives. When they are performing a peacekeeping role, outside intervention forces operate on this margin of agreement and decency.[39]

A force capable of enforcement but operating as much as possible like a peacekeeper might more readily secure cooperation than a strict peacekeeping force per se.

The fourth objection is much like the third, but differs in that it is more implied than explicit, being imbedded in the speech of practitioners.[40] It runs as follows: whether or not a middle-option operation is a practicable alternative, it is dangerous to acknowledge it as such for it will only confuse national politicians and publics. They know consensual peacekeeping is peaceful and relatively low cost and that high-level enforcement, that is, war, is very risky indeed and necessitates a major commitment of forces and the will to use them. To offer them a middle option will only encourage them to bluff and to attempt to achieve major gains on the cheap.[41]

The historical record clearly shows an unwillingness of member states to provide credible forces to back up the enforcement resolutions passed by the Security Council. Too often forces more suited for peacekeeping have been put in harm's way by being assigned enforcement tasks. The way around this problem is to insist that there be only two stark options: either commit to consensual peacekeeping and no more, or commit to war even if it does not turn out to be necessary because threats or limited violence prove to be sufficient.

This cynical argument is powerful, for it reflects the political reality of states desiring to reap the benefits of enforcement while not paying the price. But to consider only two options, nonviolent peacekeeping and full-fledged enforcement, can just as readily lead to no action at all if decision makers deem the first inappropriate and the second too bloody-minded. In other words, restricting oneself to only these choices can provide the perfect rationale to do nothing beyond hand-wringing resolutions that call upon the parties to cease and desist. A discrete middle-ground option can offer the temptation to bluff. This means being ready to resort to violence, but only if necessary. At the end of the day, the middle option may be rejected as too risky, but failing to consider it or muddling consideration by grafting it to either traditional peacekeeping or full enforcement—which could well augment the temptation to bluff—may be to foreclose action that might have made a difference. It seems clear, however, that if such action is to take place, it probably will not be in an operation directed out of New York.

A CENTRAL FEATURE OF IMPLEMENTATION

An ultimate by-product of the United Nations' difficulties when conducting peace support operations in the activist era is the recognition that potentially hazardous missions requiring Chapter VII authority generally have to be conducted by a willing state or coalition endorsed by the United Nations but not controlled by it when executing the mission. This is because most UN-controlled operations with provision for enforcement (even if only at the local level) seem almost doomed to fail. UN administrators do not have the necessary staffing and budget to plan, support, and execute large-scale, complex, and risky military operations. Member states rarely provide the necessary capabilities for such missions, which run against a general UN aversion to anything that smacks of enforcement. Most member states like neither to engage in it nor to use the term in resolutions.[42]

As the case studies illustrate, "contracting" for the services of a willing state or a coalition gets around these problems. A UN administrator noted sardonically that when Security Council members vote for operations that will remain under the organization's control, they assume the best will occur and skimp on the resources provided, but when they themselves undertake operations endorsed but not controlled by the organization, they assume the worst and provide accordingly.[43] Hence, an endorsed force usually has more robust rules of engagement, giving it greater leeway to pressure the parties, than a UN-controlled one, and it brings the wherewithal necessary to intimidate credibly and to protect its own personnel as well as others. The coalition would not have signed up otherwise. Coalitions are usually led by one or more of the Permanent Members with enough of an interest in the crisis situation to cause them to lobby for the Security Council's endorsement. For the most part, other council members (sometimes grudgingly) vote for the operation or refrain from vetoing it since the coalition (especially its leader) does the planning, takes the physical risks, and pays the bills. Where the humanitarian need is clear and pressing, they may even be quite grateful to give voting support to anyone agreeing to shoulder the burden on the behalf of the organization.

Concluding Remarks

The degree to which phenomena are recognized and labeled affects the formulation of policy options. We believe that there is a phenomenon, appropriately labeled "coercive inducement," which is conceptually and practicably distinct from both classical peacekeeping and enforcement. Table 2-1 summarizes how it differs from both in regard to consent, impartiality, and use of force. Table 2-2 compares principles of coercive inducement derived from the above discussion with the principles of peacekeeping as presented in the previous chapter and principles of enforcement suggested by logic and history.

Though coercive inducement seems not widely accepted, we speculate that the violence that plagued the activist era did increase recognition.[44] The refusal of some force contributors to move beyond consensual peacekeeping may have been less a matter of comprehension than one of volition.

Table 2-1. Comparing Options

	Peacekeeping	Coercive Inducement	Enforcement
Consent	Assumed to be wide-spread and firm.	Aim is to augment consent, assumed to be provisional at best.	None assumed.
Impartiality	More symbiotic than blind.	Blind implementation of mandate vis-à-vis all parties.	Not applicable. Mandate identifies target of UN actions.
Use of Force	Self-defense only, with mandate defense rarely exercised.	Can range from shows of force to limited, focused campaigns with any violence to be minimum necessary to influence behavior.	Sustained and wide-spread use of force if diplomatic entreaties are unsuccessful.

That is, decision makers and peacekeeping practitioners fled from the option because they realized full well that it involved risks and commitments that their domestic constituencies were not ready to undertake.

That stance is consistent with the current consensus of cutting back on peace support and avoiding hazardous missions. It heralds little enthusiasm for engaging in inducement, but as Kofi Annan has observed, the moral imperative to do so will not lessen in the future.[45] No one is predicting that conflict and its associated humanitarian disasters will be any less prevalent. Hence priority ought to be given to sorting out the operational requirements for shaping or inducing consent. We hope that the case studies presented in the following chapters will illuminate what should and should not be done when undertaking coercive inducement.

Table 2-2. Principles of Peacekeeping, Coercive Inducement, and Enforcement

Peacekeeping	Coercive Inducement	Enforcement
1. Peacekeepers function under the command and control of the secretary-general.	1. Absent an effective UN system for command and control, inducement contingents should function under the aegis of a leading state or coalition in operations endorsed by the United Nations.	1. Enforcement contingent functions within a coalition command-and-control framework in operations endorsed by the United Nations.
2. They represent moral authority rather than force of arms.	2. Coercive inducement personnel should represent both moral authority and credible force.	2. They represent force of arms applied for internationally endorsed ends.
3. They reflect the universality of the United Nations in their composition.	3. While aspiring for as much universality as possible, inducement contingents primarily reflect the capabilities that make for an immediately effective crisis response.	3. While aspiring for as much universality as possible, they must be driven more by concern to assemble units that can contribute to speedy and effective crisis response regardless of their provenance.
4. They deploy with the consent and cooperation of the parties and do not seek to impose their will.	4. Deployed personnel assume no better than provisional consent and act to impose the will of the international community on recalcitrant parties.	4. They assume active resistance to implementation of UN mandates.

5. They are impartial and function without prejudice to the rights and aspirations of any side.

6. They do not use or threaten force except in self-defense.

7. They take few risks and keep casualties to a minimum.

5. While not intending to harm anyone's interests, an inducement force must implement mandates even when doing so prejudices those of one or more of the sides.

6. If necessary, force may be used for other than self-defense, but any use should not exceed the minimum required to bring about the desired behavior.

7. Anticipating risks, inducement contingents must plan to minimize casualties while preparing for the worst.

5. Their actions are directed against the malefactors identified in UN mandates.

6. Within legal limits, they use what force is necessary to guarantee that in future a malefactor will observe the UN mandate.

7. They plan for risks and considerable casualties and support their forces accordingly.

3

BOSNIA

by Chantal de Jonge Oudraat

This chapter examines the threat and use of military force—especially, air strikes—by the United Nations and the North Atlantic Treaty Organization (NATO) in Bosnia and Herzegovina (hereafter Bosnia). More specifically, it examines how and when the United Nations and NATO used force and how this affected the behavior of the warring parties on the ground.

In response to severe violations of the laws of war by, mainly, but not exclusively, the Bosnian Serbs, the United Nations and NATO were under considerable pressure to stop the fighting in Bosnia and come to the rescue of its besieged civilians. A debate developed over how to proceed. One school of thought held that the best way to stop the violence was through diplomatic initiatives; meanwhile, humanitarian assistance efforts could alleviate the immediate plight of the Bosnian people. Another school of thought held that the only way to stop the violence and gross abuses of human rights was through coercive measures, particularly through the use of military force.

In Bosnia, an unsuccessful attempt was made to marry both approaches. A humanitarian assistance operation based on the principles of a traditional peacekeeping operation—consent, impartiality, and use of force only in self-defense—was gradually turned into a coercive military operation. However, the measures necessary to ensure its success were implemented belatedly—only after the bluff of the United Nations and NATO had been called and considerable damage had been inflicted to their reputations. The turning point came in May 1995. The humiliating images of

UN soldiers tied to possible targets and used as human shields by an irregular army of Bosnian Serbs was too much to bear. Suddenly, Western credibility was at stake. Faced with a serious rift in the Atlantic alliance, the United States finally decided to put its weight behind international efforts to stop the war in Bosnia. It was only at this point that military coercion became a serious undertaking.

After briefly recalling the origins and the development of the war in Bosnia, this chapter examines those instances when military force was threatened or used by outside powers. Six cases are analyzed in detail. They illustrate the complexity of the "use of force" debate. Although this chapter focuses on the period before the signing of the Dayton Peace Accords, it also briefly examines the experience after Dayton and emphasizes the differences between the UN Protection Force (UNPROFOR) and the NATO/ U.S.-led Implementation Force (IFOR) established under the accords.

THE ORIGINS AND EVOLUTION OF THE WAR

The breakup of Yugoslavia entered the final stages in June 1991, when two of its six constituent republics—Slovenia and Croatia[1]—declared their independence.[2] Although the ensuing war in Slovenia lasted only ten days and marked the end of the Socialist Federal Yugoslav state, fighting in Croatia continued through the end of 1991.[3] Unlike the war in Slovenia, which was between Slovenes and the Yugoslav People's Army (JNA), the war in Croatia was between Serbs and Croats.[4] This war was initially fought on Croat territory, but shifted to the territory of Bosnia in early 1992.

Indeed, by the end of 1991, the war in Croatia had come to a standstill, and Slobodan Milosevic, the president of Serbia and power broker of the Federal Republic of Yugoslavia (FRY), and Franjo Tudjman, the Croat president, had agreed to the deployment of UN peacekeepers in the Krajina and eastern and western Slavonia.[5] Under the UN plan drawn up by Cyrus Vance, the UN secretary-general's special envoy to Yugoslavia, the JNA was to withdraw from Croatia. The Krajina and eastern and western Slavonia were to be demilitarized and were declared United Nations Protected Areas (UNPAs). They were regions where Serbs constituted the majority or a substantial minority of the population and where intercommunal tensions had led to armed conflict. Under the plan, local authorities and police would continue to function under supervision of the United Nations.[6]

Figure 3-1. Prewar Bosnia-Herzegovina

As for Bosnia, plans for its partition abounded during 1990 and 1991 in both Croatia and Serbia. Tudjman thought that partition of Bosnia might stave off war between Croatia and Serbia. If he could not keep the Yugoslav Republic together, Milosevic decided he wanted to secure the creation of a Greater Serbia and annex those territories in Bosnia and Croatia where Serbs lived.[7] However, a two-way partition of Bosnia would inevitably provoke a serious political, if not violent, conflict with the Bosnian Muslims, who made up 43 percent of Bosnia's population.

Bosnia was in many ways a microcosm of the former Yugoslavia. Following the multiparty elections in November 1990, three major political parties emerged. They were organized along ethnic lines and roughly reflected the ethnic composition of the republic. To defeat the communists and other reformists, they agreed to govern in a trilateral power-sharing arrange-ment.[8] However, Bosnian Serb and Croat political parties were closely associated with Belgrade and Zagreb, respectively. Local party leaders were never allowed to stray very far from the policy lines set out by Milosevic and Tudjman. Hence, when the war between Serbs and Croats broke out in the Krajina and eastern and western Slavonia, the Bosnian tripartite power-sharing arrangement was doomed to fail.

Signs of trouble appeared in Bosnia in September 1991, when Bosnian Serbs declared several regions in Bosnia to be autonomous. The divide between Bosnian Serbs and the Muslims widened on 15 October 1991, when the Muslim Party of Democratic Action (SDA) introduced a resolu-tion on independence in the Bosnian parliament. Serbs adamantly opposed to such a course decided to leave the parliament. Ten days later they formed their own parliament, which immediately voted in favor of remaining part of Yugoslavia. In the wake of the Bosnian Serb declarations, Bosnian Croat regions in western Bosnia also declared their autonomy.[9]

Faced with the gradual breakup of the Bosnian state, Alija Izetbegovic, the Bosnian president, called in November 1991 for the deployment of UN peacekeepers in those areas being patrolled by Serb militia.[10] However, Vance advised against it in the absence of consent from all local parties.[11] Bosnia was still part of Yugoslavia and deployment of peacekeepers needed the approval not only of Izetbegovic, but also of Milosevic. The latter fiercely opposed the idea of deploying UN peacekeepers in Bosnia; his war aims there had not yet been attained.

As a gesture to Izetbegovic, the United Nations decided to establish the headquarters of the UN force in Croatia in "neutral" Sarajevo. The United Nations hoped that the mere presence of the headquarters would have a calming effect on the Bosnian situation. The commanders of the 14,000-man UN force in Croatia arrived in Sarajevo in March 1992 at a time when Bosnia was still part of Yugoslavia. However, independence was imminent and so was the start of the war.

While a cease-fire in Croatia took hold and preparations for the deploy-ment there of the UN Protection Force were under way, the paramilitary gangs that had been active in the Krajina and eastern and western Slovenia moved into Bosnia, with the JNA and Croat military forces following suit.[12] The stage was being set for a continuation of the Serb-Croat war in Bosnia.

Milosevic and Radovan Karadzic, the Bosnian Serb leader, had threatened war in the event of Bosnia's secession from Yugoslavia. Izetbegovic,
however, had little choice. Remaining part of a Serb-dominated Yugoslavia
would have meant the marginalization of Muslim national identity. Par-
titioning the country along ethnic lines had equally little appeal to Izetbegovic. Although in terms of population the Muslims were the largest group
in Bosnia (43 percent), they were mostly city dwellers, scattered around the
country, and hence not in the possession of an economically viable and
contiguous piece of territory.[13] For Izetbegovic and other Muslim leaders,
the road to survival lay in defending a unitary Bosnian state. Partition had
to be resisted at all costs.[14] Tudjman, still weak militarily, was ready to pay
lip service to the idea of a unitary Bosnian state and was willing to support
a Croat-Muslim alliance against the Serbs. By choosing independence,
Izetbegovic knew he was starting a war that he would have trouble winning on the battlefield. Moreover, he was well aware of the feeble foundation of his alliance with the Croats. But the alternative was even less appeal-
ing. By declaring Bosnia an independent state and portraying it as a victim
of Serb and, to a lesser extent, Croat aggression, he attempted, throughout
the war, to enlist international support and provoke outside military intervention on Bosnia's behalf.

1992–93: Wavering International Responses

The war in Bosnia started in earnest after the European Community (EC)
recognized Bosnia as a sovereign state on 6 April 1992.[15] That same day,
Karadzic proclaimed the establishment of the independent Serb Republic
of Bosnia and Herzegovina, later renamed Republika Srpska. Serb attacks
initially focused on northeastern Bosnia. Zvornik was among the first towns
to fall. The assaults followed the patterns of earlier attacks in Croatia—
paramilitary units would enter villages under cover of the JNA. Sarajevo had
actually come under fire two days before Bosnia had been recognized as an
independent state. The Sarajevo airport, which was a prime strategic objective, was under JNA control. Bosnian Serb attempts to take the capital failed,
but Karadzic's forces managed to divide the city and seize control of the
districts of Grabvivca and Nedzarici. The siege of Sarajevo had begun. The
city would become the symbol for the struggle of a unitary Bosnian state.

By May 1992 the situation in Sarajevo became increasingly dangerous; it
prompted the United Nations to move most of its UNPROFOR personnel

to Zagreb. A small team of UN officers remained in Sarajevo to conduct cease-fire negotiations and to carry out humanitarian activities, but it had no official mandate to carry out such tasks.[16]

During the summer of 1992, the eastern, northern, and northwestern parts of Bosnia underwent systematic ethnic cleansing. Within a few months, Serbs occupied close to 70 percent of Bosnia. Hundreds of thousands of refugees fled into Croatia and Bosnian-government-controlled areas in Bosnia. The total number of refugees rose to 750,000 by the beginning of June 1992, over 16 percent of the Bosnian population.[17] Many started to seek refuge in Western European countries, which in turn looked for ways to keep the refugees within the confines of the Bosnian Republic.[18] With this in mind, a UN humanitarian operation was launched in Bosnia in June 1992.[19] The UN force in Bosnia was part of UNPROFOR Croatia and known under the same generic name. By July 1992, 1,200 UN troops had been sent to Bosnia to secure the Sarajevo airport and keep it open for a humanitarian airlift.[20] In September 1992 the humanitarian assistance mission was expanded to encompass the whole of Bosnia, and UNPROFOR was ordered to support efforts by the UN High Commissioner for Refugees (UNHCR) to deliver aid throughout Bosnia and to protect UNHCR convoys.[21] More UN troops were deployed, but the war continued to rage.

As the indiscriminate killings of civilians, concentration camps, and organized rape became known in the West, demands for forceful military action were articulated. During the summer of 1992, several Western leaders, including U.S. presidential candidate Bill Clinton and the former British foreign secretary David Owen, called for a military action that would punish Serb aggression and stop the war.[22] Failed European—especially, French—attempts to deploy a European interposition force in the former Yugoslavia in 1991 had made a military response in Bosnia dependent on the cooperation of the United States.[23] However, those in power in Washington were prepared only to issue rhetorical injunctions. The U.S. military fiercely opposed the use of force in Bosnia. The American military doctrine that had evolved since the Vietnam War called for the use of force only in situations where victory could be assured rapidly and where important U.S. interests were engaged.[24] British military leaders and policymakers were similarly afraid of being drawn into what they saw as essentially a civil war.[25] Plans to end the carnage in Bosnia were stifled by expansive military estimates of the number of troops needed to do the job.[26] In the summer of 1992, even air strikes were considered too risky and not feasible, given the mountainous and densely forested terrain in Bosnia.[27] To respond to the public outrage over the war in Bosnia, the UN Security Council declared the establishment of a no-fly zone over Bosnia in October 1992,[28] but it took until April 1993 for NATO to begin enforcing it.[29]

Diplomatic efforts to stop the fighting were equally unsuccessful: the Vance-Owen Peace Plan presented in January 1993 had met with opposition from both Serbs and Muslims.[30] Moreover, while the Europeans and the Russians backed the plan, the new Clinton administration gave it only grudging support, and many influential U.S. commentators castigated it for rewarding Serb aggression and ratifying ethnic cleansing.[31] Lastly, none of the outside players was willing to impose the plan on reluctant local parties. It was estimated that between seventy thousand and one hundred thousand outside troops would be needed to implement it. The United States was particularly disinclined to deploy ground troops without a plan that had been accepted by all local parties.

In the absence of such an agreement, the Clinton administration began to push a "lift and strike" strategy—it called for lifting the arms embargo on Bosnian government forces, while engaging in air strikes against the Bosnian Serbs, whom the administration had identified as the aggressors.[32] The Gulf War had instilled in more than one analyst a belief in the utility of air strikes as a tool either to deter aggressive action or to punish such action.[33]

Britain and France were adamantly opposed to such a strategy. They argued that it would bring about an intensification of the war and jeopardize the safety of their troops, which by this time had been deployed in Bosnia to help deliver humanitarian aid. Also, Europeans tended to apportion blame for the conflict more evenhandedly, and were at this stage primarily worried about keeping the war from spreading. Seen from the United States, the European position was a "mosaic of indifference, timidity, self-delusion and hypocrisy."[34] Europeans, on the other hand, pointed to the persistent U.S. refusal to deploy ground troops in Bosnia and the greater risks that the European soldiers would have to bear if air strikes were launched. U.S.-European relations deteriorated sharply over the course of 1993 as this debate unfolded.

With the opening of a second front in central and southern Bosnia in April 1993 and the demise of the Vance-Owen Peace Plan in May 1993, the

Croat-Muslim alliance collapsed. Serb advances and the attack on Srebrenica in April 1993 sent thousands of Muslims into an ever more
crowded central Bosnia. Delicate ethnic balances were tipped, and ethnic
conflict spread. Mate Boban, a Tudjman vassal who had created a one-
party ethnic state in western Bosnia—Herceg-Bosnia—sent out his militias
to ensure control over those territories where Croats lived. Together with
soldiers of the regular Croat army, they launched their own vicious ethnic-
cleansing campaigns. Heavy fighting between Croats and Muslims over the
city of Mostar commenced in May 1993.

The three-sided war that now unrolled in Bosnia was bound to lead to
the defeat of the Muslims. Despite the UN arms embargo, weapons had
trickled into Bosnia and Bosnian government forces enjoyed occasional
battle successes. However, their overall strategic position remained far from
enviable. Moreover, at the end of 1993, the Bosnian government was faced
with the loss of control over the Bihac enclave in the northwestern part of
the country. Fikret Abdic, the local Muslim leader who had excellent trade
relations with neighboring Croatia, declared the establishment of his own
state in September 1993, and he reached a separate peace agreement with
the Serbs in November 1993.[35]

Throughout 1993, calls for outside military intervention became more
vociferous in Western Europe and North America. However, Western governments could not agree on a course of action, and their reaction to the
war in Bosnia remained restricted to the passing of resolutions whose
implementation proved to be highly controversial and problematic.[36]

It was not until 1994 that NATO actually carried out air strikes on the
United Nations' behalf. Indeed, none of the Western allies was prepared to
intervene forcefully in Bosnia. Consequently, diplomatic efforts to reach a
peace settlement sputtered on. The Vance-Owen Peace Plan made way for
the Union of Three Republics plan[37] and the European Union (EU) Action
Plan.[38] Each partitioned the Bosnian Republic into three entities, but each
differed on specific borders.

1994–95: Air Strikes—The Deterrer Deterred

The Croat-Muslim war greatly profited the Bosnian Serbs and consoli-
dated their positions. The United States, which from the start of the war
had been an advocate of Muslim interests, believed that any future deal
in Bosnia could succeed only if the Muslim position was strengthened

and the Croat-Muslim war put to an end.[39] A revived Croat-Muslim alliance would permit weapons to flow from Croatia to Bosnia and provide it with the necessary strategic depth.[40] Croatia was persuaded to go along in exchange for support to regain the territories it had lost to the Serbs in Croatia.[41]

The breakthrough in U.S. diplomatic efforts to repair the Croat-Muslim alliance came after the February 1994 Sarajevo market attack. In its aftermath NATO issued its first serious threat to launch air strikes, but fell short of massively intervening on the side of the Bosnian government. Indeed, its decision to establish a heavy-weapon exclusion zone around Sarajevo was aimed at all local parties, including the Bosnian government. Wittingly or unwittingly, it convinced the Bosnian government of its precarious position: Bosnian Muslims and Croats signed a cease-fire on 24 February. This was followed by a federation agreement, signed on 18 March, which stipulated that the armed forces of both sides were to be under unified command. Finally, Izetbegovic and Tudjman signed an agreement that linked the new Bosnian federation to Croatia.[42]

Although the Croat-Muslim alliance proved its worth in military terms, the use of NATO air power proved to be highly problematic. In April 1994, NATO was challenged again. After attacking Serb positions to compel them to stop their assault on the safe area of Gorazde, UN soldiers were taken hostage and NATO was deterred from carrying out further air strikes. Gorazde drove home the point that NATO air strikes were not a viable option as long as UN peacekeepers were vulnerable to attack. This had already been fully understood by France and the United Kingdom, which had troops on the ground. The United States had a different view, but since it was not willing to commit ground troops, it focused on a negotiated solution to the war.

The stalled EU-UN negotiations were replaced by a Contact Group composed of the United States, France, the United Kingdom, Germany, and Russia. It held its first meeting in April 1994 and came forward with a new peace plan in July 1994. The plan called for 51 percent of Bosnian territory to go to the Croat-Muslim federation and 49 percent to the Bosnian Serbs. If the Serbs rejected the plan, economic sanctions on both Serbia and the Bosnian Serbs would be tightened. The United States additionally threatened to lift the arms embargo on the Bosnian government. If the Muslims rejected the plan, sanctions on Serbia would be eased. Whether the Contact Group was prepared to use military force to impose the plan on the combatants remained unclear.

Milosevic quickly supported the plan and threatened to sever political and economic ties with the Bosnian Serbs if they rejected it. The Bosnian Serb Assembly nonetheless did so on 3 August 1994.[43] Although Milosevic closed the border with Bosnia the following day and accepted the deployment of 100 international border monitors in exchange for an easing of the UN sanctions, the Contact Group was unsure about what to do next, apart from the tightening of economic and financial sanctions against the Bosnian Serbs.[44]

Leave, lift, and strike—that is, withdraw UN forces, lift the arms embargo on the Bosnian government, and launch air strikes on Bosnian Serb targets—as Owen had proposed in July, was an option no one contemplated seriously. Indeed, no one wanted the arms embargo to be lifted at this stage. The Bosnian government feared that lifting the embargo would not help them win the war against the Serbs; it might even provoke preemptive strikes. Moreover, since the signing of the Croat-Muslim federation agreement, the flow of arms to the Bosnian army had picked up steadily.[45] The British, French, and Russians had always been against lifting the arms embargo, because the conflict would subsequently intensify and their troops on the ground would be placed in greater danger. They had consequently threatened to withdraw their troops should the arms embargo be lifted. That said, pulling out was not an attractive option; it was believed that this would have serious humanitarian consequences and hence devastating domestic political repercussions in the West. Even the United States, which was vocal on this issue, had no real interest in lifting the arms embargo. Going down this path might have forced the United States to come to the assistance of withdrawing UN troops and a Muslim population being overrun by Serb forces. Similarly, a suggestion by Secretary-General Boutros Boutros-Ghali for UNPROFOR to hand things over to a multinational force run by Contact Group members received no support in Western capitals.[46]

By the end of 1994, the situation in Bosnia had deteriorated. Although Fikret Abdic's state had collapsed in the face of a joint Croat-Muslim offensive in August 1994, the attempt by Bosnian government forces to break out of the Serb-surrounded Bihac enclave failed. Bosnian government forces were rolled back by an alliance of Bosnian and Croat Serbs in

November 1994. The West was once again sharply divided about what to do. Initially, the United States favored strong military action against the Serbs in the form of a sustained air campaign. The British and French objected on the grounds that the Bosnian government forces had started the fighting around Bihac. Moreover, they thought that a strong Western military response would require additional ground troops—in particular, American ground troops—to protect the UN forces already on the ground. In the absence of such support, Europeans threatened to withdraw their troops from Bosnia. The limited NATO air strikes finally decided upon proved ineffective and were quickly called to a halt to save the lives of UN peacekeepers taken hostage by Serb forces. Bihac once again underscored the contradictory requirements of coercive operations, on the one hand, and humanitarian relief operations, on the other. In the latter case, NATO air strikes had limited utility—a point that Washington finally started to appreciate.[47]

Negotiations aimed at reaching a settlement of the conflict were consequently stepped up. The United States began to understand that concessions would have to be made to the Serbs. In December 1994, former U.S. president Jimmy Carter was given the Clinton administration's blessing to set off for Karadzic's headquarters in Pale and negotiate a cease-fire.[48]

The Bihac crisis had a big impact on U.S. and Western thinking: the involvement of the Croat Serbs was a vivid reminder that the war could spread back into Croatia. It demonstrated the importance of solving the problems that remained in the Krajina and western and eastern Slavonia as well. That Tudjman was getting ready to force a solution in the Krajina became apparent when, in January 1995, he demanded the withdrawal of all UN troops from Croatia. Although a compromise was negotiated and a restructured, smaller UN force was put in place in March 1995—the UN Confidence Restoration Operation in Croatia (UNCRO)—Tudjman's call led to a significant increase in tension in the region.[49] The UN force was helpless when, on 1 May 1995, Croatia attacked the UN Protected Area of western Slavonia. Neither Milosevic nor Karadzic came to the rescue of the Serbs in Croatia. This offensive sent thousands of Croat Serbs into Bosnia, where the December cease-fire had already broken down.

Fighting in Bosnia had picked up in March 1995, when Bosnian government forces initiated offensives around Travnik and Tuzla.[50] Bosnian Serbs countered with increased pressure on Sarajevo early in May.[51] Several UN heavy-weapon collection points were overrun. In response, NATO initiated air strikes against Bosnian Serb targets. Bosnian Serbs immediately seized 350 UN peacekeepers, tied them to potential targets, and brought them before television cameras. NATO air strikes were once again called off. Even so, the humiliating images of UN soldiers being used as human shields demanded a response. In an attempt to project resolve, a 10,000-strong Rapid Reaction Force (RRF) was dispatched to Bosnia.[52]

The endgame of the UN operation in Bosnia had started. UN troops and personnel were gradually withdrawn from all Serb-held territory, and plans were made to extract all UN troops from Bosnia. The eastern safe areas—Gorazde, Srebrenica, Zepa—were written off and plans to phase out UN troop deployments in these areas were put into effect. In Srebrenica, which came under Serb attack in July 1995, thousands of Muslims were slaughtered even though Dutch peacekeepers were still in place. Faced with uproar in the West after the fall of Srebrenica, the Western powers were forced to take a stand and demonstrate that they were serious this time. On 21 July, NATO declared that any attack on Gorazde—the last remaining safe area in eastern Bosnia—would be met with a "substantial and decisive" response.[53]

Meanwhile, Tudjman agreed to come to the rescue of Bosnian government forces in Bihac, and he prepared for a full-scale attack against the Krajina Serbs. His successful campaign in the Krajina, which started on 4 August 1995, changed the configuration of forces in Bosnia as well. Within four days, the Krajina Serb state had been swept away. Milosevic did not respond. The new balance of power in the region provided new opportunities for peace. The United States quickly took advantage of them. U.S. national security adviser Anthony Lake was dispatched to European capitals with a new peace plan.

An attack on the Sarajevo marketplace on 28 August 1995 provided NATO the excuse to show its resolve. A two-week bombing campaign against Serb targets followed. The NATO air campaign also helped Croat and Bosnian government forces, which came close to overrunning Banja Luka, the Serb stronghold in the north of Bosnia.[54] Defeating the Serbs was, however, not part of the deal that was being negotiated. The U.S. plan provided for the Serbs to be allotted 49 percent of Bosnian territory, as opposed to 51 percent for the Croat-Muslim federation. The battlefield successes of the latter made such a division realistic, but they could not be permitted to tilt the balance too much their way. Milosevic, who since 1994 had been in favor of a negotiated solution in Bosnia, had regained control over the Bosnian Serbs. His unwillingness to support the Krajina Serbs sent a powerful message to the Bosnian Serbs and demonstrated that they needed support from Belgrade, lest they run the risk of being overrun themselves. All of the pieces were finally in place for a negotiated end to the war in Bosnia.

1996: Peace at Last?

A comprehensive peace settlement was negotiated in Dayton, Ohio, from 1 to 21 November 1995 and signed in Paris the following month. The agreement stated that Bosnia would continue to exist as a single state with several federal institutions, including a tripartite presidency (one Bosniac,[55] one Croat, and one Serb), a bicameral legislature, and a constitutional court. However, the agreement also stipulated that the Bosnian Republic would contain two entities—the Federation of Bosnia and Herzegovina, administering 51 percent of the country's territory, and the Republika Srpska, administering 49 percent (see figure 3-2). Each entity would be allowed to develop special relationships with neighboring countries. Strong U.S. denial to the contrary, these provisions of the agreement constituted a de facto recognition of the partition of Bosnia.

The implementation of the military aspects of the agreement was to be monitored by IFOR, a heavily armed force of 60,000 soldiers, including 20,000 U.S. troops.[56] Its tasks were to provide a secure environment, ensure freedom of movement, maintain separation of forces, and monitor the cease-fire. The force was given a one-year time limit, and was slated to depart Bosnia on 20 December 1996. IFOR's rules of engagement allowed the robust use of force to ensure compliance with the military aspects of the agreement. Its civilian and political aspects were to be monitored by the High Representative for the Implementation of the Peace Agreement on Bosnia and Herzegovina, who could call on the assistance of the 1,700 unarmed members of the UN International Police Task Force (IPTF).[57]

Implementation of the military aspects of the agreement proceeded smoothly. The civilian aspects, particularly the orderly return of refugees, did not go as planned. Preparations for the organization of free and fair elections were also marred by the continuing presence of Karadzic at the head of the Serb Democratic Party (SDS),[58] and by Serb manipulation of voter registration lists. The latter led, in August 1996, to the postponement of the municipal elections scheduled for 14 September 1996.[59]

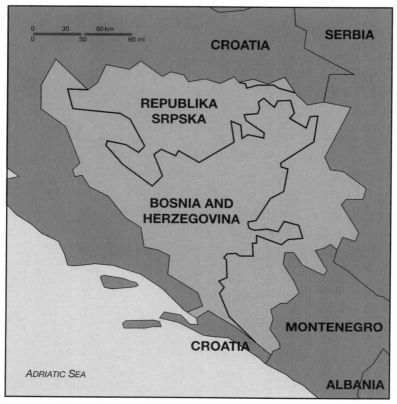

Figure 3-2. Dayton Peace Accords Partition of Bosnia

Despite increasing pressure on IFOR to assist in the implementation of the political and civilian aspects of the peace agreement, IFOR avoided getting involved in the return of refugees, the apprehension of war criminals, and other civilian law enforcement activities. The United States, in particular, was committed to a strict division between the military and civilian aspects of the agreement. Military force was to be used only to enforce the former and to stop the war from flaring up again.[60] That said, with the lack of progress on the civilian aspects of the Dayton agreement, it became increasingly likely that a follow-on force would have to be deployed after 20 December 1996 to avoid war from breaking out in Bosnia once again.

Recognizing the need for such a force, NATO decided in early December 1996 to keep a 35,000-strong Stabilization Force (SFOR) deployed in Bosnia for a new eighteen-month period.[61] Apart from its new name and its scaled-down size, the NATO-led mission remained essentially the same: deter a resumption of hostilities and provide a safe and secure environment for civil efforts. In November 1997 this force was extended indefinitely.

THE THREAT AND USE OF MILITARY FORCE IN BOSNIA

The use of military force in Bosnia was authorized by the Security Council in 1993 to enforce the no-fly zone, to defend UN personnel, and to deter attacks on UN safe areas. It was used for these purposes at several occasions during 1994 and 1995. Air strikes were also used to enforce the heavy-weapon exclusion zones established by NATO around Gorazde and Sarajevo in 1994. After briefly examining the enforcement of the no-fly zone, this chapter will focus on the use of military force to deter attacks on the safe areas and enforce the heavy-weapon exclusion zones.

Enforcement of the No-Fly Zone[62]

The first enforcement task entrusted to NATO related to the no-fly zone created by the United Nations in October 1992. In response to an aerial bombing of two villages east of Srebrenica, the Security Council decided on 31 March 1993 to extend the ban on military flights to cover flights by all fixed-wing and rotary-wing aircraft in Bosnian airspace. It also authorized NATO to use military force to ensure compliance with the ban.[63]

Before April 1993, the no-fly zone was repeatedly violated by helicopters carrying personnel. Although these violations continued after April 1993, the secretary-general could justifiably claim in 1995 that the no-fly zone had been largely successful in discouraging the use of Bosnian airspace for combat purposes.[64] Indeed, the creation of the zone had been primarily a symbolic gesture, given the limited contribution made by air forces to the fighting on the ground.[65] NATO reported few enforcement actions in response to violations of the zone. One occurred after the February 1994 market attack in Sarajevo. On 28 February 1994, four warplanes violating the no-fly zone were shot down.[66]

The blatant violation of Bosnian airspace by the Croat air force in August 1995, when it bombed positions in Serb-held Krajina, was not followed by NATO/UN reprisals. By that time, NATO had decided to take sides: its attacks on antiaircraft missile sites near Knin and Ubdina in Serbian-held Croatia were thinly disguised efforts to support the Croat offensive.[67]

Enforcement of the Safe Areas and the Heavy-Weapon Exclusion Zones

The second enforcement task entrusted to NATO was associated with the safe areas that were established following the Serb attack on Srebrenica in April 1993. The Security Council declared six safe areas in Bosnia: Bihac, Gorazde, Sarajevo, Srebrenica, Tuzla, and Zepa.[68] These cities were to be "free from armed attacks and from any other hostile acts that would endanger the well-being and the safety of their inhabitants and where unimpeded delivery of humanitarian assistance to the civilian population would be ensured."[69] UNPROFOR was to deter attacks against the areas, monitor local cease-fires, and promote the withdrawal of military or paramilitary units other than those of the Bosnian government. It would occupy some key points on the ground, and participate in the delivery of humanitarian relief.[70]

UNPROFOR's protection and deterrence role was to be based on its presence alone. UNPROFOR was not authorized to defend territory or engage in offensive military operations. It was authorized to use its weapons only in self-defense and as a last resort. Once it opened fire, it had to adhere to the principle of minimum force and stop firing when the opponent ceased fire. Retaliatory fire was prohibited.[71]

UNPROFOR's ability to carry out these tasks was restricted not only by its rules of engagement but also by the resources made available to it. Since UN member states were willing to authorize only an additional 7,950 troops, as opposed to the 34,000 requested, the operational scope of the safe area mandate had to be scaled back considerably.[72] UNPROFOR's limitations were supposed to be compensated for by the availability of NATO air power. Air strikes were authorized to defend UNPROFOR troops and deter attacks on the safe areas.

Air strikes to defend safe areas or to compel an end to attacks on safe areas were not to be confused with air strikes to protect UN personnel and troops. In UN operations, the latter were referred to as air support. Most of the air strikes that were authorized in Bosnia were in fact air support operations. These subtle differences—between protective and preemptive or punitive air strikes—were not always appreciated by those under attack. These differences were also lost on most public commentators. The problem was compounded when NATO imposed heavy-weapon exclusion zones around Sarajevo and Gorazde, in February and April 1994, and used air strikes to enforce them.

Because of deep disagreements within NATO regarding the use of air power, it took until August 1993, and only after persistent mortar attacks on civilians in Sarajevo, for NATO to formally express its willingness to carry out coercive air strikes—air strikes against those responsible for attacks on safe areas.[73] Although it was agreed that the UN secretary-general should be the one to authorize the use of Western air power in Bosnia, air strikes other than air support could be launched only with the concurrent approval of NATO's North Atlantic Council.[74] This dual-key arrangement, whereby the decision concerning the targets and the execution of air strikes was taken jointly by the military commanders of the United Nations and NATO, was a continuous source of friction between the two organizations. NATO was keen not to be seen as a subcontractor to the United Nations; the United Nations was keen not to be pushed into positions it could not sustain.

At first, air strikes were supposed to follow the same type of rules of engagement applying to UN ground troops. The principles of proportionate and minimum use of force meant that air strikes were limited to offending tanks or artillery pieces. These rules of engagement were changed in October 1994, when the United Nations and NATO agreed that only general warnings would be given to the offending party. Tactical warnings of impending air strikes would not be issued. Moreover, several targets, between three and four, would be authorized for each air strike. The principle of proportionality and the need to avoid unacceptable civilian casualties continued to be respected, however.[75]

Between 1993 and 1995, the United Nations and NATO threatened and used air power on fifteen different occasions. To assess the results of NATO's air threats and the effect they had on the behavior of the parties on the ground, six key cases from the fifteen listed in table 3-1 in which force was threatened or used are examined in detail below. These six cases responded to defining moments of the war in Bosnia and revealed major disagreements between and among Western powers on the use of military force.

Sarajevo: February 1994. The first explicit NATO air threat was issued after the Sarajevo market attack of 5 February 1994, which killed sixty-

Table 3-1. UN and NATO Air Threats and Strikes (13 April 1993–15 December 1995)

Date	Action
2 August 1993	In response to the shelling of Sarajevo, NATO issues a threat to launch air strikes.
9 February 1994	In response to the shelling of Sarajevo, NATO imposes a heavy-weapon exclusion zone of 20 kilometers and threatens air strikes in case of noncompliance.
28 February 1994	Four (Serb) planes violating the no-fly zone are shot down by NATO.
12 March 1994	After Bosnian Serbs attack French troops near Bihac, UNPROFOR requests NATO air support. The request is canceled because of bad weather.
10–11 April 1994	After Bosnian Serbs attack UN personnel in Gorazde, UNPROFOR requests NATO air support. NATO bombs several Serb targets identified by the United Nations. Serbs retaliate and take hostages. Air strikes are discontinued.
22 April 1994	In response to continuing Bosnian Serb attacks against Gorazde, NATO imposes a heavy-weapon exclusion zone and threatens air strikes. Parties reach an agreement. Despite partial compliance, no further air strikes are launched.
5 August 1994	After the seizure by the Bosnian Serb army of heavy weapons in the Sarajevo heavy-weapon exclusion zone, UNPROFOR requests NATO air strikes. NATO destroys one tankbuster. Following the air strike, Serbs return the weapons seized from the collection depot.
22 September 1994	After a Serb attack on a French armored personnel carrier near Sarajevo, UNPROFOR requests NATO air strikes. NATO attacks a Serb tank within the 20-kilometer exclusion zone.

21–23 November 1994	After attacks on Bihac from the Udbina airfield in Serb-controlled Croatia, UNPROFOR requests NATO air strikes. NATO attacks the airfield. In retaliation, Bosnian Serbs detain more than 400 UNPROFOR personnel. They are released on 13 December 1994. After an attack on NATO aircraft, NATO hits SAM sites at Otoka and Dvor on 23 December.
25–26 May 1995	In response to the Bosnian Serb seizure of heavy weapons in Sarajevo, UNPROFOR requests NATO air strikes. NATO attacks an ammunition depot at Pale. Serbs retaliate by shelling all safe areas, except Zepa. After the second NATO attack on the Pale ammunition dump, Serbs take about 350 peacekeepers hostage. The last soldiers are released in June 1995.
11 July 1995	After attacks on UNPROFOR personnel in Srebrenica, UNPROFOR requests NATO air support. NATO attacks ground targets identified by the United Nations, but the air strikes do not deter the Bosnian Serbs from taking the city.
26 July 1995	Following the fall of Srebrenica and Tuzla, NATO warns Bosnian Serb forces that further attacks on safe areas will be met with decisive force.
4 August 1995	NATO strikes two Croat Serb SAM radar sites. The U.S. Navy strikes antiaircraft missile sites near Knin and Udbina, ostensibly in self-defense; it gave a helping hand to the Croat offensive to take back the Krajina.
30 August 1995– 14 September 1995	After a Serb mortar attack on Sarajevo, NATO launches a two-week series of air strikes on a wide range of Bosnian Serb military targets (Operation Deliberate Force).
4 October 1995	NATO aircraft attack ground sites in self-defense after having been illuminated by fire control radars.
8–9 October 1995	In response to threats to UN personnel near Tuzla, UNPROFOR requests NATO air support. The attack on 8 October is unsuccessful in hitting its target. On 9 October NATO successfully attacks a Bosnian Serb command-and-control bunker.

Sources: NATO, NATO's Role in Peacekeeping in the Former Yugoslavia (NATO Basic Factsheet, no. 4, February 1996); and Boutros Boutros-Ghali, Report of the UN Secretary-General, S/1995/444.

eight people and injured over two hundred. Although the United Nations did not identify those responsible, the UN secretary-general asked NATO to "urgently prepare for air strikes to deter further such attacks."[76] Some NATO members believed that the time had finally come for NATO to act. Led by the Americans and the French,[77] NATO issued an ultimatum demanding that all heavy weapons be removed within ten days from an exclusion zone with a radius of twenty kilometers around the city, or otherwise be put under effective control of UNPROFOR.[78]

Meanwhile, the special representative of the UN secretary-general, Yasushi Akashi, and the British UNPROFOR commander in Bosnia, Lieutenant-General Michael Rose, initiated talks between the warring parties. Concurrent with NATO's ultimatum, a cease-fire and an agreement on the modalities of the withdrawal of heavy weapons, brokered by Akashi and Rose, were concluded between the Bosnian Serbs and the Bosnian government.

However, despite the agreement and NATO's ultimatum, the Serbs refused to hand over the weapons. In an attempt to break the deadlock, Rose suggested that the parties would not have to surrender their weapons as long as UN forces could keep an eye on them through electronic surveillance.[79] U.S. officials balked and insisted on a strict interpretation of NATO's ultimatum that all heavy weapons be put under "effective" UNPROFOR control.[80] Although the end of the ten-day ultimatum was rapidly approaching, compliance was far from assured.

UN officials were not the only ones dreading NATO air strikes. The Russian president, Boris Yeltsin, under severe pressure from ultranationalists at home, foresaw great difficulty justifying a NATO air attack on the Serbs. In a surprise move meant to inhibit NATO from carrying out its threat, he offered to station Russian troops in the Serb-held suburbs of Sarajevo from which the Bosnian Serb military had to withdraw its heavy weapons.[81] A meeting on 17 February 1994 between the Bosnian Serb leadership and Vitaly Churkin, the Russian deputy foreign minister and Yeltsin's special envoy to the former Yugoslavia, clinched the deal. Within hours, Ratko Mladic, the Bosnian Serb military commander, regrouped, withdrew, and handed over his heavy weapons to Russian UN peacekeepers. This allowed the United Nations to claim that all parties were complying with NATO's demands. The air strikes were called off. The crisis was defused.[82]

As David Owen has observed, the February 1994 crisis did not constitute "vindication of the threat of air strikes and a sign that Bosnian Serbs would crumble under threat." Indeed, as Owen has convincingly argued, "it was the Russians who had taken the threat of NATO air strikes seriously and . . . it was their decision to move their troops to Sarajevo which had forced Mladic to act over his heavy weapons."[83]

Some commentators have suggested that Washington's plan to go ahead with air strikes was really directed at the Russians. Russia appeared to be backtracking from its commitment to domestic political and economic reform, and some Clinton administration officials have been credited with arguing that air strikes in Bosnia could serve as a reminder to Yeltsin about the potential ramifications of military adventurism with respect to the "near-abroad."[84] This would explain why the United States considered NATO to be the ideal institution to press the issue of air strikes.[85] Indeed, although the Western allies believed that no new Security Council resolution was needed for NATO air strikes in Bosnia, the Russians, Chinese, and a number of nonaligned countries were of a different opinion. Had the decision to launch air strikes been left to the UN secretary-general, he might have felt compelled to request authorization from the Security Council, and that would have left the door open for a row with the Russians—and perhaps a Russian veto.[86]

The NATO threat was generally considered a success, and it prompted NATO and the United Nations to embark on a seemingly more robust peacekeeping campaign. The downing on 28 February 1994 of four Serb warplanes violating the Bosnian no-fly zone also contributed to this impression. For a short while, hopes that the Sarajevo model could be used in other parts of Bosnia flourished. However, the threat of air strikes was not a panacea, as Western leaders would quickly discover.

The most lasting and positive result of the NATO threat was not the weapon exclusion zone, which would be frequently violated, or the relative calm that descended on Sarajevo, but the involvement of the United States in the search for a solution to the Bosnian conflict. Its successful efforts in February 1994 to revive the Croat-Muslim alliance drastically changed the balance of power in Bosnia. U.S. acceptance, albeit reluctantly, of a plan that would divide Bosnia along ethnic lines also changed the dynamics of the negotiating process. Ever since January 1993, the Clinton administration had sought to maintain the moral high ground and had resisted the idea of partition. It had insisted that such an outcome would have rewarded Serb aggression and ethnic cleansing. Others, such as France and the United

Kingdom, were more concerned about bringing a quick end to the fighting. The latter conception started to take root in Washington as well in the spring of 1994.[87] Russia, through its clever diplomatic move, bought itself a permanent seat at the negotiating table. It also made sure that it would henceforth be consulted about possible air strikes.

Gorazde: April 1994. Gorazde was a Muslim enclave in eastern Bosnia surrounded by Serb-held territory. It had been declared a UN safe area in May 1993. The United Nations had eight military observers there. At the end of March 1994, Bosnian Serbs launched a ground offensive aimed at capturing the city. Attempts by the United Nations to stop the fighting were to no avail and did not receive strong backing from NATO. The American position was particularly ambivalent. On the one hand, the United States pushed for air strikes. On the other hand, commenting on the fighting around Gorazde and public calls for a strong NATO response, the chairman of the U.S. Joint Chiefs of Staff, John Shalikashvili, declared the threat of air power ineffective against infantry assailing Gorazde.[88] That the Americans were not willing to get militarily involved to stop Gorazde from falling was reaffirmed on 3 April 1994 when Defense Secretary William Perry stated, "We will not enter the war to stop that from happening."[89] Mladic must have been encouraged.[90]

On 10 April 1994, Gorazde was attacked from three different directions. Lieutenant-General Rose, threatening air strikes, warned Mladic to stop shelling the town; the attacks continued. In response, NATO aircraft dropped three bombs on a Serb "artillery command bunker," which consisted of a few tents. The Serbs were unperturbed and continued shelling the town. A second NATO air attack was ordered on 11 April 1994. Three armored personnel carriers and a truck were destroyed. Although a temporary lull in the shelling followed, Mladic was not deterred. He denounced the NATO air strikes, and argued that the United Nations and NATO had crossed the line of impartiality and chosen to support Bosnian government forces. To discourage further air strikes, Bosnian Serb forces took between 150 and 200 UN personnel hostage, launched an artillery and mortar attack on Tuzla, another UN safe area, and sealed off several heavy-weapon collection points around Sarajevo.

The final Serb assault occurred on 15 April 1994. Bosnian defenses collapsed quickly, and two British military observers, dispatched to Gorazde earlier to help direct NATO air strikes, were injured.[91] In order to evacuate them, Rose asked for air support, but Akashi, who had to authorize air support, denied Rose's request.[92] Akashi was in the midst of negotiations with Karadzic and might not have wanted to jeopardize his chances of reaching an agreement.[93] Moreover, he might have feared for the lives of the hostages. By 16 April, Serb troops stood at the gates of the town. Rose reiterated his request for air support in the afternoon. This time, Akashi agreed. However, bad weather forced NATO planes to fly low, and one British plane was struck by a surface-to-air missile (SAM) and crashed. The mission was abandoned. That evening, Akashi announced that the Serbs had agreed to a cease-fire and the release of the UN hostages in exchange for a halt to combat air patrols over Gorazde. The deal was brokered with the help of Churkin, the Russian deputy foreign minister who had proven his diplomatic nimbleness in February.

The cease-fire agreement notwithstanding, the following day Bosnian Serb troops entered and occupied the town. The Russians were livid. As before, they were eager to avoid NATO air strikes. However, when the Serbs moved to launch their final assault on Goradze after having promised that they would not, the Russian leadership and particularly Churkin were outraged. In defiance of nationalists back home, Foreign Minister Andrei Kozyrev publicly backed NATO's threat to bomb Serb forces if they did not withdraw from the town.[94]

Finally, on 22 April 1994 and after a request by the UN secretary-general, NATO called for (1) an immediate halt to the Serb attacks against Gorazde; (2) withdrawal of Serb forces to a distance of three kilometers from the town center by 24 April 1994; and (3) freedom of movement for all UN forces and humanitarian relief convoys. If the Serbs failed to comply with these three demands, air strikes would follow. In a separate decision, NATO also demanded the withdrawal of all heavy weapons to a perimeter twenty kilometers from the town by 27 April. It agreed that heavy-weapon exclusion zones around all of the other safe areas—Bihac, Srebrenica, Tuzla, and Zepa—could be established later if they were threatened by heavy weapons.[95]

The shelling of Gorazde nonetheless continued. NATO asked Akashi to authorize air strikes. He refused on the grounds that the Serbs had begun to withdraw their heavy weapons. Indeed, in a meeting in Belgrade, a new deal had been clinched. The Serbs agreed to a cease-fire around Gorazde and the withdrawal of troops and weapons. They also agreed to the deployment of UN troops in the area from which the Bosnian Serb troops would withdraw. Rose quickly dispatched 150 Ukrainians to Gorazde, who arrived in the night of 23–24 April.[96]

Even so, compliance remained far from complete. Small groups of Serb militia were encountered in the three-kilometer zone, and on 30 April an UNPROFOR patrol came under attack twice. The United Nations estimated that a total of 200 to 250 Serb soldiers and militiamen were present in the three-kilometer zone. UNPROFOR personnel were frequently harassed, and were from time to time detained and stripped of their equipment and weapons.[97] Bosnian Serbs were not the only culprits, in that Bosnian government forces also refused to demilitarize. No further air strikes were ordered, however. The heavy-weapon exclusion zone was difficult to enforce from the air and would have warranted a much larger number of ground troops, which nobody was willing to provide.

The offensive on the town resulted in several hundred dead and an equal number of wounded.[98] Tensions between the United States and its Western European allies were high during and after the Gorazde crisis. It brought the United Kingdom and the United States to the brink of a serious falling-out. Renewed U.S. calls for a lifting of the arms embargo did not ameliorate relations between the United States, on the one hand, and the United Kingdom and France, on the other. The latter threatened to withdraw their troops from Bosnia if the embargo was lifted. In fact, withdrawal was thought to have serious humanitarian repercussions and was, hence, not a real option for London and Paris for domestic political reasons.

Since the Americans were unwilling to get involved on the ground, the only option was to push for a diplomatic solution. The Contact Group—composed of the United States, Russia, France, the United Kingdom, and Germany—met for the first time on 26 April 1994. It seized the diplomatic initiative from David Owen and Thorvald Stoltenberg, the two cochairmen of the EU-UN Peace Conference on the former Yugoslavia that had been in existence since September 1992.[99]

Gorazde was a vivid reminder of the vulnerability of UN troops in Bosnia. The hostage-taking strategy devised by Mladic proved to be very effective in deterring the use of NATO air power. It was also the first time that UN-NATO action was undertaken against one particular side—the Serbs. Lastly, air strikes had brought the United Nations' primary mission —the delivery of humanitarian assistance—to a complete halt.

The clarity of purpose and the political unity that seemed to have emerged after the Sarajevo market attack of February 1994 blew apart when put to test. For the United Kingdom and France, Gorazde became a watershed, in that it demonstrated the differences between humanitarian relief operations and enforcement operations—peacekeepers could not be asked to engage in combat operations. France and the United Kingdom were not willing to engage in the latter without the United States, and they argued that within the confines of a humanitarian relief operation, air strikes were an inadequate and potentially dangerous military response. It put their troops on the ground at risk and made cooperation with local parties more difficult.

Bihac: November 1994. In October 1994, the Bosnian government army launched a large and initially successful offensive operation against Bosnian Serb forces in and around Bihac. However, in early November, with the help of Serbs in the Krajina, the Bosnian Serbs beat the Muslims back. By mid-November, they had regained most of the lost territory and launched an assault on Bihac itself. On 18 November, Krajina Serb forces dropped napalm and cluster bombs on southwest Bihac. Serb aircraft, which had taken off from the Ubdina airport in the UN Protected Area in the Krajina, carried out another attack the following day. In response, the Security Council extended NATO's authority to bomb targets to deter attacks on safe areas to targets in Croatia.[100] The airstrip in Ubdina was bombed on 21 November. Serb aircraft were not targeted, apparently to avoid civilian casualties.[101] In the days that followed, Bosnian Serb forces tried to shoot down NATO planes, which subsequently launched two attacks on Serb SAM sites in the area. Although Bosnian Serb forces started shelling Bihac, they stopped short of entering the town. NATO attempts to take out the Serbs' heavy weapons, which were pounding Bihac, were unsuccessful and were called off because they could have endangered UNPROFOR troops and civilian personnel. Indeed, in response to the NATO air strikes, Serb forces took 400 UN personnel hostage.[102] Moreover, a battalion of 1,000 Bangladeshi soldiers was trapped in Bihac. Humanitarian assistance efforts were brought to a halt throughout Bosnia.

At the start of the Serb counteroffensive, U.S. officials tried to persuade the French and the British to establish a heavy-weapon exclusion zone around Bihac and launch air strikes in case of noncompliance. However, Western Europeans did not believe such actions were warranted, given that Bosnian government forces had started the latest round of fighting. Moreover, the

British and the French believed that the U.S. plan would greatly endanger the lives of their peacekeepers. Indeed, the Americans had initially advocated air strikes at ammunition dumps and supply bases throughout Bosnia, not just Serb weapons in the neighborhood of Bihac.[103]

The rift over air strikes had severe repercussions on U.S.-European relations and NATO. Those with troops in Bosnia complained that the United States demanded action, but at the same time was adamant about not putting its own troops on the ground. Western European countries were also exasperated by the strong American support for the Bosnian government, which fed Muslim hopes that the Americans could be persuaded to intervene militarily, and which made the Bosnian government more difficult to deal with at the negotiating table. The French foreign minister, Alain Juppé, suggested that the United States was covertly supplying arms to the Bosnian government.[104] A particularly raw nerve was touched when the Clinton administration announced that as of mid-November it would no longer enforce the arms embargo against the Bosnian government and, more important, that it would no longer share intelligence on arms shipments with its allies, or use its ships to monitor the ban. The United Kingdom, which cherished its special relationship with the United States, was struck hard by the U.S. attitude.

Faced with the possibility of inflicting serious damage on the Atlantic alliance, the Americans backed off from their demands for air strikes and renewed their negotiation efforts. Similarly, Clinton's pledge in December 1994 to commit U.S. troops to an UNPROFOR rescue operation, if needed, helped to mollify the allies. Atlantic unity became more important than Bihac, particularly in view of the Clinton administration's interest in NATO expansion.[105] Former U.S. president Jimmy Carter was given the administration's blessing to visit Pale, and he successfully brokered a four-month cease-fire for the whole of Bosnia. At the same time, a new peace plan, based on the July 1994 plan of the Contact Group, was put on the table in January 1995.

Bihac was in many ways a repeat of the Gorazde episode, and it brought to the fore the same types of problems. The U.S. push for a strong military reaction can be explained by its frustration over the deadlock in its negotiating efforts. Since the Bosnian Serb rejection of the Contact Group plan in August 1994, nothing had happened on the negotiating front. Yet, without a willingness to share the risks that an imposition and enforcement of a heavy-weapon exclusion zone entailed, American calls for interdiction strategies were counterproductive. They deepened the split within NATO.

Sarajevo: May 1995. In March 1995 the cease-fire agreement between Bosnian government forces and Bosnian Serbs that had been concluded in January 1995 broke down. Fighting resumed first in the Bihac area, and spread gradually to central Bosnia, Tuzla, and Sarajevo. Following Tudjman's call for a withdrawal of UN troops from Croatia, military tension significantly increased in neighboring Krajina and western Slavonia. Pressure on Bosnian and Croat Serbs intensified when Tudjman attacked western Slavonia, which sent thousands of Croat Serbs into Bosnia.

Fighting around Sarajevo escalated in early May—heavy-weapon collection points were overrun, ten Bosnian Muslims were killed, and thirty were wounded following Serb mortar attacks. On 8 May, air strikes were requested by the British UN commander for Bosnia, General Rupert Smith.[106] However, Akashi and the commander of all UN forces in the former Yugoslavia, the French general Bernard Janvier, believed that air strikes entailed too many risks. They believed that they were aimed at enforcing the heavy-weapon exclusion zone rather than providing air support to protect UN troops.[107] The decision by Akashi and Janvier was challenged by the United States and the United Kingdom. The French did not voice objections.[108] When the request for air strikes was reiterated some two weeks later and following more mortar attacks that killed sixteen people and wounded at least sixty, as well as more violations of the heavy-weapon exclusion zone, Akashi and Janvier relented.[109]

On 24 May 1995 Smith called for a cease-fire and adherence to the heavy-weapon exclusion zone. When Bosnian Serbs failed to return the heavy weapons they had seized, a NATO air strike was ordered. The target was an ammunition dump near Pale. Undeterred, Serb forces surrounded more weapon collection points in the heavy-weapon exclusion zone and launched attacks not only on Sarajevo, but also on Bihac, Gorazde, Srebrenica, and Tuzla. NATO's second air attack on the ammunition dump near Pale prompted Bosnian Serb forces to take between three hundred and four hundred UN peacekeepers hostage. Some peacekeepers were used as human shields and tied to potential targets so as to discourage further NATO air strikes, which indeed they did.[110]

In response to the hostage crisis and the humiliating pictures of UN soldiers handcuffed and tied to bridges, energy facilities, and other targets, the

Western powers—pushed by the French—decided to deploy an extra 10,000 soldiers to protect their peacekeepers and to help the UN forces carry out their mandate.[111]

At first, it was unclear what the new Rapid Reaction Force was to do. Was it to prepare for a possible withdrawal of UN forces? Or, was it laying the groundwork for a more "muscular" or "robust" force that would not hesitate to use military force in response to an attack? Within UN circles it had become clear that a robust RRF could become fully operational only if vulnerable UN troops were redeployed. But the need to redeploy and concentrate troops in safe areas meant that they would be less able to carry out their primary mandate—the delivery of humanitarian assistance.

This made "muscular" peacekeeping an unattractive option to the UN secretary-general, Boutros-Ghali. In a report to the Security Council, he strongly argued against giving such a mandate to the UN troops. In his opinion, UNPROFOR could carry out only those tasks that had been agreed upon by the warring parties. If the Security Council wanted to provide the force in Bosnia with more muscle it could certainly do so, but in that case the force should come under national command, as had been the case with the UN forces in Somalia and Haiti. Boutros-Ghali argued that the United Nations had no capacity "to manage an operation that could involve combat on a considerable scale."[112] He was not willing to see the United Nations blamed for yet another round of Western mistakes.

The Western powers did not follow the suggestions made by the UN secretary-general. They were unwilling to take a decision at this stage—either to withdraw or to engage in a potential combat mission. For Clinton, both options posed problems. In December 1994, the United States had promised its allies to provide U.S. ground troops in case UNPROFOR had to withdraw from Bosnia; few believed that such a retreat could be carried out peacefully. By deciding that the RRF would become an integral part of UNPROFOR, the United States and the Western Europeans bought some time during which diplomatic efforts to halt the war by "peaceful" means could be continued.[113] Meanwhile, UN forces were redeployed to more defensible locations.

Once more, air strikes proved ineffective. However, unlike previous occasions, the allies seemed determined this time to solve the problem that had undercut their efforts in Bosnia. The endgame of the UN force—and the war in Bosnia—had started. Three main factors shaped the endgame. First,

Croat and Bosnian government offensives would change the balance of power in the region. Second, the realization in Washington that the problem in Bosnia would not go away on its own and that it could damage Clinton's chances in the presidential elections of November 1996 pushed American officials to take action. Third, Jacques Chirac, the new president of France, adopted a tougher stance toward the Serbs and called for stronger military measures to enforce Security Council resolutions.[114]

Srebrenica: July 1995. While the RRF was being deployed and UNPROFOR forces were being reconfigured, the Bosnian Serbs launched a full-scale assault on the safe area of Srebrenica. The fall of Srebrenica and the ensuing massacre of thousands of Muslim men under the gaze of the Dutch peacekeeping force was the most traumatic failure of the UN peacekeeping efforts in Bosnia to date.

The NATO air strikes that were finally authorized on 10 July came too late to stop the slaughter. By that time, the Serbs had entered the town and threatened to kill thirty Dutch peacekeepers who had been taken hostage.[115] Zepa, another UN safe area, fell soon thereafter.[116] The weak international response to the fall of the eastern safe areas is to be explained by the fact that the Western powers had given up on them: they were seen as indefensible, and they complicated efforts to devise a territorial settlement to the conflict. Even so, the United Nations and the Western powers could not just walk away from the enclaves. Such a retreat would have been a political humiliation and a public relations disaster. Moreover, the Muslims would have prevented such a retreat.[117]

Following the public outcry in the West over the Srebrenica massacre, troop-contributing countries met in London on 21 July 1995 and declared that any attack on Gorazde would be met with "a substantial and decisive response." The details of NATO's response to further attacks against the remaining safe areas were worked out later between NATO and the United Nations.[118] It was decided that NATO would respond "firmly and rapidly" if faced with an attack and that it would initiate air strikes following the direct request of the UN force commander on the ground.[119] Authorization from the civilian UN representative was no longer needed.

The French were a driving force behind NATO's response. Chirac had made strong public appeals for firm action. He even floated the idea of recapturing Srebrenica.[120] Although the latter idea was not pursued, his public declarations helped to spur the Americans along and to speed up the endgame decided upon in May.[121] Unlike other occasions when air strikes were used, Srebrenica highlighted dissension between the United Kingdom and France, on the one hand, and the smaller troop contributors, on the other. Indeed, the latter had no control over the operation in Bosnia, let alone over when and where to use air strikes. The smaller European countries, which had traditionally been at the forefront of UN peacekeeping operations, suddenly saw their influence diminished. Air support was rarely available to them when requested. Had a British or French battalion been based in Srebrenica, a "stand" might well have been taken there, and not in Gorazde where British troops were stationed. The lives of thousands of Muslim men might have been spared.

Sarajevo (Operation Deliberate Force): August 1995. On 28 August 1995, a mortar attack hit the Sarajevo marketplace in almost the same spot as in 1994. It was the pretext NATO had been waiting for. After having established that the attack came from Serb positions, NATO, as it had promised in July, responded "substantially and decisively" with a series of strategic air strikes designed to make Bosnian Serbs withdraw their heavy weapons from Sarajevo and lift the siege of the city.

Operation Deliberate Force dropped the West's pretense of impartiality. The United States finally decided to impose a peace. This was possible because UN troops had quietly been redeployed so as to make them less vulnerable to hostage taking. Moreover, by this time Croatia had successfully reconquered the Krajina and driven the Serbs out with the silent acquiescence of Milosevic and the Western powers.[122]

During the two weeks of Operation Deliberate Force (30 August– 14 September), NATO flew 3,400 sorties, including 750 attack missions against 56 ground targets.[123] Bosnian Serb air defenses, ammunition depots, artillery sites, and military communication facilities were among the first targets. While the NATO campaign took place in the eastern part of the country, Croat and Bosnian government forces began advancing and recovered huge chunks of terrain in the western part of the country. At the same time, negotiations in Geneva continued and an Agreement on Basic Principles for Peace was signed on 8 September 1995 by the foreign ministers of Croatia, Bosnia, and the Federal Republic of Yugoslavia.[124]

Despite the tough response, which bore no resemblance to the anemic strikes NATO had previously resorted to, NATO was not attacking the

Bosnian Serbs with overwhelming force. NATO officials insisted that their air strikes were graduated in nature. They were careful to avoid civilian casualties, and they steered clear of targets that would alter the strategic balance between Serb and Muslim-led government forces too dramatically.[125] NATO leaders insisted that air strikes would halt as soon as Bosnian Serb heavy weapons surrounding Sarajevo were removed. Even so, Mladic refused to withdraw these weapons for two weeks. Finally, on 14 September, he acquiesced, the Sarajevo airport was reopened, the siege was lifted, and the air strikes were suspended.

The cease-fire around Sarajevo did not immediately affect the rest of Bosnia. Fighting continued in the north, where Muslims and Croats were pushing the Serbs back.[126] At the end of September, the situation on the ground started to resemble the map drawn up by the U.S. team led by Richard Holbrooke, the assistant secretary of state and chief U.S. negotiator since August 1995. At this point, the Croat and the Bosnian government forces had to be reined in; they were not allowed to overrun the Serb stronghold of Banja Luka. The deal signed in Geneva on 8 September had promised 49 percent of Bosnian territory to the Serbs; it had not demanded Serb surrender. After a successful counteroffensive by the Bosnian Serbs in early October, a general cease-fire took effect on 12 October. A comprehensive peace settlement was negotiated in Dayton, Ohio, from 1 to 21 November and signed in Paris in December 1995.

The conventional wisdom about the September air strikes is that they were necessary to bring the Serbs to the negotiating table.[127] However, before the start of Operation Deliberate Force, Bosnian Serb leaders had already agreed to allow Milosevic to represent them in the negotiations.[128]

Milosevic had long been ready to cut a deal. UN economic sanctions were crippling Serbia. Milosevic wanted to see them lifted and was willing to compromise on Bosnia to bring this about. While air strikes were hitting Bosnian Serb targets, negotiations continued. Why Milosevic did not order Mladic to withdraw his heavy weapons sooner, especially after 8 September, may have been related to the Serb desire for assurances that Muslim Bosnian government forces not attack Bosnian Serbs from Sarajevo; Mladic was not going to withdraw his heavy weapons without such assurances. Another reason may have been that Milosevic was not adverse to having the Bosnian Serbs bombed as long as Karadzic paid the political price for this; his relations with the latter had deteriorated considerably.[129]

NATO itself had a stake in being seen as strong and decisive. The end of the Cold War had thrust NATO into an identity crisis. Its first attempt to adopt peacekeeping as a new mission had failed miserably. NATO's reputation had been damaged by its involvement in the former Yugoslavia, and it needed to be bolstered. A two-week bombing campaign served this purpose well.

Lastly, air strikes boosted Clinton's political domestic image. Bosnia had become "a cancer on Clinton's entire foreign policy—spreading and eating away at its credibility."[130] As a symbol of U.S. foreign policy, Bosnia projected negative images of U.S. power in the world. The time had come to act. Moreover, Clinton was pushed by a Senate that, under the guidance of Senator Bob Dole, had passed a resolution on 26 July 1995 that requested the president to unilaterally lift the arms embargo on the Bosnian government. Although Clinton could veto the Senate resolution, he was not certain he could sustain a veto.[131] A unilateral lifting of the arms embargo would send the United States on a new collision course with its NATO allies.

In sum, many factors came into play when the decision was made to launch sustained air strikes. The two-week air campaign was designed primarily to restore NATO's credibility and to reestablish American leadership. Had the latter's credibility not been so tattered, it is possible that the mere threat to use force could have obtained the same result. Indeed, once the United States decided to get involved and once it articulated a clear objective —to end the war—the conflict moved toward resolution.

Implementing Dayton: IFOR and SFOR

IFOR, the NATO Implementation Force of the Dayton Peace Accords, was composed of 60,000 heavily armed troops, including 20,000 U.S. soldiers.[132] Under overall military command of NATO's Supreme Allied Commander Europe (SACEUR), General George Joulwan, its task was to monitor the military aspects of the Dayton Peace Accords. These included providing a secure environment; ensuring freedom of movement; monitoring the ceasefire; and effecting the withdrawal and separation of forces. The Implementation Force was given a one-year time limit to carry out these tasks.

IFOR's rules of engagement provided for robust and immediate use of force to ensure compliance with the military aspects of the peace agreement. To demonstrate that IFOR was different from UNPROFOR, it knocked down checkpoints and moved into Serb-held areas in which

UNPROFOR had not previously been allowed to venture, within hours of its deployment. NATO also made clear that force protection was a top priority and that the decision to use force was delegated to the senior soldier present. Additional ships in the Adriatic and increased air activity over Bosnia emphasized that the protection of forces on the ground was a high priority.[133] In the event, IFOR never had to resort to such use of force.

The military aspects of the Dayton agreement were carried out with few difficulties. The most serious instances of noncompliance occurred in July and August 1996 when undeclared weapons and ordnance were discovered in the Republika Srpska. IFOR reacted to these situations by publicizing its preparations for a military operation and by engaging in talks with the responsible political authorities.[134] By redeploying its troops to larger bases and by advising UN and aid workers to go to those bases, or leave Bosnian Serb territory, IFOR paved the way for possible air strikes. In the end, the use of force was avoided. Most other noncompliance incidents involved the confiscation of small arms.

The only other significant difficulty concerned the departure of all organized foreign forces from Bosnia, particularly two thousand foreign Islamic fighters. It was a condition of the Dayton Peace Accords and of the U.S.-inspired program to equip and train the Bosnian army. Although these Islamic forces were to have left by 19 January 1996, it was only on 26 June 1996 that the United States declared that all foreign fighters had either left Bosnia or been removed from the government's army and security services. Moreover, while it was recognized that several hundred foreign Islamic fighters remained in Bosnia after that date, their potential for disturbing the peace was downplayed by IFOR officials.[135]

With the completion of its military tasks, IFOR increased its assistance to the UN International Police Task Force, the Office of the High Representative for the Implementation of the Peace Agreement on Bosnia and Herzegovina (OHR), and the Organization for Security and Cooperation in Europe (OSCE), the latter being responsible for the preparation of the September 1996 elections. Indeed, the implementation of the civilian aspects of the accords was problematic. Numerous human rights violations were reported by the OHR, there was no freedom of movement for civilians, and little headway was made with respect to the return of refugees. Although IFOR would assist these civilian agencies in areas such as planning, logistics, and communications, or by providing protection, it fell short of engaging in civilian law enforcement activities or apprehending war criminals. The U.S. military, weary of "mission creep" and worried about reliving its failed attempt to apprehend Mohammed Farah Aideed in Somalia in October 1993, stuck to a narrow interpretation of the force's mandate.

As a result, the high representative, Carl Bildt, was left to deal with the political and civilian aspects of the peace accords and to address the numerous human rights violations that took place with a small and unarmed police force. War criminals remained at large and "the forces of ethnic separation [remained] stronger than the forces of integration."[136] Given this climate, a continued security presence was believed necessary by most observers. However, the United States, in the midst of a presidential campaign, announced its willingness to continue to deploy troops in Bosnia only one month before its troops were slated to depart.

IFOR was on the whole a success—in that it suffered no casualties from combat, elections took place, and war was suppressed. Its success can be attributed to the clarity of its mission; the international community's political will to use military force in the event local parties became hostile; the consensus among the allies on the purpose of the mission and the means to achieve that purpose; and the availability of sufficient and adequate resources. These factors combined to make the threat to use force extremely credible. The involvement of U.S. ground troops also added immeasurably to IFOR's success. Last but not least, the interest of the local parties to cooperate and their desire to separate their military forces meant that IFOR encountered very little opposition while carrying out its tasks.

That said, Bosnia remained a volatile place. The September 1996 elections repeated the experience of the November 1990 elections and provided the nationalist parties with overwhelming victories. The persistence of problems with the civilian implementation of the Dayton Peace Accords fueled debate regarding the purpose of the mission. One school of thought held that IFOR's mandate needed to be extended to include the supervision of the civilian aspects of the agreements. It was argued that this would demonstrate that the international community was determined to see the accords succeed. It would also solve the chronic resource problems the civilian side of the operation faced. Another school of thought argued that people cannot be coerced into forming a cooperative relationship and that the most the international community could do was silence their guns. The fact that the peace agreement did not make a clear choice between rebuilding the Bosnian state and partition complicated the debate about the purpose of the mission. The political repercussions of this debate were serious; wavering would undermine political support for the peace process.

The NATO-led mission in Bosnia may ultimately fail because, from the beginning, it lacked a true exit strategy, linked to strategic and political conditions, not timetables. Even before U.S. troops were deployed in Bosnia, the Clinton administration insisted that they would have to leave on 20 December 1996. By announcing this exit schedule, Washington created a perverse incentive system. In the absence of progress on the civilian side, the U.S. exit timetable simply gave the warring parties a one-year rest period and an invitation to resume fighting once IFOR was withdrawn. The problems associated with this policy were not really recognized in Washington in November 1996, when the United States announced its participation in a follow-on force. Indeed, the United States again announced its exit timetable—June 1998. It was only in November 1997 that the United States realized exit strategies should not be driven by dates, and that it proposed the indefinite extension of SFOR.

On 21 December 1996, IFOR handed command to the NATO-led Stabilization Force (SFOR). SFOR involved initially up to 35,000 troops, 8,500 of whom were American.[137] Its mandate was similar to IFOR's. Its main mission was to deter the resumption of hostilities and provide extra time—eighteen months—for political reconciliation and economic reconstruction. As was the case for IFOR, SFOR was a NATO-led force authorized by the Security Council under Chapter VII of the UN Charter.[138] Like IFOR, it operated with the formal consent of the local parties.[139]

Even so, IFOR and SFOR were not peacekeeping forces. They were sent to Bosnia because the United States decided to impose peace on the combatants, not because the parties invited the West in. The consent of the local parties was obtained through coercive diplomacy and forceful persuasion. Hence, once the international force is withdrawn, it is likely that the consent and cooperation of the parties will evaporate.

SFOR will have to contend with the same types of problems that confronted IFOR. Pressure for it to participate in the apprehension of war criminals increased. This question was closely linked to the larger question of the viability of a multiethnic Bosnian state and the willingness of outside powers to keep their troops in Bosnia to prevent war from breaking out again. Without any clear choices, international troops will likely need to remain in Bosnia indefinitely.

CONCLUDING REMARKS

The threat and the use of force in Bosnia have been both a failure and a success. Initially, the threats and actual use of military force in Bosnia were a failure, primarily because military force was used in a halfhearted way and without a clear political goal. Different and shifting analyses of the conflict in the former Yugoslavia, and its impact on European and international security, led to different and conflicting policy recommendations and to confusion about the type of operation the United Nations and NATO should undertake—peacekeeping, peace enforcement, "muscular" peacekeeping, humanitarian assistance, or none at all.

European powers were unable to create a consensus among themselves on the different policy options, the United States was unwilling to act in Bosnia, and the United Nations could do little without the support of its member states. Without a clear political goal, assembling a coalition that could carry out and sustain the operation in Bosnia proved difficult.

Consequently, UNPROFOR was chronically understaffed and underequipped. Unlike IFOR, UNPROFOR was never endowed with forces that could generate a credible deterrent. To deter attacks against the safe areas, the Security Council in June 1993 authorized an increase of only 7,950 troops in UNPROFOR's force level—34,000 additional troops were deemed necessary by UN military commanders.

To compensate for the lack of UN troops on the ground, NATO air strikes were made available to the United Nations. However, commanders on the ground were leery of air strikes, which risked dragging them into a war they were not given the means to fight. They knew that their troops were highly vulnerable to attack—they were dispersed and incapable of securing their lines of communication. Hence, UN commanders requested air support only in the last resort and primarily to protect their own troops. Pressure to request air strikes to help defend the safe areas was, however, always strong. NATO had set a precedent for such strikes in February 1994 when it established a heavy-weapon exclusion zone around Sarajevo. However, preemptive or coercive air strikes were not without risks—as the UN forces found out in April and November 1994.[140] UN ground forces were easy targets for attack, a point that was not lost on the Bosnian Serbs. By taking UN personnel hostage, the Bosnian Serbs managed to deter most future air strikes and made the idea of safe areas a farce.

In July 1995, after the fall of Srebrenica and after the extent of the slaughter of Muslim men became known, the belief that UN troops contributed to better local conditions could no longer be sustained. At that point, the international community's policy options were reduced to two choices: withdrawing all UN troops or imposing a peace settlement on the warring parties. The latter option had become far less risky, because the Croatian offensives in the summer of 1995 had cleared the way for such a settlement. Moreover, the United States had finally committed itself to end the war in Bosnia.

For the first time, a clarity of purpose emerged. The deployment of IFOR left no doubt about the type of operation the troops were engaged in. IFOR commanders stated clearly and loudly that implementation of the military aspects of the Dayton Peace Accords was nonnegotiable. While deployed with the formal consent of all local parties, IFOR's robust assets meant that, unlike UNPROFOR, it could coerce any recalcitrant party to abide by the agreement. Indeed, whereas UNPROFOR had been a peacekeeping force unable to function as a combat force, IFOR was a combat force that was to function mainly as a peacekeeping force. Threats to use force by IFOR leadership were credible and effective.

The military strategy devised before August 1995 was flawed in that it depended on air power to carry out a job for which air power was ill suited. This problem was overcome when sufficient numbers of ground troops were sent to Bosnia as part of IFOR. The fact that IFOR was not challenged militarily by the local combatants shows how important it is to have troops on the ground and in sufficient numbers.

However, as 1996 drew to a close, and as the implementation of the civilian and political aspects of the Dayton Peace Accords lagged, questions regarding the objectives of the mission of the IFOR force resurfaced. They were temporarily laid to rest with the decision to deploy a follow-on force, but they did not disappear. Without active cooperation by all parties, and without a clear choice for either partition or integration, the requirement for a strong outside military presence remained to deter the outbreak of hostilities.

In sum, international intervention in Bosnia, after the summer of 1995, was a success. However, this success continued to be undercut by an arbitrary exit schedule imposed on the NATO-led operation. Successful operations are more likely to be guided by true exit strategies than by arbitrary timetables. International interventions should be driven primarily by the strategic and political requirements of the local situation—not by domestic political concerns of the intervenors. In November 1997 the United States finally acknowledged as much when it proposed an indefinite extension of NATO forces in Bosnia.

4

SOMALIA

In 1992 Somalia became one of the first victims of post–Cold War chaos.[1] This was a distressing turn of events since its birth as a nation in 1960 (when colonial British Somaliland merged with Italian Somalia) had been greeted with hope and optimism. Unlike many other states emerging from colonialism, Somalia was a pastoral society whose people generally shared common ethnic, linguistic, and religious (Sunni Muslim) identities. Unfortunately, neither Britain nor Italy had prepared the Somalis for independence, and this ultimately led to the dissatisfaction of the populace as the fledgling government failed to meet rising expectations. Somalia's prospects for a successful transition to democracy dimmed even further when President Abdirashid Ali Shermarke was assassinated by a bodyguard in October 1969. The power vacuum was quickly filled when General Mohammed Siad Barre, Somalia's army commander, initiated a brutal coup and assumed control of the government.

During the Cold War, Barre simultaneously courted both superpower camps. He was most successful in these efforts with the Soviet Union, and in 1974 leaders of the two countries signed a friendship and cooperation agreement. Barre also maintained relations with China and with other Islamic countries (joining the League of Arab States in 1974). Relations with the West quickly cooled, and eventually all aid from the United States was stopped when Somali-flagged vessels were discovered delivering Soviet arms to Vietnam. When in 1977 the Soviet Union sided with Somalia's longtime antagonist, Ethiopia, during a border dispute, Barre ejected the Soviets and began courting the United States. Unfortunately for Barre, whose regime had a terrible human rights record, President Jimmy Carter was in the White House and he had made human rights one of the mainstays of his foreign policy.

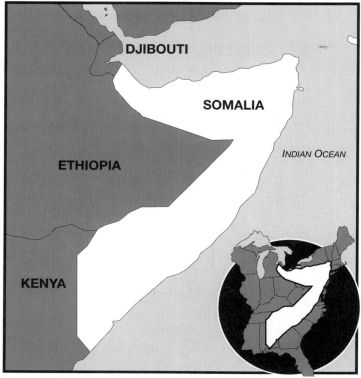

Figure 4-1. Somalia

Barre's fortunes changed, however, when a combination of factors—including the overthrow of the Shah of Iran and the Soviet invasion of Afghanistan—resulted in the Carter Doctrine, which stated that the United States would defend the vital oil reserves in the Persian Gulf. This doctrine made Somalia's geographical position (see figure 4-1) strategically important. (Slightly smaller in area than Texas, Somalia has a coastline nearly three-fourths as long as the U.S. eastern seaboard.) Somalia fared even better under the ideologically driven Reagan administration, receiving a major portion of U.S. aid in Africa between 1980 and 1987—most of which was stolen or misspent by the corrupt Barre regime. Warming relations between the United States and the Soviet Union, and mandatory cutbacks stemming from Gramm-Rudman-Hollings deficit reduction ceilings, resulted in a drastic cut in aid to Somalia in the late 1980s.

CIVIL WAR BEGINS

Without a major source of money to fund patronage and keep rivals in line, Barre became a prime target for rebel forces. Centered around clan and sub-clan structures (see figure 4-2), these rebel militias began to define civil order in Somalia. The first organized movements began in 1981 among the clans in the north (the Majerteen and the Isaaq), which had been particular targets of Barre's brutality. The Majerteen clan formed the Somali Salvation Front (SSF), which later became the Somali Salvation Democratic Front (SSDF),[2] while the Isaaq formed the Somalia National Movement (SNM) in London. Both groups were supported by Ethiopia. They were later joined by disaffected groups in the south. The most powerful of these southern groups was the United Somali Congress (USC), which was formed in 1989 by the Hawiye clan, the country's largest. It split in 1991 into sub-clan groupings. One group consisted of moderate businessmen and political leaders from the Abgal sub-clan who attempted to find a peaceful solution to the growing crisis.[3] One of the businessmen, Ali Mahdi Mohammed, soon found himself thrust into a leadership role and contending for power with the Habr Gadir sub-clan faction headed by General Mohammed Farah Aideed. Despite these internecine power struggles, the push to oust Barre intensified. Fighting in the capital of Mogadishu became so fierce that the United States abandoned its embassy in early January 1991 and three weeks later Siad Barre fled the capital.[4] For the most part, however, these events were overshadowed internationally by Iraq's invasion of Kuwait.

Even more chaos ensued after the rebel factions began fighting among themselves. In 1992, following Barre's ouster, Aideed formally launched the Somali National Alliance (SNA) with headquarters in Mogadishu. In fact, the four strongest Somali factions were all centered in major cities. Aideed and Mahdi divided Mogadishu between them, while Bardera was controlled by the Somali National Front (SNF), led by Barre's son-in-law, General Mohammed Hersi Morgan, and Kismayo was controlled by the Somali Patriotic Movement (SPM), led by Colonel Ahmed Omar Jess. Hoping to isolate themselves from the fighting in the south, northern Somali clans

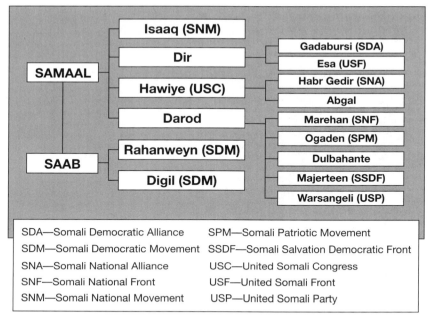

Figure 4-2. Somali Clan Structure and Associated Factions

declared their independence—a status that was never recognized by the international community.

The bloodshed in the south, which cost an estimated 30,000 lives in less than four months, spread outward, engulfing the countryside and killing tens of thousands more Somalis. It was particularly brutal in the area known as the Triangle of Death, between Kismayo, Bardera, and Baidoa (figure 4-3). Roving bandits began to systematically pillage farms and villages, taking crops, livestock, and other possessions. Local economies were destroyed; hundreds of thousands of Somalis were displaced; and the civil society of the country completely collapsed. The food supply, which had been disrupted by thieves, was further exacerbated by a two-year drought that gripped east Africa.

Under these circumstances, food became a source both of power and of conflict, since it had replaced currency as the major source of wealth and

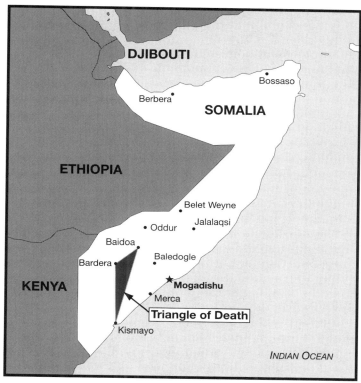

Figure 4-3. Somalia's Triangle of Death

exchange. Relief agencies were overwhelmed with the extent of the disaster and helpless to deal with the banditry. Often a mother would obtain food only to be shot dead and robbed shortly after leaving a food station. Weapons were everywhere. Somalia became an armed camp because of its Cold War legacy and as a result of intense clan fighting. The most deadly and mobile weapons were "technicals"—light trucks carrying mounted assault rifles. They received that designation because relief organizations were forced to pay protection money to local hoodlums in order to get any supplies to areas of great need; for the record, such payoffs were written off as "technical assistance."[5]

The roads to neighboring countries were soon clogged with walking corpses looking for refuge and food. During late 1991 and 1992, the most vulnerable—women, children, and the elderly—died by the hundreds of thousands. Nevertheless, the Organization of African Unity (OAU) opposed UN intervention because there was no Somali government to request such assistance. Others, such as the Organization of Islamic Countries, did press Secretary-General Perez de Cuellar for action. With the approval of his newly appointed successor (Boutros Boutros-Ghali), the secretary-general dispatched the under secretary-general for political affairs James Jonah as a special envoy to Somalia. Shortly after taking office, Boutros-Ghali visited Somalia and, upon his return to New York, encouraged the Security Council to take urgent measures to end the fighting.

In January 1992 the council adopted Resolution 733, which established a total arms embargo, urged an immediate cease-fire, established a humanitarian relief effort, and resulted in an invitation to interested parties from the secretary-general to come to New York for discussions. Aideed and Mahdi had emerged as the principal leaders in the most war-torn part of Somalia, and both laid claim to the presidency. Mahdi had had himself sworn in as the interim president shortly after Barre fled the capital. Aideed claimed national leadership because he saw himself as Somalia's liberator, and he believed this entitled him to be its future leader. Mahdi accepted Resolution 733, but Aideed expressed reservations. Nevertheless, both factions accepted the invitation to New York and sent representatives to consultations held in February. None of the principals attended.

Getting Aideed and Mahdi to the negotiating table was not easy, especially since they had carved out for themselves the same political territory and ambitions. From January to October 1991 they prepared to fight, but according to Mohamed Sahnoun, who was appointed the secretary-general's special representative to Somalia in 1992, Aideed and Mahdi were waiting for an outside mediator to broker a compromise. When no mediator appeared, fighting broke out in Mogadishu with a vengeance. The capital was gutted, a thousand people per week were killed, and all municipal government and services were destroyed. The fighting went on for more than a year before Aideed and Mahdi met face to face in December 1992. Although "they embraced warmly and seemed genuinely dedicated to ending the civil war," personal rivalry and a desire for power made all attempts at negotiating a peaceful solution futile.[6]

With Yugoslavia and Cambodia drawing most of the world's attention, fighting continued to rage in Somalia. Although six Security Council resolutions were passed and two major conferences about Somalia held during 1992, no action was taken because of OAU opposition. Exacerbating the problem, in 1991 all UN agencies fled Somalia, leaving behind only four humanitarian relief agencies—the International Committee of the Red Cross (ICRC), Save the Children UK, the International Medical Corps, and Médecins sans Frontières—to deal with the growing tragedy. This perceived abandonment by the United Nations soured all UN-Somali relations from that time forward.

In addition, Aideed harbored personal animosities toward the new secretary-general, Boutros Boutros-Ghali, whom Aideed believed was behind Egypt's strong support of Siad Barre while Boutros-Ghali was Egyptian minister of state for foreign affairs. The secretary-general was equally unenamored with Aideed. These powerful animosities complicated the United Nations' role in Somalia over the next two years. The fact that the world generally, and the United Nations specifically, focused on the problem in Mogadishu alienated factional leadership in the hinterlands and intensified the rivalry between Aideed and Mahdi. Because of his superior strength and military expertise, Aideed believed he could achieve a military victory and therefore opposed any cease-fire or UN involvement. Mahdi understood his weaker position and favored both a cease-fire and a UN role.

In February 1992 the two sides agreed in principle to a cease-fire, which was signed in March. Enforcement of this agreement, like many others that were to follow, was sporadic. The following month, the Security Council passed Resolution 751 authorizing the secretary-general to deploy fifty UN military observers to Somalia to monitor the cease-fire and pave the way for a larger 500-man contingent, which would help secure the passage of relief convoys. It also allowed the secretary-general to appoint a special representative to Somalia and (as noted earlier) he chose Mohamed Sahnoun, a respected, but highly outspoken, Algerian diplomat. Sahnoun was effective, but too independent for UN headquarters in New York. "In the seven months of his tenure Sahnoun held meetings with almost all of the faction leaders; he believed he would be able to win their confidence by responding seriously to their concerns and offering the perspective of a sympathetic outsider."[7] Sahnoun's primary focus was on reconciliation, and he attempted to include clan elders and women's groups as well as those who controlled the militias.

UNOSOM I

The mission authorized by Resolution 751 was designated the UN Operation in Somalia (UNOSOM) and was approved as a classical peacekeeping mission. In principle this meant that consent by all parties was required. In reality it meant obtaining the consent of Aideed and Mahdi. Aideed still believed that UN involvement interfered too greatly with Somali sovereignty (not to mention his freedom of action). As a result, he opposed the deployment of UN observers if they were authorized either to wear uniforms or to bear arms. He finally relented, however, giving his permission for the operation in June. Unfortunately, in mid-June a Russian aircraft bearing UN markings crashed after delivering arms and newly printed Somali currency to Mahdi in north Mogadishu. Suspecting a UN conspiracy, Aideed immediately withdrew his consent for the UN mission. The crisis was averted only after he was convinced that the aircraft, which was under lease to the UN's World Food Program, was pursuing an entrepreneurial venture arranged by its owners.[8] The incident nearly derailed the entire peace process. The fifty Pakistani observers finally arrived in July in the midst of a worsening crisis and with Aideed limiting their freedom of movement.

The secretary-general reported in July that 4.5 million people, including 1 million children, were suffering from malnutrition and at risk of dying. There were now 350,000 refugees in Kenya and thousands more in Ethiopia. Over 300,000 people were internally displaced within Somalia and, along with food, they lacked basic sanitary facilities and potable water. An unimaginable health crisis was looming on the horizon.[9] UN efforts, often criticized as being disorganized, slow, and insufficient, were hindered because so many of its assets were involved in humanitarian crises elsewhere, such as in Bosnia, Bangladesh, and northern Iraq.

In the United States, politicians began concentrating on presidential and congressional campaigns. They soon learned that the domestic economy, not foreign policy, dominated the minds of most of the electorate. Even though President George Bush was forced to concentrate on domestic issues, he was not unmoved by the situation in Somalia. The U.S. ambassador to

Kenya, Smith Hempstone, Jr., graphically cabled Washington about conditions in the area.[10] Pressured by Congress,[11] the media, and an activist African UN secretary-general, Bush dispatched the U.S. director of the Office of Foreign Disaster Assistance, James R. Kunder, to Somalia. Kunder reported that the crisis in Somalia was the "single worst humanitarian crisis in the world."[12]

OPERATION PROVIDE RELIEF

Spurred to action, the UN Security Council passed Resolution 767, which called for the urgent deployment of the troops authorized in Resolution 751, approved airlifts of emergency supplies to Somalia, and sent an advisory team there to make further recommendations. President Bush authorized a U.S. airlift to deliver humanitarian relief supplies and to transport the 500 peacekeepers. In August 1992, U.S. Central Command (USCENTCOM) began Operation Provide Relief. During the next seven months, U.S., German, Canadian, and Belgian aircraft flew nearly 2,500 missions delivering 28,000 metric tons of food and supplies.[13] Also in August 1992, the Security Council adopted Resolution 775 authorizing an additional 3,000 personnel, bringing the total to 3,500, to protect the movement and distribution of relief supplies.[14]

The initial contingent of 500 Pakistanis finally was deployed to Somalia during September and October, but the battalion found itself sequestered at the airport, only moving when granted permission by local authorities (that is, Aideed). It soon became clear that airlifts alone would not end the crisis. Bandits continued to loot supplies and, despite the increased food arriving in country, the portion of assistance actually reaching the people who needed it most dramatically dropped. Lawlessness was aggravated by the fact that no police or judiciary system was functioning in Somalia. To address this situation, Mohamed Sahnoun convened a September meeting of twenty Somali clan leaders and intellectuals in the Seychelles. They discussed practical ways of improving the flow of relief supplies as well as addressing longer-term national reconciliation.

That same month Jan Eliasson, the new under-secretary-general for humanitarian affairs (UNDHA), led a UN fact-finding delegation to Mogadishu. As a result, a donors conference was called in Geneva to develop an action plan. Presented by Sahnoun, the Hundred-Day Plan for Accelerated

Humanitarian Assistance outlined methods of increasing relief assistance and reenergizing Somali agriculture. The plan had two broad purposes: to deal with the refugee problem and to strengthen Somali civil society. The plan was adopted and Philip Johnston, president of CARE USA, was asked to implement it. By now over twenty-five nongovernmental organizations (NGOs) were operating out of Mogadishu, and coordinating their efforts was a major challenge. When Johnston arrived in October, he confronted this challenge by establishing a collaborative organization where NGOs could meet to discuss common plans and objectives.

In the meantime, Sahnoun worked actively to develop clan and community leadership, but tensions grew between him and UN headquarters. He answered to three under-secretaries—for peacekeeping operations, political affairs, and humanitarian affairs—and received a letter from the secretary-general instructing him to stop criticizing the United Nations. Frustrated by this situation, as well as by UN bureaucracy, Sahnoun resigned. His replacement, Ismat Kittani, was never able to develop the same trust and relationships with the feuding factions, thus exacerbating the crisis. It soon became clear that UNOSOM I was doomed to failure.

THE UNIFIED TASK FORCE

With the U.S. presidential election just around the corner, President Bush, in his October 1992 address to the UN General Assembly, responded to widespread criticism of U.S. inaction in Somalia and Bosnia by promising a more proactive relationship with the United Nations. Even though he lost the election the following month, he made good on his promise by offering to send U.S. troops to Somalia to stabilize the situation and provide a secure environment for the delivery of humanitarian assistance. On 3 December 1992, the Security Council, in Resolution 794, accepted the U.S. offer to lead a coalition force and authorized member states, operating under Chapter VII of the UN Charter, to help secure delivery of relief supplies. The coalition would fall under U.S. not UN control, and its troops could act (including forcefully) without local consent if necessary. The following day, President Bush, Secretary of Defense Dick Cheney, and Chairman of the Joint Chiefs of Staff General Colin Powell indicated that the United States was ready to commit U.S. forces to what it designated Operation Restore Hope. Lieutenant General Robert Johnston of the U.S. Marine

Corps was immediately designated Commander Joint Task Force (CJTF), Somalia, and assigned overall command of the multinational mission, termed the Unified Task Force (UNITAF). President Bush also appointed Robert Oakley, a former U.S. ambassador to Somalia, as a U.S. special envoy. En route to his new assignment, Oakley first met with the secretary-general and then attended a humanitarian conference in Addis Ababa convened by Jan Eliasson the first week of December. At the conference Oakley was able to explain the upcoming U.S.-led operation.

For most of the relief workers in Somalia, the announcement about UNITAF was good news. Since early fall, "virtually every field representative suggested a multilateral armed intervention, although some did not want a unilateral U.S. intervention."[15] One exception was the International Committee of the Red Cross, which "has an immutable rule, of great long-standing, that any vehicle bearing its emblem may carry no arms or weapons whatsoever."[16] The ICRC cast a jaundiced eye at the upcoming intervention and "was obliged to hire Somali guards for their personnel and facilities and to reject UNITAF military protection."[17]

Almost immediately differences arose between the United States and the United Nations over the exact mission of UNITAF forces. From the U.S. perspective the mission was twofold: establish a secure environment for the delivery of humanitarian aid, and then expand that environment into a framework that would allow turnover of the mission to a UN force. The United States intended to do this using only enough force that faction leaders would realize that order would be restored with or without their assistance. The Unified Task Force eventually involved twenty nations and reached a troop strength of more than 38,000. Even so, the United Nations believed the U.S. approach was too circumscribed, and in an 11 December letter to President Bush, Boutros-Ghali called for UNITAF to conduct a full-scale disarmament program, which the United States resisted. In February 1993 the United Nations rejected a compromise U.S. proposal that would have allowed UNITAF to begin a broad program of "voluntary" disarmament that had been agreed to by all of the Somali factions. The proposal was rejected by the United Nations on the grounds that UNITAF should implement it on its own authority without involving the United Nations. Had agreement been reached, many of the unfortunate events that occurred later might have been prevented since Aideed's militia, as well as others, would have been much weaker. Acting on its own, however, would have reinforced the faction leaders' belief that U.S. leadership had made the UN role moot. Ismat Kittani, the secretary-general's special representative, was still officially charged with the responsibility of negotiating a settlement. Oakley found himself having to constantly remind the Somalis that Kittani's role was crucial since the United States would be leaving the United Nations in charge.

UNITAF operations began with the landing of 1,300 Marines to secure Mogadishu's port and airfield on the night of 8 December. Oakley had labored the previous two days with faction leaders to ensure there would be no opposition to the landing. It was during these meetings that he first made use of coercive inducement tactics. In urging them not to interfere with the landings, he reminded "them [about] the massive firepower used so effectively by the United States during Operation Desert Storm."[18] Except for the embarrassment of having fully combat-equipped Marines hitting the beaches in the glare of media lights, the landing proceeded flawlessly.

At a meeting called by Oakley on 11 December, Mahdi, Aideed, and their followers embraced and there seemed to be genuine relief that the United States had done for them and the Somali people what they could not do for themselves—stop the cycle of death and destruction. At that meeting, the two antagonists developed and signed the Seven Point Agreement. One of the goals of UNITAF then became holding the parties to it by "using the implicit threat of coercion . . . as well as persuasion [and] pressure."[19]

UNITAF forces operated using a liberal set of rules of engagement (ROE), which allowed them to determine when and how much force should be used to guarantee mission success. "ROE embody two of the most important principles from operations other than war—restraint and legitimacy—because the use of force must be seen as supporting the ends for which the operation was begun in the first place."[20] In addition to self-defense, UNITAF ROE listed four basic "noes" its troops could enforce: no technicals, no banditry, no roadblocks, and no visible weapons. UNITAF commanders were authorized to use "all necessary force" to carry out their mission, but in keeping with the humanitarian aspects of the operation, this did not translate into "shoot on sight" authorization. General Johnston instructed his troops "to challenge and approach" those breaching UNITAF rules and to use appropriate force only if offenders failed to voluntarily comply with them. The rules for self-defense included the following:

When U.S. forces are attacked by unarmed hostile elements, mobs and/or riot-
ers, U.S. forces should use the minimum force necessary under the circumstances and proportionate to the threat.[21]

In order to avoid serious confrontations, UNITAF's leadership believed
the first step in establishing a secure environment for the movement of
relief supplies, as well as for the forces themselves, was to remove all heavy
weapons from the streets of Mogadishu. Oakley clearly explained the ROE
to faction leaders and threatened that any technicals spotted after December 26 were subject to immediate capture or destruction. Both factions
complied by moving most of their technicals into compounds.

That does not mean UNITAF went unchallenged. In mid-December
1992, three technicals decided to test UNITAF's will by firing on a
patrolling Marine helicopter on the outskirts of Mogadishu. They were
immediately eliminated by Cobra helicopter gunships. Shortly after
Christmas one of the smaller factions tried to take advantage of the restrictions imposed on Aideed and Mahdi and unleashed an artillery barrage
into the Mogadishu suburbs. The faction's weapons were located and eliminated by Marine helicopter gunships. Following each of these incidents,
UNITAF leadership conferred with the factions and explained why their
weapons were eliminated. At no time were lines of communication closed.
Thus, UNITAF leadership complemented political dialogue with balanced
and limited applications of force.

In February, Mahdi, who preferred the political path to peace, turned his
technicals over to UNITAF. Aideed, on the other hand, quietly moved his
out of cantonment and into the countryside. The ROE were also used as jus-
tification to confiscate weapons encountered during the course of UNITAF
operations. "These rules combined with the demonstration of overwhelming force by UNITAF, resulted in few challenges to forcible confiscation
efforts—and surprisingly few acts of violence directed against U.S. forces."[22]

This remarkable accomplishment was enhanced by a "joint security
committee," which the factions themselves established. It met daily until the
United Nations took over the operation on 4 May. At these meetings, not
only were the factions able to continue their peace dialogue, but UNITAF
personnel were able to explain what was going to happen or why certain
events (such as the confiscation of weapons) had occurred. These meetings
took place even when the situation between Aideed and UNITAF became
tense. Although Aideed exploited any opening, he generally respected the

rules and disowned as bandits any of his men who were captured by UNITAF for breaking them. The success of this approach was noticeable immediately. By the end of December, Mogadishu, which had been a ghost port, was the second-busiest harbor in Africa.

The fact that UNITAF did not aggressively seek to disarm the factions caused some difficulties. Since its headquarters was in the southern portion of Mogadishu, very near to Aideed's headquarters, it was rumored that UNITAF had a special relationship with Aideed—a rumor he encouraged. A complaint concerning this favoritism was raised at a January conference on national reconciliation held in Addis Ababa. When on the following day UNITAF attacked Aideed's forces and destroyed a weapons storage compound that had fired on Marine Corps patrols despite repeated warnings, the rumors of favoritism were put to rest—at least temporarily. Aideed soon started complaining that attacks against his compound and weapons caches were aimed at weakening him relative to Mahdi. "However, UNITAF was careful to balance raids on Aideed's weapons caches with similar raids on those belonging to Ali Mahdi and other factions in the Mogadishu area."[23]

Outside Mogadishu UNITAF secured the abandoned Soviet airstrip at Baledogle, the second longest in Africa. From that base UNITAF forces were much closer to the heart of the famine and away from the chaos and fighting in Mogadishu. With facilities in both locations under UNITAF control, forces from other coalition partners were soon deployed.[24] General Johnston also built upon the NGO collaborative group started by Philip Johnston (no relation), and formed the Civil-Military Operations Center (CMOC) in late December. It helped, but coordination between the military and NGOs still proved difficult. Later, when the CMOC became too large to successfully discuss high-level policy decisions, Oakley formed a separate group, the Executive Steering Committee, to deal with policy.

UNITAF's original plan was to deploy into the countryside in about fifty days. Many NGO field representatives, however, pressed for a much quicker deployment, noting that local violence and banditry were increasing. General Johnston, however, refused to act prematurely and moved only when conditions and available forces permitted. Even so, deployment was completed a month ahead of schedule. UNITAF divided its forces into eight humanitarian relief sectors (HRS) centered around major cities: Mogadishu (United States), Baledogle (Morocco), Kismayo (United States and Belgium), Baidoa (United States), Bardera (United States), Oddur

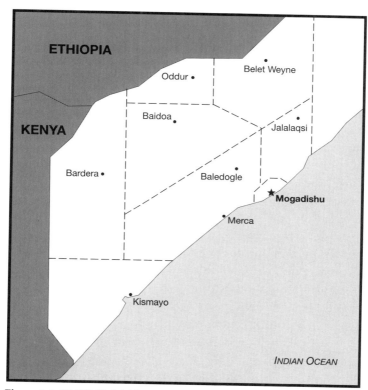

Figure 4-4. UNITAF's Initial Humanitarian Relief Sectors

(France), Belet Weyne (Canada), and Jalalaqsi (Italy). A ninth HRS was later added at Merca under U.S. command. As figure 4-4 shows, the area covered by these nine sectors was less than a third of the country. This deployment pattern reflected the limited scope of UNITAF's mission, which was to end the famine and stop the dying in the south. Conditions were much better in central and northern Somalia.

UNITAF was able to accelerate its deployments because it established a formidable military reputation and because advance political preparation created a near absence of organized resistance. Oakley, assisted by the U.S. Liaison Office (USLO) and USAID's Office of Foreign Disaster Assistance

(OFDA), was instrumental in preparing the sectors to receive forces. The first sector established was around Baidoa, and the U.S. team flew in a day ahead of the Marines to explain why they were coming. Once in place, UNITAF forces followed the pattern established in Mogadishu of banning technicals and confiscating arms caches belonging to local bandits. No attempts were made to confiscate personal firearms from nonthreatening civilians. UNITAF also encouraged the people to establish local rule and instituted a series of town meetings to facilitate this goal.

During one of the town meetings held ten days after UNITAF's arrival, local Somalis, including members of Aideed's SNA group, urged the Marines to eliminate a group of heavily armed "bandits" operating out of a walled compound on the outskirts of Baidoa. UNITAF forces went to confront the group, which surrendered without a fight, and confiscated four technicals along with dozens of lighter weapons. Two days later Aideed dispatched a representative who admitted to Oakley that the group had been an ill-disciplined SNA militia and asked for the weapons to be returned. Oakley refused. After that, the SNA identified its heavy weapons to UNITAF and placed them in approved cantonment areas to avoid confiscation. Within weeks the chaotic situation in Baidoa had turned around, and it became the model for expansion into the other humanitarian relief sectors. From Baidoa, UNITAF forces moved north and west to Oddur, Belet Weyne, and Jalalaqsi, then moved southward to Kismayo and Bardera.

Not all areas were as successful as Baidoa. In the Kismayo sector, fighting continued to erupt between Morgan's SNF militia and SPM allies of Aideed led by Colonel Jess. On 24 January 1993, Morgan attacked SPM troops who were guarding their weapons in a UNITAF-approved cantonment area thirty-five kilometers outside Kismayo. UNITAF leadership decried this violation of the Addis Ababa agreement, which the SNF had signed, and the following day UNITAF helicopter gunships and armor counterattacked, destroying technicals and artillery and forcing SNF forces to withdraw. Throughout this period, U.S. officials maintained discussions with Morgan, who appeared reconciled to keeping his forces outside the city. But on 22 February, a number of his men, disguised as herders bringing animals to town, slipped past UNITAF forces, recovered hidden weapons, and attacked SPM leaders in Kismayo. Oakley and Johnston then issued ultimata to Morgan and Jess telling them to withdraw their forces from the area. Even though both sides complied, it was erroneously reported that Morgan had defeated UNITAF forces and occupied Kismayo.

Aideed, knowing that UNITAF forces were superior to Morgan's, believed the reports and suspected UNITAF complicity. As a result, his supporters attacked the Nigerian contingent in Mogadishu.[25] The attack was conducted at a busy intersection near the headquarters that housed personnel from UN agencies, NGOs, and numerous media, all of which thought the attack was proof that the operation was coming apart. This was exactly the impression Aideed wanted to promote. He saw UNITAF's encouragement of local councils and the disarmament of his and allied militias as weakening his position. Within two days, however, order was restored in the capital. "The real message, Oakley told the press, was that Somalia and UNITAF had proved strong enough to withstand the confrontation without losing their primary focus on reconciliation and reconstruction and without being dragged into renewed factional conflict."[26] Aideed was then told that he would be held personally accountable for further anti-UNITAF disturbances —there were none.

The cat-and-mouse game played with Aideed reflects the balancing act that must be accomplished during any coercive inducement operation. The desired objective is to obtain a specified behavior without having to revert to force. The pressure applied must be delicate and subtle. Therefore, force should be applied only "as the direct result of carefully considered command decisions, decisions that calibrate the nature of the threat with the balance that must be struck between often competing requirements of restraint and the security of the force."[27] As one group of analysts noted about Somalia:

> [W]hile it was an old peacekeeping dictum that a show of force can avoid the need to use force, it was also true that to be credible there had to be a willingness and competence to use force and threaten it on an on-going basis.[28]

They also noted that U.S. strength not only "evoked fear, but also confidence in its capability."[29] This confidence in U.S. competence was important for both sides. For the factions, knowing that threats can be carried out under most circumstances makes compliance easier and inducement much more effective.[30] The perception of competence also makes it easier to attract more and better-equipped coalition partners since they understand their own forces will not be subject to as much risk as they might be otherwise.

By almost all measures of effectiveness, UNITAF was an unqualified success in meeting the first portion of its original mission—securing the distribution of relief supplies and stopping the dying. Others (especially at the United Nations) wanted to build on this success and saw the moment as an opportunity for Somalia to sort out its political future and end the chaos that had resulted in the total collapse of the country. A widespread concern of the population, the United Nations, and NGOs was that pre-UNITAF conditions would return as soon as the U.S.-led operation was handed to the United Nations. "It would be a tragedy," Boutros-Ghali stated to the Security Council, "if the premature departure . . . of the Unified Task Force were to plunge Somalia back into anarchy and starvation."[31] Hence, there was tremendous UN foot-dragging in arranging for a turnover of the operation.

One criticism that has been raised concerning UNITAF, and that ultimately had a tremendous negative effect on UNOSOM II, was that UNITAF was remiss in not tying its humanitarian mission to a broader political objective. The United States viewed UNITAF as a paramedic mission, which could offer first aid and apply a tourniquet until the patient could be placed in the care of a competent physician. The United States was not interested in getting involved with Somalia's long-term rehabilitation.

By concentrating its operations in southern Somalia (especially around Mogadishu), UNITAF made Aideed and Mahdi the prominent players in Somalia. This was resented by faction leaders outside Mogadishu as well as by much of the rest of the population of Somalia. The unintended result was a growing opposition to the intervention by individuals who might have otherwise supported it. Walter Clarke decries this fact and avers:

> Fundamental to all [peace operations] plans is the need to establish a political dynamic that seizes political initiative from warlords and other miscreants and places it under the control of positive elements of society. . . . Just as humanitarian policy must focus on the victims of chaos, so must international political doctrine be just and favor political victims rather than their oppressors.[32]

Since the purpose of using military force is to buy time for the other instruments of policy to work, one group of analysts recommends that the focus should be above the level of the factions.[33]

One final comment needs to be made about UNITAF; it concerns "mission creep." This pejorative term first appeared in the military's lexicon during the Somalia operation, and refers to requests to carry out activities not specifically mentioned in the mission's mandate. The importance of avoiding mission creep has garnered such widespread support within the military that it has quickly achieved the status of an operational principle. When one looks at how the term has since been applied, however, it has more often than not been used as an excuse to avoid having to do something that appears difficult or distasteful (like disarmament). Mission tasks have always had to be adjusted during the course of an operation, and this will not change. Unfortunately, those planning complex emergencies are now so focused on avoiding mission creep that it has resulted in "mission shrink."[34] The military would do well to delete "mission creep" from its terminology.

Transition to UNOSOM II

The wrangling between the United States and the United Nations did not go unnoticed by potential contributor nations. It had been anticipated that most of the forces assigned to UNITAF would transition to UNOSOM II. But the Australians and Canadians announced withdrawal dates in May and June, and participation by the Belgians and Indians remained uncertain. Pakistan's participation depended on a congressional waiver allowing U.S. military assistance to be given to its troops. The United States, France, and Italy all appeared ready to stay the course. With little progress being made toward transition, the United States began pressing the United Nations to name a force commander.

The UN Secretariat was well aware of Congress's growing displeasure with the United Nations and its unwillingness to have U.S. forces assigned under foreign command. To allay some of these fears, the well-respected Turkish lieutenant general Çevik Bir was designated as the force commander in February 1993. The United States promptly insisted that Major General Thomas Montgomery, U.S. Army, be appointed as his deputy. As February rolled into March, transition planning remained stalled. With the United States picking up more than 75 percent of the cost of the UNITAF operation, and with UN resources already strained to the limit with large operations in the former Yugoslavia and Cambodia and smaller missions in Angola, Mozambique, and elsewhere, UN hesitancy to take on another large peace enforcement operation was understandable. As one group of analysts noted, "The US had genuinely unrealistic expectations that the UN could replace it in the field. This mistake was fatal for UNOSOM II and for the United States, which not only would be unable to withdraw, but would be drawn more deeply into Somalia under a much more complex mandate."[35]

For its part, the United States offered to keep some of its logistical resources in place during the transition and contribute a 1,300-man Quick Reaction Force (QRF) to provide protection for UNOSOM II troops. Unfortunately, the QRF was not placed under General Bir's command but reported directly to USCENTCOM in Florida. Supplemental U.S. forces, which would arrive later, also used a similar command arrangement, which proved both confusing and disastrous. The United Nations did not receive prior notification of their operations (which were often at cross-purposes with those of the United Nations), and, as a result, the United Nations was unable to conduct contingency planning to support those operations (which would prove fatal in the October Ranger fiasco). By mid-March, transition planning had begun in earnest as Bir and Johnston began a six-week, side-by-side turnover.

On 26 March 1993 the Security Council passed Resolution 814, a Chapter VII mandate officially authorizing the creation of UNOSOM II. The new mandate was broader than that of either UNOSOM I or UNITAF. Not only was UNOSOM II supposed to protect the delivery of humanitarian relief, it was also supposed to consolidate, expand, and maintain a secure environment for the advancement of economic assistance and the political reconciliation of the government. In other words, the United Nations was "to assist Somalis in rebuilding their nation from the ground up."[36] As was noted earlier, the secretary-general had lobbied unsuccessfully to get UNITAF to disarm the country, and Resolution 814 specifically addressed the need for disarmament and demobilization of militia units. In recognition of the fact that this was an ambitious mandate and that continued U.S. support was essential to its success, retired U.S. Admiral Jonathan Howe was selected to replace Kittani as the secretary-general's special representative.[37]

UNOSOM II was also to help implement the agreement reached at the National Reconciliation Conference held in Addis Ababa in March. The conference achieved two major results—it renewed the commitment by all fifteen Somali factions in attendance to implement the nationwide cease-fire and disarmament plan, and it agreed to a framework establishing the Transitional National Council (TNC).[38] The transition period was to last two years. As always, however, the devil is in the details, and the Addis

Ababa Accords failed to determine TNC membership, the geographic definitions of political regions, or the future of northern Somalia, which was still pressing for independence. The success achieved by UNITAF could be continued only by a rapid and effective follow-up plan (including expanding into areas where UNITAF had not deployed), but the accords were not self-enforcing and, at the time of the agreement, a follow-on UN force was authorized but not yet assembled.

Because the accords lacked crucial details and its enforcement was questionable, the consent given by the factions at Addis Ababa was at best provisional and at worst ineffectual. "The factions, each watching and waiting for the other to disarm, were either too suspicious and frightened to do so or, in some cases, had no real intention of doing so. They feared both serious attacks from their enemies and the loss of future power and position, and Aideed's SNA prepared to challenge the UN peacekeepers as soon as U.S. forces had departed."[39] In addition to these internal challenges, differences between the United States and the United Nations about what needed to be done before UNITAF could transition to UNOSOM II were growing.

The United Nations was convinced that only the United States had the wherewithal to effectively disarm and demobilize the militias—a condition the United Nations felt was necessary to guarantee both the safety of follow-on personnel and mission success. In addition, Boutros-Ghali wanted the United States operating throughout Somalia, not just in the south. In fact, the secretary-general did not even want to start planning for UNOSOM II until the United States accepted this broader mandate and began carrying it out. But despite a change in administrations, the U.S. course of limiting the geographical scope of the operation and avoiding general disarmament activities was set and would not change. As a result, Boutros-Ghali continued to insist until late April 1993 that it was premature and dangerous to begin planning for a UN takeover. He was so certain that UNITAF could be pressured into implementing a "coercive disarmament" plan that the United Nations never prepared a plan of its own.[40]

The United States continued to resist forceful disarmament and only collected weapons it believed posed a significant threat to friendly forces. The result was a stress on eliminating heavier weapons. Thus, between December 1992 and February 1993, UNITAF collected 1.27 million rounds of light ammunition along with 2,255 small arms. UNITAF also confiscated 636 heavy weapons, including tanks, mortars, grenade-, rocket- and missile-launchers, and surface-to-air missiles. Ambassador Robert Oakley insisted that "had UNITAF pursued a policy of full-scale disarmament, it would have needed a much greater force for the mission and would almost certainly have become embroiled in a series of local clashes."[41]

Boutros-Ghali was generally right about disarmament, and at least the heaviest weapons should have been confiscated and destroyed. "Successful disarmament did not require the removal of every weapon in the country; sufficient disarmament could have been conducted to weaken the warlords enough to make them more reliant on a process of political reconstruction."[42] The fact that UNITAF generally eschewed disarmament "diminished the impact of powerful forces as a credible threat and Somalis then felt both free and compelled for survival to continue to live by the gun."[43] In other words, UNITAF's policy helped undermine the credibility and effectiveness of follow-on forces.

Howe's arrival and Oakley's departure signaled a sea change in how events would transpire. Howe sided immediately with the secretary-general and attempted to convince his high-level contacts in Washington to keep UNITAF forces in place until June and expand their mission. The UNITAF commander, however, insisted that his mission was complete and that his forces were not equipped to handle a new, broader mission. He was supported by USCENTCOM, General Joseph Hoar, the Joint Chiefs of Staff, and, eventually, the president. UNITAF forces that were not being reassigned to UNOSOM II began their withdrawal. The last 340 U.S. combat troops departed on 3 May, leaving behind over 3,500 U.S. service personnel involved in support roles (mainly in communications and logistics). UNOSOM II was officially under way.

Unfortunately, as UNOSOM II took over, all its personnel had not deployed and many of those in place were ill equipped to meet the challenges they faced. There had been virtually no guidance from either the secretary-general or the Security Council on how to proceed. Even though it was assumed that UNOSOM II forces would operate using the same ROE as UNITAF, precise rules of engagement had not, in fact, been agreed upon.

The military situation was not entirely bleak, however. General Bir actually had more troops under his command in Mogadishu than had General Johnston. The areas that were most in need were between Kismayo and Bardera and from there over to the Kenyan border. Admiral Howe, however, found himself in much worse shape on the civilian side. His staff was small and demoralized, and he immediately asked for help from both the United States and the United Nations. The United States responded by sending a personnel management team from Washington, but the United Nations knew nothing about the team until just before it arrived in Mogadishu. Howe's unique access to both Washington and New York eventually resulted in confusion among members of the Security Council, troop contributors, and Somalis as well as in Washington and New York. It was never clear who exactly was calling the shots—Howe, New York, or Washington.[44] In the long run, it was ironic that Howe's access, which should have been a strength, became a liability. This occurred because, by the time Howe arrived, the United States was focusing on its withdrawal from Somalia and Howe was placed in the uncomfortable position of trying to help the United Nations persuade the United States to delay its departure. Thus, Howe admits that "whether the United States should have provided the SRSG [special representative of the secretary-general] for the period of transition between UNITAF and UNOSOM II is open to question. . . . With the United States trying to uncouple itself from this obligation and to decrease its visibility in the country, another nationality as SRSG made sense."[45]

Just as significant to the eventual outcome of the UNOSOM II operation was the fact that close coordination among civil, military, and humanitarian relief organizations evaporated. The CMOC and the joint security committee disappeared with the withdrawal of UNITAF. There was a growing uneasiness that the United Nations would soon be challenged. In fact, "the perception among the Somalis, particularly the SNA, [was] that the operation was probably weak and could be pushed around."[46] A test of strength between the two was inevitable.

Aideed was certain that the United Nations was biased against him. This perception stemmed from the lingering animosity between him and the secretary-general and from the fact that Howe had repudiated the results of a May "peace conference" sponsored by Aideed in Mogadishu. Howe believed Aideed was trying to advance his own political ambitions by sponsoring a conference that conflicted with a parallel UN-sponsored conference. UNOSOM leadership was convinced that "Aideed's ambitions could never be satisfied by genuine power sharing and compromise. They concluded that he should be politically marginalized rather than engaged in continued high-level dialogue."[47] This was a dangerous course of action.[48] As John Hirsch and Robert Oakley later wrote:

Given Aideed's well-known vision of himself as the man who saved Somalia from Siad Barre and the man destined to assume national leadership, his equally well-known capacity for devious violence when opposed, and his demonstrated hostility to earlier attempts to marginalize him and the SNA, UNOSOM and the United States should have better appreciated the dangers along the path they had chosen.[49]

Concerned about confrontation, Pakistani patrols in south Mogadishu were sharply reduced. Seeing this as a sign of weakness, Aideed reintroduced much of his weaponry back into the city and started broadcasting scathing anti-UNOSOM attacks over his radio station. UNOSOM countered his military buildup by deciding to inspect his weapons compounds and announced on 4 June that it would begin to do so the next day. UNOSOM's leadership also decided to close down Aideed's radio station.

Although an SNA official warned against conducting the inspections, six weapons storage sites were scrutinized. One of them was collocated with Aideed's radio station. When a Pakistani patrol entered the station the morning of 5 June, angry crowds of Aideed supporters began to gather. The patrol then came under attack by SNA militia members who took cover behind rock-throwing women and children. By early afternoon the Pakistanis were pinned down and taking casualties. The U.S. Quick Reaction Force and Italian armored units were detached to end the fighting. When the dust settled into the dry Mogadishu streets, twenty-four Pakistanis were dead and dozens more injured. Many of the victims had been savagely mutilated or otherwise abused.

Convinced that this was a preplanned, deliberate attack, the Security Council passed Resolution 837 on 6 June, which specifically identified the SNA as the aggressors and authorized "all necessary measures" to arrest, detain, and prosecute those responsible. Resolution 837 changed the entire premise upon which UNOSOM had been operating. The United Nations was now at war.[50] The decision to go after Aideed and his supporters was based primarily on the belief that a deliberate attack against UN peacekeepers could not go unpunished because doing so could have broad repercussions in other ongoing and future UN operations.[51] Not all participating countries were happy with this new direction. Paris and Rome began issuing directions to their contingents that often directly conflicted with orders given them by General Bir.[52]

Over the next several months the confrontation continued to escalate. UNOSOM personnel immediately started to collect Aideed's heavy weapons and were frequently confronted by anti-UNOSOM demonstrations. Dozens of UNOSOM troops were injured as were hundreds of Somalis. Twelve days after the attack on the Pakistanis, Moroccan peacekeepers took heavy casualties after they attacked Aideed's enclave in southern Mogadishu. The same day, Howe offered a $25,000 reward for Aideed's capture and issued an arrest-and-detention warrant. Aideed was so incensed he reportedly offered a million dollar reward for Howe's assassination. All hope of continuing a political dialogue had ended.

UNOSOM attacks on SNA weapon storage sites continued through June and July. One of the most controversial attacks was conducted by QRF helicopter gunships against Aideed's command and control center. Inside the compound clan elders and SNA leaders were holding a meeting. Dozens were killed and, following the withdrawal of the QRF gunships, angry mobs surrounded journalists covering the event and killed four of them—displaying their bodies for television cameras. The effect of this raid on the Somalis was electrifying. Many who had not previously supported Aideed became sympathizers, and he began to assume mythical proportions to many in the country.

On 8 August the SNA exploded a remote-controlled device under a U.S. Humvee, killing four soldiers. Fourteen days later six more U.S. troops were killed by a land mine explosion. For weeks Howe had requested Washington to send special forces to Somalia to track down Aideed. After the mine incident, President Clinton relented and ordered Delta Force commandos, Army Rangers, and a helicopter detachment airlifted to Mogadishu. These forces, however, would remain under USCENTCOM command and control, a fact routinely overlooked in subsequent criticisms of UNOSOM. Their orders were simple: capture Aideed and any of his senior SNA leaders, and help pacify southern Mogadishu. As Hirsch and Oakley put it, "In effect, the Rangers and Delta Force became a posse with standing authority to go after Aideed and his outlaw band."[53]

As this new force was being deployed, military leaders in the United States were having second thoughts about the war that was now being waged. General Hoar had opposed the deployment of the special forces, and General Colin Powell, chairman of the Joint Chiefs of Staff, had only reluctantly approved the operation, believing it would provide an extra measure of security for other U.S. forces. As the commandos and Rangers went about their search-and-detain missions, clashes continued between the SNA and UNOSOM. Hundreds of Somalis were killed and UNOSOM forces from Italy, Nigeria, and Pakistan suffered casualties. The Security Council unanimously adopted Resolution 865 on 22 September confirming previous resolutions and commending UNOSOM II for its activities—presumably including the pursuit of Aideed. It also called for national elections in March 1995.

That same week, Secretary of State Warren Christopher personally discussed with the secretary-general the growing unease of the United States with the military course the operation in Somalia was following and provided a memorandum recommending a new, more political, approach. Boutros-Ghali remained unpersuaded and in a strongly worded rebuttal warned that U.S. forces were essential for UNOSOM success and that the pursuit of Aideed was the only rational course. The differences between the United States and the United Nations increased when Aideed's militia shot down a U.S. Army helicopter on 25 September, killing three more soldiers. Congress immediately passed a nonbinding resolution asking the president to seek its approval for further operations in Somalia.

The irony of the situation was that even as Washington was recommending to the United Nations a less militant approach in Somalia, it had special forces actively pursuing Aideed. The issue finally came to a head when, on 3 October, the Rangers launched a surprise attack against the Olympia Hotel in central Mogadishu in another attempt to capture Aideed. Twenty-four suspects were arrested, including several key aides, but not Aideed. As the Rangers were preparing to withdraw, they came under fierce attack. Two U.S. helicopters were shot down and those who came to their rescue were soon pinned down. The QRF and other UNOSOM forces came to their assistance, but by the time the fighting ended, eighteen U.S. soldiers were killed, seventy-eight were wounded, and one was captured. On the Somali side, between five hundred and one thousand people were either killed or wounded. What really sparked outrage in the United States, however, was the degrading treatment given to one dead soldier's body—a scene which was shown dozens of times on television. This event proved to be the catalyst for changing U.S. policy, and it also changed how forces would thereafter be deployed in Somalia.

On 6 October Clinton ordered the military to stop any further pursuit of Aideed and to use force only in self-defense. The following day he reappointed Oakley as a special envoy and tasked him to reopen political channels with Somali factions. The president also announced a new U.S. policy, said he was sending additional troops to bolster force protection,[54] and recommended keeping forces in Somalia until 31 March 1994. Congress eventually enacted this new policy into law, cutting off all funding for Somali operations after 31 March. Like a row of dominoes, other contributing states followed suit and announced withdrawal dates.[55] Ironically, this occurred shortly before UNOSOM II reached its peak in mid-November 1993, when it achieved an end-strength of nearly 30,000 soldiers from twenty-nine countries.[56]

Aideed greeted this new U.S. policy warmly and declared a unilateral cease-fire. When Oakley arrived in Mogadishu on 9 October, he set up a series of meetings with UNOSOM officials and with the factions. His first tasks were to consolidate the cease-fire, get a new political process under way, and obtain the release of two captives being held by the SNA, U.S. Army pilot Michael Durant and Nigerian soldier Umar Shantali. Oakley reverted to the coercive inducement tactics he had used so successfully during UNITAF. He told SNA representatives that the United States would not make any hostage deals, preferring to mount an armed rescue attempt if the prisoners were not released. He also noted that with reinforcements on the way, any opposition to such an action would cause south Mogadishu to suffer badly. As a sign of good faith, Aideed released Durant and Shantali on 14 October, having received assurance from Oakley that the release of SNA prisoners would be discussed with President Clinton upon Oakley's return to Washington.

The UN Secretariat was unhappy with this new policy because it left the Secretariat little room to maneuver. On 16 November the Security Council adopted Resolution 885, which established an international commission to deal with Somali reconstruction and suspended the call for Aideed's arrest. Although these events pleased Aideed, he refused to meet with Howe and had reservations about taking part in a fourth humanitarian conference that had been called in Addis Ababa in late November. He finally relented on the condition that he be flown there in a U.S. aircraft. Oakley, without informing the president, arranged this transportation, a decision that captured headlines, riled New York, and caught Washington off guard. However, the president supported Oakley's actions.

By January the secretary-general had resigned himself to the new situation and announced that the new focus of the UNOSOM II operation would be to promote "Somali initiatives in the political, security and nation-building process."[57] Its forces were to engage in "voluntary disarmament" should any Somali so choose, as well as the protection of "ports, convoys and refugees."[58] Although UNOSOM II would remain organized under Chapter VII of the UN Charter, it "would not use coercive methods but would rely on the cooperation of the Somali parties."[59] Thus, UNOSOM II had become a de facto traditional peacekeeping operation.

Planning began immediately for covering the U.S. withdrawal. On 4 February 1994 the Security Council adopted Resolution 897, which formally dropped forced disarmament from the mandate and reduced troop strength by 25 percent. As the deadline approached for the withdrawal of U.S. forces, the United States and the United Nations were still bargaining with other contributing states to keep their forces in place. Some countries that stayed, such as Pakistan and Egypt, agreed to do so only after the United States agreed to provide them with equipment, such as armored personnel carriers. Others, such as Botswana, India, Italy, Malaysia, Morocco, and Zimbabwe, agreed to stay without conditions. In order to demonstrate that a new policy was in effect, different leadership had to be put in place that had not been associated with the old. Bir and Montgomery were replaced by Malaysian general Aboo Samah Bin-Aboo Bakar and Zimbabwean general Michael Nayumbua. Howe was replaced by his deputy, Ambassador Lansana Kouyate. Aideed responded to this change in leadership and indicated his willingness to renew cooperation with UNOSOM.

As Aideed had promised, no organized interference with the withdrawal emerged, and on 25 March the last U.S. forces left. The remaining UNOSOM II forces were much less active than any of their predecessors and they basically "hunkered down." There were several isolated incidents of violence involving the Indians near Kismayo, and five Nepalese were killed when they were caught in the middle of a firefight with feuding factions. But for the most part, UNOSOM II forces remained sequestered because of their concern for self-defense. That meant they provided less and less protection to relief operations, which had also been drastically reduced because of renewed violence.

By mid-July technicals had returned in large numbers to the streets of Mogadishu, and the SNA had once again started to ambush UN convoys. Later that month, a Zimbabwean unit preparing to withdraw from Belet

Weyne was surrounded for a week by an SNA force. When UNOSOM II headquarters failed to send help, the Zimbabweans surrendered and the SNA stole their weapons. Attacks continued to intensify during August and September. Ten Indian peacekeepers were in killed in ten days near Baidoa. By the end of September, only Mogadishu, Baidoa, and Kismayo had UNOSOM units stationed in them. The situation was so bleak, and the Somalis so unwilling to accept outside help, that 31 March 1995 was selected as the final withdrawal date of UN forces. The Marines who provided protection for the withdrawal, many of whom had served in Operation Restore Hope, wanted to label this final ignominy Operation Abandon Hope—instead it was called United Shield.

The differences between UNITAF and UNOSOM II could not have been more stark. UNITAF succeeded in its limited operation because it was partial only to its mission. It confronted any individual or faction that threatened its mandate. It avoided surprises. It issued the same ground rules to all sides and then held them equally accountable for obeying them. Nevertheless, UNITAF personnel took great care to minimize the use of force. William Shakespeare could well have been penning the ROE for UNITAF when he wrote, "O, it is excellent to have a giant's strength, but it is tyrannous to use it like a giant."[60]

The set of ROE that UNITAF personnel drew up for UNOSOM II forces to use was nearly identical to its own. Unfortunately, contributing states were never able to agree upon them. In the end, each contingent used whatever rules with which it felt most comfortable. For some, this meant strictly self-defense ROE; for others, it meant more aggressive rules. This mixing and matching of ROE increased tensions between the contingents and put a number of troops at risk. UNITAF leadership concluded early on that using the right ROE was critical. As Hirsch and Oakley wrote:

> It became clear that a severely minimalist approach to the use of force was far more likely to hamper a peacekeeping operation, inviting challenge by appearing weak, rather than inspiring cooperation by demonstrating both strength and peaceful intent. . . . The will and ability to use overwhelming force—as the Weinberger-Powell doctrine recommends—offers the greatest possibility of successfully completing a peacekeeping mission and minimizing casualties on all sides.[61]

At the same time, however, they note the importance of downplaying the "overwhelming force" aspect of such missions and stressing their containment role.

> The purpose of UNITAF's and [the U.S. Liaison Office's] maintaining dialogue with all the faction leaders was not to legitimize them or their actions but to seek nonviolent solutions. A peacekeeping or peace enforcement operation may involve a strong military presence, with authority to use force if necessary, but it has of necessity been a maxim of peacekeeping that every effort must be made not to make enemies, or to be seen as taking sides in an internal confrontation. Even if some immediate military reaction should be necessary—for example, in response to an attack on peacekeepers—it should not lead to long-term hostility with any group.[62]

UNOSOM II was challenged, not simply because it was ill equipped to conduct combat, but because it appeared weak. Its contingents were feuding, its objectives were unclear, and it had not demonstrated the political will necessary to carry out a conflict against Aideed, even though it in effect declared war on him.

There were also lessons learned from Somalia by anyone wishing to challenge the will of the international community, the most important of which is to determine a country's (or coalition's) willingness to accept casualties. Aideed guessed right. He watched CNN and knew there was an enormous debate in Congress over whether the United States had any national interests in Somalia. He reached the conclusion that the Americans had no tolerance for body bags coming home from a distant and politically insignificant land. When the Rangers were killed in October 1993 and their bodies were shown being desecrated on American television, the cries to get out of Somalia were legion and loud. Even the perception of unwillingness to accept casualties undermines force credibility and effectiveness.

CONCLUDING REMARKS

"It is my belief," wrote Mohamed Sahnoun, "that if the international community had intervened earlier and more effectively in Somalia, much of the catastrophe that has unfolded could have been avoided."[63] The Somalia case demonstrated—and not for the first time—that early international intervention is unlikely. By the time the United Nations is called upon to put together a peace operation, crises are often intractable. Nevertheless, Sahnoun's point is well taken. The earlier an intervention can be mounted the better. Even though the timing of when to get involved is a political decision, its consequences for military success are enormous. When political will exists, cases such as the Congo in 1960 and Operation Turquoise demonstrate that things *can* happen quickly.[64] For Somalia, had "political doctrine on international humanitarian intervention . . . been available at the time, it would probably have indicated that mid-1992 was the proper time to introduce a substantial military force. Many more lives would have been saved, and opposition to effective international political action would have been weaker."[65]

Following the failure of UNOSOM I, Somalia became a laboratory for what was later called peace enforcement. The primary focus of the experiment was to determine whether significant military power could be effectively applied in the morass between peacekeeping and warfighting. Secretary-General Boutros-Ghali would later acknowledge, "There was no model for the United Nations to follow in its efforts."[66] Unfortunately, the final failure of the UNOSOM II mission colored how most media and politicians eventually judged the entire effort. Many believe that Somalia was not a genuine test of peace enforcement.[67]

While there were numerous failures in Somalia, the use of coercive inducement by UNITAF was not among them. Ambassador Oakley demonstrated time and again that skillful diplomacy backed by political will and credible force can be used to achieve desired objectives. Those failures that did occur were often the result of command-and-control problems. Such problems did not go unnoticed by the leaders of contending factions, who saw them as signs of institutional weakness that could be exploited.

Another challenge faced by all three operations in Somalia was how to achieve mission credibility. For UNOSOM I, which at its height consisted of 500 Pakistani peacekeepers armed primarily with moral authority, a Security Council mandate was simply not enough. "There was no military option at this initial stage," wrote Mohamed Sahnoun. "The UN mission had to rely to a large extent on moral suasion to get things done."[68] When belligerent cooperation did not materialize, the mission failed.

UNITAF's credibility was never seriously questioned. The operation demonstrated that a significant synergy can be created by political and diplomatic dialogue that is backstopped by credible force. Nevertheless, UNITAF had its critics. The U.S. concern with force protection, and the fact that UNITAF operated in southern Somalia, meant that its leadership concentrated their attention on Aideed and Mahdi, which gave these warlords a stature some believed was not justified.[69] UNOSOM II lost its credibility in the eyes of some Somalis when it became a party to the conflict.

Consequently, the foundation of coercive inducement was eroded. Then UNOSOM II went to war. It identified an enemy and targeted him. Unfortunately, UNOSOM II was not equipped to fight a war—having neither the doctrine, resources, nor political backing.

In order to retain its credibility, a coercive inducement operation must demonstrate that it is interested in all and biased against none of the parties. Credibility, in this context, has two dimensions. First, it must be legitimate (that is, it must have the backing of the international community as demonstrated by a Security Council resolution). Second, a coalition's activities must be consistent with the mission's stated objectives. The combination of legitimacy, threat, and sufficient coercive power establishes the credibility of an intervention force in the eyes of those in a targeted state. Both Sahnoun and Oakley conducted legitimate negotiations (that is, they were backed by Security Council resolutions) and worked hard at keeping lines of communication open with all parties. The differences in the results they achieved can be explained primarily by the fact that Oakley was backed by a large military force and Sahnoun was not.

That does not suggest that the diplomatic and political dimensions of a complex emergency are not important. In the long term, they are extremely important, since they guide participants toward a common goal. Unfortunately, Oakley's skill notwithstanding, the overall political dimension of UNITAF was ultimately inadequate. "The initial intervening force in Somalia," wrote Walter Clarke, "avoided the establishment of a political agenda for its actions. . . . The collapse of the subsequent UN political and military efforts was probably rendered inevitable by the narrow construction of the UNITAF mandate."[70] If one of the lessons from Somalia is that success is dramatically enhanced when a decisive and powerful force is rapidly deployed, a second lesson is that whatever measure of success a force achieves, it will be short-lived unless it is guided by a comprehensive concept of operations and a clear political objective.

Force must be complemented by open communications with feuding factions and other sectors of the populace and relief community. This dialogue helps sustain mission momentum, which is an extremely difficult challenge. Expectations about what a force will accomplish (especially if it is U.S. led) will usually exceed what is realistically attainable. Oakley underscored the importance of this synergy between dialogue and military credibility: "Continuing dialogue can reduce casualties and increase chances of military success. The converse is also true: The leverage of political efforts to broker peace agreements is bolstered by sufficient military strength."[71]

The Somalia case study demonstrates vividly why coercive inducement is necessary. From the beginning of the Somali crisis, "agreements with Ali Mahdi and Aideed on access and other issues were often broken within hours—if not at their orders, at least with their acquiescence."[72] Coercive inducement applied early on might have had lasting effects. Walter Clarke asserts:

> Later tragedies might have been avoided if UNITAF had been authorized to use its overwhelming advantages in military force, command and control, logistics, and communications to support a political agenda. This would have required political tactics to undercut the power of the warlords in favor of normal Somalis who were striving against mighty odds and a lot of firepower to reinstate local authorities, create self-help groups, open schools, reopen farms and shops, and restore community services.[73]

The political strategies that were followed tended to strengthen warlord legitimacy rather than marginalize it. Eventual attempts to marginalize or eliminate warlords were uneven and too late. The lack of an overarching political framework resulted in disjointed and unsuccessful applications of force.

> The military is most effective when it has clear objectives devised by a political authority and is employed in this limited manner, as it was in the first UNITAF phase of delivering humanitarian assistance. When this task or set of objectives is completed, the military requires on-going political direction; if it is left without this and becomes the principal decision-making authority in the field, its decisions are likely to be based on military imperatives, which are characteristically short term and limited in scope.[74]

The importance of a clear political objective or mandate cannot be overemphasized. Although ambiguous resolution language is easier to adopt in the Security Council, it can cause confusion and ineffectiveness in the field. As one anonymous UN commander lamented on his way to an unspecified mission:

> None of the political leadership can tell me what they want me to accomplish. That fact, however, does not stop them from continually asking me when I will be done.[75]

In the Somalia case, if the mandates for UNITAF and UNOSOM II were not well written, the blame cannot be laid entirely at the steps of the

Security Council. In an unprecedented departure from normal procedures, the first drafts of the Security Council resolutions that authorized UNITAF and UNOSOM II were written in the Pentagon.[76] When the United States then proved unwilling to provide UNOSOM II with the wherewithal to achieve its mandate, the United Nations was justifiably nettled.

The ultimate outcome of events in Somalia notwithstanding, coercive inducement can work. Oakley knew this and he was able to get the factions "to do things they didn't want to do."[77] But this lesson was not learned by the United Nations: "the drive for an enforcement capability . . . obscured the need to develop the third option, the middle road in use of force, the original context of a 'peace-enforcement' concept of operations, which was not enforcement at all costs. Simply connecting enforcement powers and a political mandate could not produce the concept needed."[78] This led Kofi Annan, then UN under-secretary-general of peacekeeping operations, to conclude:

> I don't think the member states have the stomach for this type of operation. It's going to be a very long time before the United Nations as an organization takes on a peace enforcement mission and manages it itself.[79]

UNITAF, however, demonstrated that when such missions are subcontracted, and when they selectively use force to achieve international goals, they can be successful, at least in the near term, without drawing a mission into the conflict itself.

5

RWANDA

Although Rwanda lies less than a thousand kilometers from Somalia—roughly the distance between Chicago and Washington, D.C.—the differences between them could hardly be more striking.[1] Unlike Somalia, whose population is homogeneous (in ancestry, language, and religion), Rwanda's population is sharply divided between two groups, the Hutu (90 percent) and the Tutsi (9 percent);[2] its religious beliefs are split among Catholic (65 percent), traditional (25 percent), Protestant (9 percent), and Muslim (1 percent) faiths; and it has two official languages, French and Kinyarwanda, and a commercial language, Kishwahili. Despite its overwhelming Hutu majority, the region was dominated by the Tutsi minority for centuries. Although this situation would have inevitably led to dissatisfaction and possible revolt, the bitterest seeds of conflict took root with the arrival of Europeans.

Traditional history, much of it invented by European scholars and priests, asserted that the Tutsis were originally from Ethiopia (although Egypt was also mentioned) and were considered "black Caucasian" conquerors by the Hutus because of their tall stature and thinner noses.[3] The Europeans, who were struck by these physical differences as well as by the fact that Tutsis were in control, fostered the notion that the Tutsis were a superior race to the Hutus. Unfortunately, both groups, having been indoctrinated in this myth for decades, began to believe it with devastating results. As one scholar noted:

> In the last resort, we can say that Tutsi and Hutu have killed each other more to upbraid a certain vision they have of themselves, of the others and of their place in the world than because of material interests. This is what makes the killing so relentless. Material interests can always be negotiated, ideas cannot and they often tend to be pursued to their logical conclusions, however terrible.[4]

There remain few real distinctions between most Tutsis and Hutus as a result of hundreds of years of intermarriage.[5] Physical appearance is a completely unreliable determinant. Rwandans follow a patriarchal lineage and are thus labeled as either Tutsi or Hutu depending on the tribe of their fathers. The reality is that many of Rwanda's population are "Hutsis," people of mixed lineage. The insistence that there is a distinction between the two has been unnecessarily fostered by the requirement for each Rwandan to carry an official identification card that lists tribal affiliation. This practice started during colonial times to benefit the Tutsi, but remarkably, it continued following independence at the insistence of the Hutu.[6] The Catholic Church also played a significant role in the unfolding Rwandan drama. The church, which fostered Tutsi membership during its early years in the country, eventually switched its allegiance from the Tutsi elite "to helping the Hutu rise from their subservient position towards a new aspiring middle-class situation. . . . Independence was just around the corner and the changes which had been initiated were going to proceed at an accelerated pace under pressure of circumstances, with people's consciousness definitely not keeping up with the speed of social change—a gap which was to have tragic implications."[7]

THE HUTUS COME TO POWER

Tutsi domination was broken when the Hutus seized control during a civil war fought between 1959 and 1961. This fighting resulted in a "legal coup" arranged by Colonel Guy Logiest, a de facto military governor in Rwanda, and Grégoire Kayibanda, a Hutu schoolteacher turned journalist-cum-political activist.[8] Kayibanda's ascent to the presidency ended the civil war, Tutsi rule, and the monarchy system, and eventually led to Rwanda's independence on 1 July 1962.[9] During the succeeding decades, Hutu leaders conducted numerous pogroms against the Tutsis, creating a major refugee problem for neighboring Tanzania, Uganda, Burundi, and Zaire.[10] When Major General Juvénal Habyarimana seized power in a 1973 coup, he adopted a policy that prevented refugees from returning. He and his Mouvement Révolutionnaire National pour le Développement (MRND) ruled for over two decades, a reign that ended when the aircraft he was flying in was shot down in April 1994.[11] Events leading to this incident, and the resulting tragedy it sparked, form the backdrop of this chapter.

During the early Habyarimana years, Rwanda benefited from several sources of income: bananas, coffee, tea, tin, and international relief and development funds. Beginning in 1977, however, coffee prices began to fall and they bottomed out in 1986. Tin prices collapsed shortly after and all mining ceased. Since Habyarimana's fragile administration was propped up by patronage, "the regime started to melt down as the resources shrank and internal power struggles intensified."[12] Habyarimana was forced by the World Bank and International Monetary Fund to make drastic changes to the Rwandan economy, but the structural adjustment program failed to stop further financial declines. These internal problems opened the door for diaspora Tutsis to begin planning for their return to Rwanda.

CIVIL WAR: THE RISE OF THE RWANDAN PATRIOTIC FRONT

The roots of the 1994 Rwandan crisis can be traced to the 1980s when a militant group of Tutsi refugees joined with Ugandan rebels and helped bring Yoweri Museveni to power in Uganda. Museveni's revolt began when he led a small group of twenty-six companions against the Kabamba Military School on 6 February 1981. Among that group were two young Rwandan refugees, Fred Rwigyema and Paul Kagame, who were later to play an important role in the exile movement. Flushed by this success— and eventually finding their presence in Uganda less welcome—the Tutsis formed the Rwandan Patriotic Front (RPF) in 1988 and two years later attacked northern Rwanda. The RPF's military arm was briefly headed by Rwigyema, who had risen to the rank of major general in the Ugandan army before being eased out as a foreigner. The initial RPF attack launched on 1 October 1990 did not go well, meeting stiff resistance from government troops aided by Belgium, France, and Zaire. Any chance for an RPF victory quickly evaporated when Major General Rwigyema was killed on the second day. The RPF was forced to retreat and its strategy transformed from winning a force-on-force campaign into protracted guerrilla warfare.[13] Major Paul Kagame, who had been attending military training in the United States, was called back to assume leadership of the movement.[14]

By the end of 1993, the structural adjustment program mentioned earlier had collapsed and donor nations started to drastically reduce or suspend financial assistance. In addition, Habyarimana was forced, particularly by the French, to make tentative moves toward a more pluralistic political system.[15] These events weakened Habyarimana's internal political position, and he felt compelled to sign a series of cease-fires with the RPF—none of which lasted long. The first was signed on 26 October 1990 in Gbadolite, Zaire, and was confirmed and extended on 20 November 1990 at a meeting in Goma, Zaire; another cease-fire agreement was signed on 29 March 1991 in N'sele, Zaire, but repeated violations caused it to be amended on 16 September 1991 at a meeting in Gbadolite and again on 12 July 1992 at a meeting in Arusha, Tanzania. At the conclusion of the Arusha negotiations on 18 August 1992, the government of Rwanda and the RPF signed the Protocol of Agreement on the Rule of Law. Over the next year, they signed five additional protocols.

During this period, the Forces Armées Rwandaises (FAR) grew from approximately 5,200 soldiers to nearly 50,000 and the RPF grew from 5,000 to 12,000,[16] which is where they stood when one of the most important of the cease-fire agreements was signed in July 1992. The agreement charged the five most prominent parties in Rwanda with forming a broad-based transitional government and negotiating a peace agreement with the RPF.[17] By early February 1993 the latest cease-fire had collapsed and ongoing talks in Arusha were suspended. On 8 February the RPF initiated a successful attack against Ruhengeri. In response, the French sent 300 troops to Rwanda to support beleaguered FAR troops. Nevertheless, the RPF pushed within thirty kilometers of Kigali. Hope for a new settlement was sparked on 21 February when the RPF unilaterally declared a cease-fire. The next day the Rwandan government followed suit and with Uganda requested the Security Council to deploy military observers along their common border.

UN OBSERVER MISSION UGANDA-RWANDA

On 4 March 1993 the Rwandan government again requested the Security Council to consider the situation in Rwanda. In response, the secretary-general dispatched a goodwill mission to Rwanda and Uganda. As the UN mission was gathering facts, the Rwanda government and the RPF met in Dar es Salaam, Tanzania, and agreed to reinstate the cease-fire beginning 9 March. Three days later the Security Council adopted Resolution 812, calling on the parties to observe the cease-fire and directed the secretary-general to examine the possibility of deploying a military observer force along the Rwanda-Uganda border. Peace talks resumed on 16 March in Arusha and continued into June. On 20 May the secretary-general proposed the establishment of a military observer mission. Following the signing of another protocol concerning the repatriation of Rwandan refugees, the Security Council passed Resolution 846 in June 1993, which established the UN Observer Mission Uganda-Rwanda (UNOMUR), whose mandate was to ensure that no military assistance reached Rwanda through Uganda. The governments of Rwanda and Uganda strongly supported the operation, which was primarily aimed at stopping RPF incursions and resupply. Even though RPF consent was not formally sought since the mission was to observe an international border, the truth was that the RPF controlled about four-fifths of the border. Its leaders informed the UN technical mission that the RPF "was opposed to the deployment of observers on the Rwandan side of the border, but did not object to a deployment on Ugandan territory"; therefore, UNOMUR forces were mostly stationed in Uganda.[18]

UN ASSISTANCE MISSION FOR RWANDA

On 4 August 1993 the Habyarimana government and the RPF agreed to a comprehensive peace agreement that was signed in Arusha, Tanzania.[19] The Arusha Agreement was made up of a number of different protocols that had been brokered during the preceding twelve months. They included the initial cease-fire agreement signed on 12 July 1992; the power-sharing agreements that defined the broad-based transitional government signed on 30 October 1992 and 9 January 1993; the protocol on the repatriation of refugees signed on 9 June 1993; and the armed forces integration agreement signed on 3 August 1993. The United Nations was expected to play a major role during a twenty-two-month transitional period leading to new elections at the end of 1995, a development that the secretary-general asserted was "welcomed" by both parties.[20] In the interim, a broad-based transitional government was to be installed (with Habyarimana remaining as president, but stripped of virtually all power), transitional institutions were to be established, a neutral international military force was to be deployed, and the expatriate community was to be protected. In addition, all foreign troops in Rwanda (except for UN peacekeepers) were to withdraw, and both sides were to disengage, disarm, and demobilize.

A new, integrated National Army of 13,000 troops and a gendarmerie of 6,000 personnel were to be established.[21]

Just as the Arusha process was looking the most promising, the extremist Hutu political party Coalition pour la Défense de la République (CDR) established Radio Télévision Libre des Mille Collines (RTLMC) to counter both the official government station (Radio Rwanda) and the RPF's Radio Muhabura. It almost immediately began a campaign intended to incite hatred for Tutsis and to lay the groundwork for a "final solution" for dealing with them. The importance of this development cannot be overstated. As one analyst noted:

> In a country like Rwanda where more than 60% of the population could not read or write, the existence of a free press only had meaning for the literate sector of the population, who were already politically aware anyway. The audiovisual scene was a tremendously important battlefield and here the government still reigned supreme: its version of events was the one carried out to the hilly countryside by radio. The license given to "free" extremist radio RTLMC (and to nobody else who might have supported a more moderate line) only made things worse.[22]

In a show of support for the Arusha process, the Security Council adopted Resolution 872 in October 1993 authorizing the UN Assistance Mission for Rwanda (UNAMIR) consisting of approximately twenty-five hundred personnel. UNAMIR's mandate was multifaceted and was to be carried out in four phases. During phase one, which was scheduled to last approximately three months, the installation and operation of the broad-based transitional government was to begin. UNAMIR was to assist in demilitarizing the area around Kigali as well as ensuring the security of the capital itself. It was also to help with mine clearance, provide security for repatriation efforts, coordinate humanitarian assistance and relief operations, investigate complaints of noncompliance with the peace accords, and monitor security leading to democratic elections.

The second phase, which was to take place over ninety days, involved preparations for disengaging, demobilizing, and integrating rebel forces. During this phase, the operation was to have reached its peak manpower. Phase three, which was supposed to last approximately nine months, was slated to implement the actual disengagement, demobilization, and integration. Once this was accomplished, mission end strength was to be reduced to 1,240 persons. During the final phase, anticipated to last four months,

UNAMIR forces were to provide security during the run-up to general elections. Force levels during phase four were to be reduced to under a thousand troops.

UNAMIR's commander, Canadian major general Roméo Dallaire, arrived in Kigali on 22 October. The situation he found was tense. The previous day Melchior Ndadaye, the moderate Hutu president of Burundi, had been assassinated by extremist Tutsi army officers. The CDR and its sympathizers pointed to the assassination as another proof that Tutsis could not be trusted and that the Arusha Agreement should be resisted. A month later the secretary-general's special representative, Jacques-Roger Booh-Booh, the former minister for external relations of Cameroon, arrived in the country. By early December, UNAMIR consisted of a battalion of Belgian and Bangladeshi troops stationed in Kigali. UNOMUR, which was still functioning, had its mandate extended when the Security Council adopted Resolution 891 on 20 December. By the end of December 1993, UNAMIR forces had effectively completed all phase one tasks, including ensuring the safe passage to Kigali of an RPF battalion consisting of some six hundred troops.[23] Unfortunately, no transitional government was in place even though on 10 December all parties had renewed their agreement to do so by 31 December.[24]

On 5 January 1994 Habyarimana was sworn in as president of the transitional government, as agreed to at Arusha, and there was some hope that the peace process would get back on track. The following day the Security Council passed Resolution 893 strongly urging all parties to cooperate and fully comply with the Arusha Agreement, especially the establishment of a broad-based transitional government. Optimism was short-lived, however, and the process started to unravel when militants within Habyarimana's MRND party and the Hutu-supremacist CDR party objected to the power-sharing arrangements detailed in the agreement. Political opposition was exacerbated by the fact that these parties had established, and were arming and training, unauthorized militias. The two most virulent, the MRND Interahamwe ("those who work together") and CDR Impuzamugambi ("the ones who have only one goal") militias, "were being trained and armed by the army in camps set up in 1992 and 1993."[25] When Dallaire requested permission to mount a military operation to seize suspected arms caches, UN headquarters refused to grant it and noted that such a mission went beyond UNAMIR's authorized mandate. In fact, the UN

Department of Peacekeeping Operations cautioned Dallaire to "avoid entering into [any] course of action that might lead to the use of force and to unanticipated repercussions."[26] UNAMIR leadership found this situation extremely frustrating. As the Kigali sector commander noted:

> The irony was that we knew exactly what and where the problem was, but our hands had been effectively tied. The consequence of all this was that the population lost confidence in us. They also knew of the existence of arms caches and concluded that the UN was unable to act and to impose its will.[27]

Habyarimana continued to stall implementation of the peace agreement throughout January. In February 1994 two prominent politicians, Félicien Gatabazi and Martin Bucyana, were assassinated. With political violence on the increase, no broad-based transitional government in place, and Habyarimana accused of interfering with the transitional process, UNAMIR's ability to fulfill its mandate was in serious jeopardy. In January and February UNAMIR had prevented delivery of four planeloads of arms into Rwanda, but uncovered evidence that arms were nevertheless being imported and distributed among the populace. Although the United Nations protested these obvious violations of the Arusha Agreement, the situation continued to deteriorate. As with all traditional peacekeeping missions, the success of UNAMIR was predicated on the cooperation of the disputing parties. But mistrust, fed by centuries of ethnic feuding and abuse, led to delaying tactics, shifting political alignments, and an undermining of the peace accord's implementation.

Frantic efforts to recapture the initiative by the secretary-general and his special representative failed. As a result, in February Booh-Booh warned all parties of a possible UN withdrawal.[28] This threat was repeated during Security Council debates in March and April over whether to conditionally extend the mandate for four months. During this period, UNAMIR reached it peak strength of just over 2,500 personnel.[29] On 5 April the council passed Resolution 909, which granted the extension, but expressed deep concerns about delays in implementing the Arusha Agreement. Hoping to break the stalemate, the Organization of African Unity (OAU) and the president of Tanzania, Ali Hassan Mwinyi, who had helped facilitate the Arusha Agreement, called interested parties together for a one-day summit in Dar es Salaam.[30] Any hope that the summit might have generated evaporated when the aircraft in which the presidents of Rwanda (Juvénal Habyarimana) and Burundi (Cyprien Ntaryamira) were traveling was shot down approaching the Kigali airport. No group stepped forward claiming responsibility for the shoot-down, but theories about who the guilty parties were run the gamut from French-equipped Hutu extremists within the Presidential Guard to Belgian-assisted RPF forces. The overwhelming belief is that extremist Hutus, not Tutsis, shot down the aircraft.[31] Regardless of who was to blame, the incident unleashed an unprecedented massacre of civilians and reignited the civil war.

THE GENOCIDE

In the hours immediately following the crash, opposition Hutu politicians and ethnic Tutsis were slaughtered by government troops, Presidential Guards, armed militias, and roving gangs. The worst perpetrators were the Interahamwe and Impuzamugambi militias. Among the victims were Prime Minister Agathe Uwilingiyamana, who was with child, and Supreme Court President Joseph Kavaruganda. A ten-member Belgian unit had been detached to guard the prime minister. After the Hutus had killed her, they seized the Belgian guards, disarmed them, and took them to an army barracks. There they were stripped, displayed in front of the troops, accused of killing Habyarimana, and then slaughtered by inflamed troops. Kigali descended rapidly into chaos and its streets began to smell of rotting flesh.

An "interim government," headed by former speaker of Parliament Theodor Sindikubwabo, was set up by Hutu extremists. The government denied any involvement in the massacres, claiming the killings were uncontrollable expressions of popular rage against the RPF, whom they blamed for President Habyarimana's death. Nevertheless, numerous human rights groups investigating the genocide concluded that it appeared to follow a preconceived plan.[32] One indication that the genocide was preconceived was the fact that within forty-five minutes of the president's death, Interahamwe roadblocks were in place throughout Kigali and house-to-house searches for specific victims were already being conducted. The RTLMC began inciting common citizens to take up arms to avenge the president's death by filling up mass graves and completely eliminating the Tutsi population.

Within forty-eight hours, France and Belgium organized an evacuation of foreigners from Rwanda, but little protection was afforded to most Tutsis.[33] Over the next week, an estimated twenty thousand people were massacred in and around Kigali. By the end of the month, the death toll was estimated to have reached nearly two hundred thousand. Ordinary civilians, coerced by militias and incited by extremist radio propaganda, eventually joined the fray. Because the army remained largely engaged with the RPF, most of the slaughter was carried out using machetes, knives, axes, and cudgels.[34]

The RPF battalion, which had been safely escorted to Kigali by UNAMIR, was able to break out of its quarters and engage government troops. Other RPF units advanced on the capital from the north and were in control of the northeast portion of the country by the end of the month. Under these conditions, calls for a cease-fire made no sense to the RPF. As events unfolded, the international community wrung its hands on the sidelines, both unwilling to act and refusing to recognize the genocide as something more than a frightful renewal of the civil war. The world's refusal to separate the civil war from the genocide allowed the killing to continue nearly unabated for six weeks. Only the RPF's advance into Rwanda brought the killing to an end. Once the RPF had victory in sight, a cease-fire was unthinkable. The interim government and its troops were forced to flee to Gitarama in central Rwanda (figure 5-1). Since the RPF held the interim government responsible for the genocide of Tutsis, it refused to negotiate with it and called for the perpetrators to be brought to justice. Although atrocities were committed by both sides, RPF incidents, unlike those of the Hutus, were isolated and spontaneous.

The primary reason that RPF troops did not participate in widespread retaliation was their leader, Major General Paul Kagame. Although only in his thirties during the crisis, Kagame was "demanding" and "obsessed with discipline in the ranks."[35] Kagame's stress on discipline may have been a result of the fighting in 1990 when "both sides behaved atrociously, murdering civilians of the wrong tribe and inciting villagers to do likewise."[36] Although there were some reports of RPF executions and retaliatory killings, Kagame was able to maintain generally good control by being "constantly on the move [and] traveling with a satellite phone."[37] It was reported that "during the war, the RPF rebels lived by a strict code of conduct. Murder and rape carried the death penalty."[38] As one young guerrilla, whose parents had been massacred, stated, "I have a feeling of revenge, but the code prevents it."[39] Because Kagame was convinced that RPF troops were not generally involved in massacres, he lost confidence in Special Representative

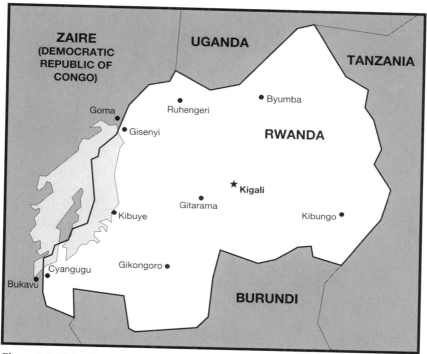

Figure 5-1. Major Rwandan Cities

Booh-Booh when the latter tried to maintain his neutrality by holding both sides equally responsible for the killing fields.[40]

THE COLLAPSE OF UNAMIR

UNAMIR forces found themselves in an impossible position during these weeks of chaos. Operating under traditional peacekeeping rules of engagement, they could use force only in self-defense. Even had their mandate been changed to allow them to stop the fighting, the 2,500 troops, many of whom were poorly trained and ill equipped, had little chance of opposing some 60,000 government and rebel forces, let alone the thousands of others involved in either militia or mob action. Appalled at what was occurring, General Dallaire believed that something could be done, and he pressed the secretary-general for new rules of engagement that would allow him to protect citizens as well as his own forces—the request was denied.[41] Even so, there were numerous acts of heroism among UNAMIR forces.[42] Several thousand refugees managed to get inside Amahoro stadium where they were protected by UNAMIR troops, although FAR artillery shells did cause some fatalities. Concerning this situation, General Dallaire noted, "At best, U.N. presence provided local security for the roughly twenty thousand Rwandans caught between the lines, helped preserve truces and cease-fires, assisted both civilian agencies and nongovernmental organizations (NGOs), held ground, and prepared the way for a new force and an increased humanitarian effort."[43] The extremist Hutus no longer saw the UN force as impartial, especially the Belgians, who were deliberately targeted.[44] Every foundation for a successful traditional peacekeeping mission eroded. The peace agreement was no longer recognized by the signatories, and they subsequently withdrew their consent for the United Nations to assist in implementing the moribund accord.

This grim situation soon became worse. Belgium decided to withdraw its forces and was followed by Bangladesh and Ghana. Recognizing the untenable situation of the UN contingent, the secretary-general advised General Dallaire to prepare withdrawal plans. Concerning the circumstances he then faced, the general later wrote:

> The situation was also exacerbated by decisions on the part of some contributing countries to either withdraw military personnel from UNAMIR unilaterally or not amend the mandate under what were significantly changed circumstances, namely a state of war instead of peace. Thus as the United Nations debated a new mandate and increases in personnel, the UNAMIR force—with little or no ammunition and barely a third of the minimum operational equipment needed in theater, hardly any defense stores, and one of its major contingents (Belgians) deliberately targeted by one of the warring factions—actually decreased from 2,500 to 450 troops through a decision by the Security Council which reinforced the impression of the United Nations as a paper tiger.[45]

This reduction in force level and adjustment of UNAMIR's mandate was formalized by the Security Council in Resolution 912 (21 April 1994). Although this resolution was unanimously approved by the council, its African members supported it only after it became clear that their call for a more robust UNAMIR force had fallen on deaf ears.[46] Refugees who had fled to UN military bases for protection were left to their fate, and the UN withdrawal became an international scandal (see, for example, figure 5-2).

Figure 5-2. Cartoon published in the *International Herald Tribune*, 22 April 1994.
Published by permission, Erhan Turgut/Cartoon & Writers Syndicate.

Within a week, however, the secretary-general asked the Security Council to revisit its decision in light of the killings, which continued unabated, and the movement of refugees who had reached into the hundreds of thousands.[47] In a 29 April letter to the Security Council, Boutros-Ghali noted that the United Nations had lost its credibility with the Rwandan parties and that only a forceful response to restore law and order could regain it. He fully understood that "such action would require a commitment of human and material resources on a scale which member states [had] so far proved reluctant to contemplate."[48] The Security Council remained reluctant and directed the secretary-general to consult with the Organization of African Unity on ways to restore stability. The OAU responded by saying that "since the UN is already engaged in Rwanda, the accent should be put on strengthening and expanding that engagement instead of transferring responsibility elsewhere."[49]

UNAMIR II ESTABLISHED

The United Nations, hoping that some accommodation would eventually be reached, continued to plan for the dispatch of a 5,500-person force into Kigali. The Security Council, after lengthy debate, eventually relented and on 17 May passed Resolution 918 (followed three weeks later by Resolution 925), which increased UNAMIR to 5,500 troops and expanded its mandate, along the lines that General Dallaire had recommended, to include the protection of civilians as well as security for humanitarian relief operations. Although Chapter VII was mentioned in the resolution, it only referred to enforcing an arms embargo. Hence, UNAMIR II was to operate as a classical peacekeeping mission. As the secretary-general noted, the "rules of engagement for this force [UNAMIR II] would not include enforcement action, as provided by Chapter VII of the [UN] Charter; the force would instead depend primarily on deterrence to carry out its tasks."[50] General Dallaire was not happy with either the mandates or implementation of these resolutions. The situation in Rwanda called for rapid and effective action, but just the opposite occurred. UNAMIR II's classical peacekeeping mandate meant that the force would be reactive—not proactive—and the United States insisted on an incremental upgrading of the force. The United States recommended the deployment of 150 unarmed military observers, whose task would be to assess the military situation, and a Ghanaian battalion, which would guard the airport in Kigali. Dallaire had hoped for the immediate deployment of properly trained and equipped troops. Among other things, Dallaire wanted a robust force that could silence

> the inflammatory broadcasts from the nominally independent Radio Télévision Libre des Mille Collines which was . . . largely responsible for spreading panic that, in turn, drove large numbers of people to refugee camps in neighboring states, thereby spreading instability throughout the region. The broadcasts also excited the Hutu population to take up arms against Tutsis and Hutu moderates to exterminate them and, also, regularly targeted UNAMIR in general and its senior officials in particular.[51]

One of the main reasons for the U.S. position was its new peacekeeping policy (Presidential Decision Directive 25), which had just been released. This directive required the United States to proceed cautiously before mounting any new peacekeeping missions.[52] To have ignored the policy the first time it could be applied would have been politically disastrous for the Clinton administration since it had wrangled for months with Congress and the Pentagon to get it approved. Hence, the United States had no sooner supported the mandate for a more muscular UNAMIR II than it turned around and asked that it be implemented incrementally.[53] When the United States finally did agree to the immediate deployment of forces (Resolution 925, 8 June 1994), it insisted that UNAMIR II not act as a buffer force or attempt to compel the parties to stop fighting, preferring it to concentrate on protecting refugees and distributing aid.

Another problem with implementing the UN resolutions was that finding troop contributors proved difficult.[54] Even the Africans were slow to pledge forces. They were still disgruntled that the UNAMIR force had been allowed to be reduced in the first place and that when the decision was reversed they were not properly consulted. When they did offer forces, their pledge came with a long list of demands. Nevertheless, within a month, nine African states had promised to send troops.[55] By the time the force was ready in July, most of the killing had ended and the RPF had defeated the interim government. During the delay from April to July, nearly eight hundred thousand men, women, and children were slaughtered. The secretary-general lamented:

> The delay in reaction by the international community to the genocide in Rwanda has demonstrated graphically its extreme inadequacy to respond urgently with prompt and decisive action to humanitarian crises entwined with armed conflict. . . . We all must recognize that, in this respect, we have failed in our response to the agony of Rwanda, and thus have acquiesced in the continued loss of human lives. Our readiness and capacity for action has been demonstrated to be inadequate at best, and deplorable at worst, owing to the absence of the collective political will.[56]

RPF spokesmen insisted that after the April massacres began the RPF resumed its offensive only because it saw no alternatives for stopping the genocide. Governments and NGOs were focused on getting a new UN force into the field but did little else to stop the killing. Even had a UN force been immediately fielded, the RPF had doubts the United Nations would have ended the genocide. The United Nations had already endured a humiliating conflict with General Mohammed Aideed in Somalia, and neither its leadership nor that of its member states had the stomach to take on a new adversary. Many in the Secretariat and elsewhere were calling for a retrenchment to traditional peacekeeping with its stress on consent and neutrality. In Rwanda's case, those who did not want to get involved used these arguments as an excuse for inaction. Shamed into silence by their lack of political will, leaders expressed dismay but not moral outrage over the killing, and even some NGOs were oddly quiet. The predominant feeling was expressed by one NGO staff member who stated that "there is no point expressing moral outrage without being able to take practical action."[57] Exacerbating the problem was the fact that most of the Hutus who could have had a moderating effect on the situation had themselves been killed. Faced with a desperate and deteriorating situation, the RPF took the only action it believed available: it pressed its offensive to ultimate victory.

In its quest for victory, the RPF was actually aided by international delays in reinforcing UNAMIR. Had Dallaire been rapidly reinforced, he might have been tempted to stop the RPF advance.[58] With momentum clearly on its side, the RPF captured Kigali on 4 July and Gisenyi, the last interim government stronghold, two weeks later. On 19 July, the RPF established a broad-based Government of National Unity with Faustin Twagira-mungu, a Hutu, as prime minister, and Pasteur Bizimungu, another Hutu, as president. The highest-ranking Tutsi in the unity government was Major General Kagame, who was appointed vice president and minister of defense.

From the beginning, the RPF declared its opposition to a reinforced UNAMIR operation. An RPF spokesman averred, "The R.P.F. hereby declares it is categorically opposed to the proposed U.N. intervention force and will not under any circumstances cooperate in its setting up and operation."[59] The reasons for this strong anti-UN sentiment are legion. First and foremost, however, was the fact that UNAMIR had not stopped the slaughter (a criticism that ignores the fact that UNAMIR was neither equipped nor tasked for such an operation). Even worse, as far as the Tutsis were concerned, the United Nations had turned tail and run. Manzi Baku-ramutsa, the new government's representative to the United Nations, later noted, "In Rwanda we have films of people begging to be protected in the genocide. And the peacekeepers left."[60] Another reason was their distrust of the secretary-general's special representative, Jacques-Roger Booh-Booh, who they believed was biased in favor of the interim Hutu government. The RPF was also wary of the UN Security Council. France, a permanent member, had been a longtime supporter of the Hutu regime, and the Hutu government itself had maintained a seat on the council throughout the genocide. Naturally, any plan supported by that representative was suspect in the eyes of the new government.

With the RPF firmly in control of northern Rwanda, it made little sense for UNOMUR to continue functioning along the Uganda-Rwanda border. Therefore, on the recommendation of the secretary-general, the Security Council passed Resolution 928 on 20 June ending the UNOMUR operation by the end of September. In an attempt to reignite the negotiation process, the secretary-general replaced his special representative, whose life had been threatened, with Mohammed Shahryra Kahn. By this time, it was clear that the deployment of UNAMIR II was faltering. In the month and a half since its mandate was adopted, UNAMIR's strength had only risen from 444 to 503. It became apparent that another, interim, approach was required.

OPERATION TURQUOISE

The RPF campaign launched one of the largest population movements in history as more than 2 million Rwandans flooded across the Zaire border and another 2.5 million were internally displaced. It was estimated that by the end of the third week in June 1994, roughly 5 million of Rwanda's 8 million people had abandoned their homes.[61] An acute lack of potable water resulted in the rapid spread of cholera among the refugees, who died at the rate of one a minute during the peak of the crisis. Under these conditions, France decided in early May to mount an effort to stop the dying and stabilize population movements. Since by that time the RPF was well on its way to victory and since the French had a long history of blindly supporting the former administration, it was assumed by most that the French mission, dubbed Operation Turquoise, was "an attempt to protect the extremist Hutu regime and its supporters."[62] But the French insisted their motives were strictly humanitarian. Gérard Prunier, an African expert but frequent critic of French foreign policy, was asked to assist in the operation's planning and did so only after he was convinced there were no official hidden agendas.[63]

In fact, even the declared agenda was unclear. Exactly what the French hoped to accomplish was never detailed beyond broad statements about the operation's humanitarian nature to protect lives. The French prime minister, Edouard Balladur, set five conditions for French intervention: a UN mandate; a clear time limit for the operation; no in-depth penetration of Rwandan territory; a strictly humanitarian purpose; and allied involvement. Condition three made no sense. At-risk populations could not be protected from the periphery and the French ended up controlling the southwest quarter of Rwanda. Furthermore, condition five was never achieved. Although the French received token support from some African states, no serious assistance was ever offered by any of France's Western allies.

The French understood that without UN sanction, the earnestness of their intent would be questioned. In a 19 June letter to the president of the Security Council, the secretary-general suggested that "the Security Council may wish to consider the offer of the Government of France to undertake, subject to Security Council authorization, a French-commanded multinational operation in conjunction with other Member States, under Chapter VII of the Charter of the United Nations, to assure security and protection of displaced persons and civilians at risk in Rwanda."[64] The Security Council accepted the French offer by adopting Resolution 929 on 22 June, which authorized their operation until 21 August.[65] The next day Operation Turquoise was launched and would eventually include 2,555 French and 350 African troops.[66] Although UNAMIR received only twenty-three hours' notice of the arrival of French troops, "close cooperation at all levels between UNAMIR and Operation Turquoise" took place from the beginning.[67]

The RPF opposed the French intervention. As mentioned earlier, France had been a strong supporter of the former regime and one of its major arms suppliers. RPF supporters viewed the French as foreign invaders coming to wrest the country from them so that it could be turned back over to Hutu extremists. To ensure their effectiveness, the French deployed with more than a hundred armored vehicles, a battery of 120mm mortars, two Gazelle and eight Puma helicopters, and eight warplanes (four Jaguar and four Mirage aircraft). The heft of this force enhanced French military effectiveness but also added to RPF suspicion that French motives were not strictly humanitarian. The French, however, reiterated their determination to make Operation Turquoise a strictly humanitarian mission of limited duration. The French cause was not helped when spokesmen for the deposed Hutu interim government called for the French to expand the mission into RPF-controlled territory and its radio station announced that the troops were coming to help kill the Tutsis.

The coalition's first mission, conducted on 26 June, helped allay some fears by protecting nearly eight thousand Tutsis surrounded by militia forces near Cyangugu. Buoyed by the protection, one of the Tutsis declared, "We want them to stay for a long time, because if they leave we will be killed."[68] The French took every opportunity to underscore the liberal rules of engagement under which they were operating. The commander of the French paratrooper unit guarding the Tutsi camp declared, "Now, if any militia tried to enter the refugee camp, we will kill them; it is very clear."[69] General Jean-Claude Lafourcade, the commander of Operation Turquoise, underscored the point by stating, "My mandate is to put an end to the massacres by using force if necessary against the troublemakers who have carried out all these crimes."[70] Two days later, the French narrowly avoided a clash with Hutu militiamen while protecting a Tutsi refugee camp near Gisenyi. On 2 July the French announced they would be establishing a "humanitarian protected zone" in southwestern Rwanda (figure 5-3) and the force started moving into position on 5 July. As they roamed the countryside in machine gun–equipped vehicles, they did not hesitate to confront personnel manning roadblocks, and insisted that all such obstacles to movement in the protected zone be dismantled. The French also did not hesitate to use force on one of the few occasions they were challenged by RPF forces. The confrontation occurred while the French were evacuating 270 Rwandan civilians (including orphans) and a dozen European clerics from Butare. At the time, the "use of force was instrumental in ensuring the safe passage of the convoy."[71] Nor did they hesitate to *threaten* force when it seemed appropriate. "In one situation, following the killing of some 50 Hutus in an RPF mortar shelling, French jet fighters flew immediately over the insurgents' stronghold, leading to a cessation of the attacks."[72]

Despite French promises that the protected zone would not be used for military or political purposes, Hutu militia and government officials found their way into the area and began unauthorized operations. This occurred despite the fact the French had established control posts, which disarmed soldiers and collected intelligence on human rights abuses to pass along to the United Nations. On several occasions, the RPF threatened conflict with the French coalition over the fact that Hutu criminals were receiving sanctuary in the protected zone; but the threats were never carried out.

Realizing that they could not disarm former government soldiers and then leave them unprotected in the face of an RPF advance, the French decided to draw a line in the sand. On 4 July, the commander of French paratroopers in Rwanda, Colonel Didier Thibaut, declared, "If the R.P.F. comes here [i.e., into the French protective zone] and threatens the population, we will open fire against them without hesitation, and we have the means."[73] Following the same pattern that proved so successful for the United States

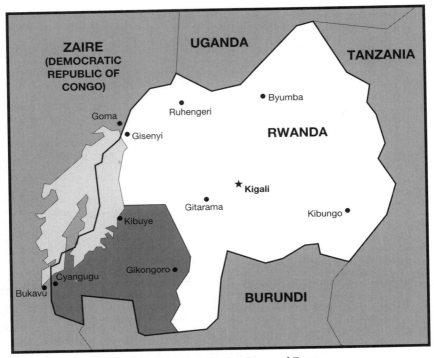

Figure 5-3. Operation Turquoise's Humanitarian Protected Zone

during UNITAF, senior French military officials conducted high-level dis-cussions with RPF leaders even as threats were exchanged.[74] "I explained to Kagame my intention of not allowing any military into the Safe Humani-tarian Zone," remarked General Lafourcade. "When we did have clashes with the RPF and other groups not under control, we solved these prob-lems through the established channels."[75] General Dallaire was also busy shuttling between General Lafourcade, Major General Augustin Bizimungu, the former Rwandan army chief of staff, and General Kagame. The RPF unilaterally declared a cease-fire on 18 July that effectively ended the civil war. The following day, as noted above, they set up the Government of National Unity.

The French presence was not enough to stop or even slow down the Hutu exodus from RPF-controlled territory into either neighboring countries or the protected area. French forces distributed leaflets urging people to stay in Rwanda and promised them food supplies if they did. They even emptied their own stocks to demonstrate their commitment. Despite moderate talk coming from Kigali, which included pleas for reconciliation, the Hutus feared Tutsi reprisals. They were encouraged in their fears by radio propaganda sponsored by the deposed government. "Radio Mille Collines was telling Hutus that the rebel government and the French forces could not guarantee their security and they should cross into Zaire immediately."[76] The French admitted they did not have enough forces to prevent lawlessness. Nevertheless, they continued their efforts to disarm militia members entering their protected area. Once they realized that RTLMC was undermining their efforts, they deployed the means to shut it down and did so on 17 July. General Lafourcade noted, "I also requested the means to spread positive information, but, be assured, we are now very much aware of the importance of a counter-radio situation."[77]

As July came to a close, France reiterated its determination to depart on 21 August when its mandate ended. Although this was good news to the new Rwandan government, it created fear and trepidation in southwest Rwanda and among international agencies trying to cope with the flood of refugees. To bolster deteriorating conditions in refugee camps in Zaire and the French safe area, the United States decided to send in troops to help distribute humanitarian relief. This operation, Support Hope, will be discussed later.

During a 21 July meeting with the new Rwandan prime minister to discuss Operation Turquoise, the French informed him that the Rwandan government would have to request French authorization to enter its protected area. As expected, the prime minister reacted sharply to this demand, noting that it was illegal for a third party to insist that a legitimate and independent government obtain permission to enter its own territory. Five days later the new Rwandan president stated, "France has intervened in our conflict on the side of the former government and their intervention led to some misunderstandings. We do not want the situation to get worse, so the sooner they disengage themselves the better."[78]

Despite the RPF's feelings, the French managed to avoid large clashes with either side. This was due in large part to the force structure that they brought to support their troops, which included Jaguar and Mirage aircraft as well as artillery and light armor. The message was clear—these were combat troops, not peacekeepers. French rules of engagement allowed force to be used "in circumstances where there was: a threat to own forces, a threat against the protected population, obstruction of the mission and, in a conflict situation with refugees, weapons were to be used only as a last resort."[79] On the other hand, to reinforce the notion that they did not want or expect a fight, "the French were not to wear helmets or anti-shrapnel jackets except when engaged or in immediate danger."[80]

To deflect growing tension, the French force commander pointed out that Operation Turquoise had continued to disarm Hutus, be they thugs, militiamen, or soldiers, within its humanitarian protection zone as well as in Zaire. He went so far as to assert, "I can say that there are currently no weapons with the troops of the [former Rwandan army] who have taken refuge in Zaire."[81] Zaire also claimed its armed forces were helping in the disarmament effort.[82] This was not entirely true. "While certain arms had been confiscated at the border, some were sold back to the [soldiers] once they were inside."[83] Former government supporters started to hide caches of weapons and to exert intimidation tactics within the refugee camps. As one report noted:

> It became clear that Rwanda's former government was re-creating a replica of its defeated regime, from former ministers down to the tiniest cell leader of a few hundred peasants. . . . Each day . . . aid workers [had] been handing over food, medicine and other supplies to these erstwhile officials. . . . Former soldiers, officials and militiamen [were] living well, hoarding donated food and blankets and selling these supplies at high prices. At the same time, nearly half the camp population—notably the elderly, women and children—were not getting enough food to ward off malnutrition.[84]

While the international community dithered, NGOs were left to deal with the mounting humanitarian crisis. But as the former Hutu government leaders garnered more and more power in the camps, they started exerting their influence against any NGO official who threatened to change the system. Just as in Somalia, NGOs and their staffs became targets of thugs. It is little wonder that under these conditions NGOs focused on quickly getting a UN force into the field that could offer them a modicum of security.

On 29 July the first of the French troops began to withdraw, despite UN pleas for them to remain until UNAMIR II could fully deploy. As the final August withdrawal date approached, it became evident that the French were not going to change their minds and tensions began to mount. Only in Kigali was the French pullout welcomed. French prime minister Edouard Balladur hinted that an invitation from the unity government might have persuaded them to stay, but such an invitation was never considered since the government was "still furious at what it called the French 'colonisation' of the zone."[85]

Extremist radio broadcasts increased their warnings for Hutus to flee before the French left and the United Nations took over. As one humanitarian relief worker, Mike McDonagh, declared, "It is going to be chaotic now. The French were a protection force and drew the line, and everyone knew not to cross it. Everyone knows that the U.N. has no spine, that's the bottom line."[86] The abandonment felt by many Rwandans was demonstrated as they threw sticks and stones and shouted at departing French troops. Even many relief organizations that had opposed the French intervention were reluctant to see them go. McDonagh spoke for many of them when he stated, "I was against them coming. I thought they came for all the wrong reasons. But they put something in place—the protected zone —which worked quite well."[87] Whatever the French motives for intervening, there is no denying they saved thousands of lives. Even the pragmatic U.S. ambassador who worked so successfully in Somalia, Robert Oakley, praised the French:

> Despite criticism that there were ulterior motives or that they would end up at war with the opposition Rwandan Patriotic Front, the French peacekeepers avoided the political pitfalls. They saved thousands of Hutus and Tutsis from slaughter and stemmed much of the refugee outflow from that part of Rwanda where they were present.[88]

Despite the overly sanguine views of the French about the effectiveness of their disarmament efforts, former members of the Rwandan government and military were able to smuggle weapons into Zaire and take control of the refugee camps where they operated with impunity. As a result, Operation Turquoise left a dangerous legacy for follow-on UN forces.

Unfortunately, the refugee flow once again became a flood as the French departed. As one UN official lamented, "The majority of the people have no confidence in the U.N. troops."[89] The commander of the UN contingent from Ethiopia that was guarding the border felt helpless and claimed "his troops had no mandate to use force to maintain order. The French used force sparingly but whenever necessary, and the threat of force was thought to be a major deterrent to violence in the security zone in southwest Rwanda."[90]

Emissaries from the deposed Hutu government scoured the country-side persuading people to leave Rwanda. Those who refused were branded Tutsi collaborators. The aim of this depopulation of Rwanda was to under-mine the legitimacy of the unity government and create such a massive humanitarian disaster that all aid would flow into the refugee camps and away from Kigali. The Hutus believed that the only way for the unity gov-ernment to combat this strategy was to offer them a power-sharing deal in the new government. Such an offer never materialized.

OPERATION SUPPORT HOPE

It was clear, as soon as the French announced in late July their determina-tion to withdraw, that the humanitarian crisis was once again going to assume major proportions. At one point over five hundred Hutus a minute were crossing over the border into Zaire. The United States was the first country to offer noncombat military support to help deliver relief. President Clinton, on 22 July, ordered General George Joulwan, the com-mander in chief, United States European Command, to assist the Rwanda relief effort. Joulwan, in turn, assigned Army Lieutenant General Daniel Schroeder to command the Joint Task Force operation dubbed Support Hope. The United States was followed quickly by other countries including the United Kingdom (Operation Gabriel), Australia (Operation Tamar), Canada (Operation Lance), and Japan. General Dallaire was not notified of the arrival of foreign troops and obtained information concerning the U.S. contingent only by visiting its force commander. Together they worked out a concept of operations for humanitarian relief. The secretary-general urged countries to place their forces under UNAMIR command, and all but the United States and Japan did so.

On the very day he received orders to assist, General Joulwan began deploying troops into the area to help with relief efforts and encourage refugees to return to Rwanda.[91] The force consisted of just over three thou-sand troops (both regulars and reserves) spread over a number of sites in Rwanda, Uganda, and Zaire. For political reasons, the decision was made to establish a joint headquarters for participating countries in Kigali and to use the Kigali airport as the hub of a relief network. The operation had two goals: stop the dying and turn relief efforts over to private organizations. Within four days of deployment, U.S. troops were producing 24,000 gallons of potable water a day in eastern Zaire, a figure that soared to 431,000 gallons a day by mid-August. "After August 11, water purification efforts begun by the U.S. military were taken over by the UN, to whom the U.S. military donated its equipment."[92] Although they received no special humanitarian support training, General Schroeder observed that troops were able to perform well because they came from "standard military units [and were] executing their wartime skills in a disciplined manner."[93]

At the start of U.S. relief efforts, deaths from disease were averaging as many as six thousand per day; they had dropped to approximately five hundred per day by the end of August. This rate was sufficient for General George Joulwan to declare, "The emergency for the most part is over. There are still a lot of problems, but they are [private relief groups' and the UN's] problems and not U.S. military."[94] Joulwan's statement clearly reflected America's new caution toward peace operations. As one observer noted, "So intent were the Americans on preventing mission creep that ultra-caution led to mission shrink."[95] By the end of the mission, which officially concluded on 30 September, the United States had flown over twelve hundred missions, delivered almost fifteen thousand tons of humanitarian relief supplies, and produced millions of gallons of potable water.[96]

FADING HOPE AND FINAL WITHDRAWAL

With the French departing, Rwandan unity government officials being posted in the former protection zone, alarmist propaganda once again being broadcast over the radio, and UNAMIR forces not yet up to strength, the United Nations was unable to convince hundreds of thousands of Hutus to remain in Rwanda. In addition, the United Nations was viewed suspiciously by the new government, which believed the United Nations was still there to help bring the deposed government back into power. The task of dealing with this deteriorating situation was left to a new UNAMIR force commander, Canadian major general Guy-Claude Tousignant, who assumed command on 19 August. Gradually UNAMIR started to build its strength, deploying nearly 4,300 troops by early October into six sectors (see figure 5-4).

In addition to protecting at-risk populations, one of the first major tasks undertaken by UNAMIR II was to coordinate the deployment of Rwandan Patriotic Army (RPA) units into the former French sector. It was

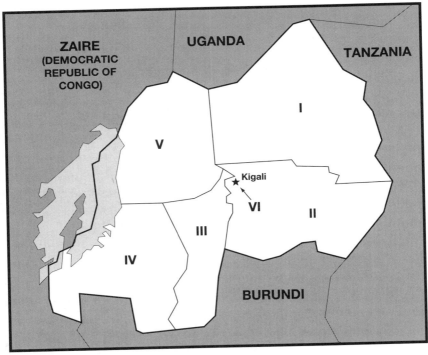

Figure 5-4. UNAMIR Operating Sectors

critical at this juncture for the United Nations to demonstrate that it was capable of following through where the French had left off. "General Lafourcade tried to persuade his Ghanaian [UN] counterpart to adopt the tactics which the French had found to be so successful. 'I impressed upon him the necessity of scattering units so as to cover the ground, and to conduct night patrols, but I believe that as soon as we left, they crept back into their shells.'"[97] UNAMIR was not idle, however; it transported refugees, collected arms surrendered by the gendarmerie, and occasionally dispatched teams to investigate genocide sites. To improve its image, explain its objectives, counter Hutu propaganda, and encourage repatriation, the United Nations also deployed an FM broadcasting capability. However, the United Nations received little cooperation from the government in the initial stages of this or any other endeavor. In fact, the government had turned the tables on foreign forces and insisted that UNAMIR obtain written authorization from the minister of defense for all deployments. Nevertheless, by October the secretary-general reported to the Security Council that there were signs of increasing stability in the country.

Despite UNAMIR's best efforts, the security situation remained volatile through the end of the year, especially along the borders where refugee camps were being used to harbor militia members and store arms. Zaire had all but reneged on its promise to disarm the Hutus, and some twenty thousand former government soldiers and militia members were said to be in the refugee camps with their arsenals intact. The unity government and the RPA became increasingly impatient with the slow process of trying to bring those responsible for the genocide to justice. The RPA began to make mass arrests, which inevitably resulted in some human rights abuses, and it was eager to close down the refugee camps. As violence became more frequent, UNAMIR forces made several December raids on camps to disarm and detain Hutu extremists.[98]

As noted above, the deposed government had entrenched itself in the camps and was exercising almost total control within their confines. NGOs were unable to defeat the monster they had inadvertently helped to create. In an 18 November report to the Security Council, Boutros-Ghali noted that the only way to reverse the situation was to separate the leaders and soldiers from other refugees and disarm them. He proposed three options to accomplish this. The most effective, he believed, would be a Chapter VII deployment of 10,000 to 12,000 troops, either UN controlled (option 1) or UN authorized (option 2), which could simultaneously move into the camps to forcibly disarm, collect, and escort former government forces into cantonment areas. A more realistic option in his view was a smaller force of 3,000 to 5,000 personnel who could sequentially accomplish the same task. As expected, the Security Council favored the latter alternative and directed the secretary-general to consult with possible troop contributors. Of the sixty nations approached, only one responded favorably.[99] In the interim, on 30 November the Security Council extended UNAMIR's mission until 9 June 1995 and enlarged its mandate to include protection for personnel assigned to the international commission dealing with war crimes in Rwanda. UNAMIR was also to assist with training a new, integrated national police force.

Encouraged by the lack of international interest in stopping them, Hutu guerrillas launched their first major cross-border attack at the beginning of the new year. Also during January 1995 an RPA unit attacked a displaced persons camp, killing eighteen people, including women and children. This was a major test for the unity government, which immediately decried the unauthorized attack, launched an investigation, and detained some of the soldiers reportedly involved. Guilty parties were later tried and executed. Skirmishes between guerrillas and RPA forces continued throughout 1995, and the unity government grew more skeptical that UNAMIR was doing anything to improve the situation. A guerrilla attack on RPA forces in September 1995 resulted in the death of a lieutenant and the RPA immediately undertook a search-and-destroy mission. By morning they had killed more than one hundred Hutus including women and children. Again Kagame promised to punish those who used excessive force. As the year ended, the RPA attacked a rebel stronghold on the island of Iwawa in Lake Kivu, killing approximately three hundred Hutus and seizing a number of weapons.

As the new year began, Rwanda's unity government insisted it neither needed nor wanted UNAMIR to stay. However, after weeks of debate, the mission was extended for three months but the number of forces involved dropped by a third. The UN flag came down at the end of the mandated period, but troops remained in hopes of revitalizing the process. But that was not to be. UNAMIR troops finally withdrew from Rwanda on 19 April 1996, bringing to a close one of the saddest and most difficult operations in UN history.

Rwanda demonstrated that early warning cannot prevent a crisis in the absence of political will. The international community was inundated with warnings about what was going to happen in Rwanda. The only surprising thing about events as they unfolded was the enormity of the slaughter. Events in Rwanda left little room for doubt that the United Nations is more often doomed to react to disasters than given the opportunity to prevent them. As General Dallaire lamented:

> The hands of the United Nations were . . . tied; and since it possesses no power akin to that of a sovereign state, it could only act with the consent of the international community under the auspices of the Security Council. As long as the individual members of this body procrastinated and pursued national agendas, the organization remained relatively powerless.[100]

Another analyst noted, "political will remains the most crucial determinant of whether or not states will or will not act collectively in a particular case."[101]

CONCLUDING REMARKS

The international community was given ample warning of the storm clouds gathering in Rwanda, and had been advised that the situation was changing from one of peacekeeping to something more pernicious—it chose to ignore those admonitions. The United Nations went into Rwanda to implement the Arusha Agreement, believing it had the consent of all parties.[102] In hindsight this belief appears naive. Stunned by the rapidity and brutality of the genocide, UNAMIR I troops were powerless to influence events. It was not simply a matter of trying harder. "Military effectiveness is the product of discipline, training, leadership, equipment and a mandate which relates to the mission."[103] General Dallaire insisted from the beginning that he could have stopped the slaughter had he been given 3,000 to 5,000 well-armed troops and permission to use them. The effectiveness of the 2,500 French troops in preventing additional slaughter during Operation Turquoise provides at least circumstantial evidence that Dallaire was correct. The French troops were well armed and had operated using liberal rules of engagement. Dallaire had neither. Hence, when UNAMIR I was confronted with genocide, to no one's surprise but everyone's regret, it failed to stop it. Faced with the stark alternatives of changing the mandate and reinforcing UNAMIR I or withdrawing, the Security Council opted for withdrawal. Unfairly or not, this poisoned the well for follow-on UN operations.

When moral imperatives made a robust intervention inevitable, it came too late to save the more than three-quarters of a million people who were slaughtered. Although arriving late, the French demonstrated admirable resolve given the lack of international political will; and Operation Turquoise did accomplish some good. France's ability to move its forces quickly into Rwanda was a damning indictment against the international community's inability to act earlier. International leaders had visions of dead soldiers being dragged through the streets of Mogadishu still fresh in their minds, and they simply were not eager to risk more casualties in a small central African country.

Because its motives were highly suspect, France entered the fray with little credibility. No one doubted that Paris still favored the deposed French-speaking Hutu government over the English-speaking leadership of the RPF. Over time, however, French credibility was enhanced because its rhetoric was supported by its actions. The mission deployed under a Chapter VII enforcement mandate, came equipped for the task, and followed rules of engagement that permitted it to back up threats with force. A willingness to threaten force and judiciously apply it, if necessary, constitute the essence of coercive inducement. It has been observed of Rwanda that "a mandate and willingness to use force contributed to *Opération Turquoise* success. Many concur with General Lafourcade's view that such interventions should be grounded in Chapter VII of the UN Charter, allowing the use of force and providing the necessary deterrent means."[104] The fact that the French routinely eschewed wearing helmets and flak vests enhanced the notion that they came ready but did not want to fight. One study concluded:

> While French troops, acting with discipline and restraint, applied such force sparingly for preventive and protective purposes, their willingness to do so was an effective deterrent. Having skilled troops who are able to use proportionate force proved indispensable.[105]

Few critics believed the French overplayed their hand, although some thought their actions were too constrained. In fact, future historians may point to Operation Turquoise as the classic tourniquet operation of the late twentieth century.

The long-term value of tourniquet operations remains an open question, but their short-term value is self-evident. While the humanitarian agencies were handing out relief supplies, the refugees were looking for something even more basic—security.[106] The French, to a large extent, managed to accomplish this in their protected zone. Thus, "one important lesson to be derived from Rwanda is how the application of force, even the most modest of means, bore results out of proportion to the effort made."[107] Providing human security is the single most critical factor leading to normalcy, and it cannot be a false security.

In contrast to Operation Turquoise, UNAMIR provided a false sense of security that ultimately discredited the United Nations. As General Dallaire wrote:

> The [UNAMIR] mission and the Rwandans which the operation was intended to secure fell victim to inflated expectations that the United Nations could not fulfill. This explains in part how a classical peacekeeping mission degenerated into a resumption of the conflict and how new human rights abuses based on political decapitation degenerated into genocide.[108]

The greatest challenge that faced the French was overcoming false expectations on both sides. Members of the deposed government not only consented to the intervention, they welcomed it, believing, as did the RPF, that the French intended to put the deposed government back in power. This made the operation doubly difficult. The French had to convince both sides that France had no intention of interfering with the outcome of the civil war.

The RPF victory had made the Arusha Agreement moribund, and no group stepped forward to offer options that might have helped reconcile Rwanda's political problems. The French did prove, however, that it was political will—rather than a shortage of money, a lack of time, or the possibility of failure—that prevented the international community from responding to the genocide. "France's soldiers did a good job, first protecting Tutsis in south-western Rwanda, then—for a time—keeping the Hutu there from fleeing into exile."[109] Then, as suddenly as the French appeared, they were gone.

In contrast to Operation Turquoise, UNAMIR II had to labor under the worst of conditions. It was established prior to Turquoise, continued its employment during that operation, and was expected to relieve it even though its mandate was seriously circumscribed by comparison. It had been a lack of UN resolve that resulted in the population losing confidence in UNAMIR I, even before the genocide started. Once the French departed, UNAMIR II did nothing to regain the confidence of either the new government or the dispersed population.

UNAMIR II was simply incapable of taking over from the French—its forces were not all in place, its motives and commitment were questioned by the new unity government, and it operated under a Chapter VI mandate even though there existed an undeniable possibility that widespread violence could be renewed. The greatest challenges for UNAMIR II, and for NGOs, were found in the refugee camps. Extremist Hutu leadership had managed to turn them into little fiefdoms, which the extremists ruled with a heavy and bloody hand. NGOs recognized too late that by allowing the Rwandans to determine who would distribute food to the needy, they had empowered the very people who created the crisis in the first place. When they finally realized that criminals were in charge of the camps, they had no means of correcting the situation. The international community was equally culpable since it could not muster the resolve to correct the situation either. Although the UN Secretariat wanted to mount operations

against the camps, contributing states were loath to let their troops participate, even had they been authorized by the mandate.[110]

Although UNAMIR II leadership was both courageous and dedicated,
the mission was rendered ineffective by the legacy of UNAMIR I and a lack
of international resolve. UNAMIR II troops felt and acted vulnerable. An
overemphasis on force protection shackled operations, including America's mission in Rwanda, Support Hope. One critic lamented, "It cannot
be acceptable for the world's superpower to be so demonstrably '*timid
and tentative*.'"[111]

There were other challenges as well. Although the Rwandan countryside
was littered with dead, the first battles there had been for the hearts and
minds of the people. The reason neighbor killed neighbor was that the vit-
riol broadcast by Radio Télévision Libre des Mille Collines encouraged them
to do so. There are two sides to conducting a public information campaign:
silencing those who incite hate and violence, and getting the mission's
message to the public. In Cambodia, the mass distribution of portable radios
in combination with a highly successful UN radio station proved a boon to
that operation;[112] but Radio UNAMIR did not start functioning until well
after the critical junctures had passed. Somalia had already taught the
United Nations that allowing hate-mongering, inaccurate radio broadcasts
to air could prove fatal to a mission, and General Dallaire would have
loved to have had a jamming capability assigned as part of his command—but he did not. One observer believes a coordinated public information campaign should go beyond silencing bad and promoting friendly
media to include criminal punishment for perpetrators of violence:

> There has to be an implicit understanding that those who use the airwaves
> (and newspapers) to foment riot and murder, seemingly with impunity, will
> be brought to account before an international court. There are few deterrent
> measures more effective than assured accountability.[113]

In the end, none of the international efforts set the stage for a long-term
solution to Rwanda's problems. Following the RPF's victory, the secretary-
general stressed time and again that "the new Government of Rwanda must
be assisted in creating conditions inside the country under which large-
scale repatriation and reintegration of refugees and internally displaced
people could take place."[114] The conditions that needed to be addressed,
but that were addressed inadequately if at all, included the following.

- *Rehabilitation of the basic economy.* All aid being funneled into the Rwanda crisis went into the refugee camps. None of it was earmarked for rebuilding Rwanda.
- *Reactivation of the public sector.* Although the unity government did manage to fill important posts and establish a National Assembly, much of the civil bureaucracy remained constrained by lack of resources. When the interim government fled, it took everything with it and emptied the banks. The unity government found itself facing shortages of telephones, computers, transports, office equipment, and fuel. Cash reserves were inadequate to pay salaries or meet other essential payments. Even public utilities were not able to be restored.
- *Establishment of a fair and effective judicial system.* Although an international tribunal was set up, the enormity of the task it faced was overwhelming. Over sixty thousand prisoners were incarcerated in overcrowded and inhumane conditions in Rwanda, and, as was noted above, there was no money available to pay police officers, lawyers, and judges.
- *Resolution of property rights.* Between the slaughter of Tutsis and the displacement of virtually the entire population of Rwanda, the issue of property rights became an issue of unheard proportions. Hutus moved onto property once owned by murdered Tutsis. When they were displaced, that property, along with most Hutu property, was seized by RPF supporters. Those people who were persuaded to return generally found their property occupied, raising rival claims. The government declared that wrongful occupation of another person's home or property was unlawful; but this policy became almost impossible to enforce.
- *Land mine clearance.* Land mines have become the single most debilitating aftermath of conflict. In Rwanda, it is believed that more than a million mines were planted in the countryside.

The Rwanda case highlights the fact that having a peace agreement in hand does not mean that peaceful conditions exist or that risks have been eliminated. The failure in Rwanda must be laid at the doorstep of the politicians who lacked the will to respond. The French saved lives, but were unable to establish lasting security conditions. Thus, international efforts amounted to little more than small bandages placed over gaping wounds —necessary but not sufficient remedies for the ills they confronted.

6

HAITI

by Chantal de Jonge Oudraat

On 31 July 1994 the United Nations Security Council authorized a U.S.-led multinational force "to use *all necessary means* to facilitate the departure from Haiti of the military dictatorship and establish and maintain a secure and stable environment."[1] The Security Council, defining the situation in Haiti as a threat to international peace and security, permitted the United States to forcefully remove the junta which had usurped power on 30 September 1991 from the democratically elected Jean-Bertrand Aristide.

The response of the international community to the military coup in Haiti was spearheaded by the United States and went through three phases. Phase I lasted from September 1991 to September 1994. It was characterized by a failure to bring about the return of the democratically elected government. Negotiations conducted under the auspices of the Organization of American States (OAS) and the United Nations lacked clarity of purpose and were not backed by sufficient political will. The coercive measures taken during this phase consisted of incremental and ill-defined economic sanctions that hit poor Haitians hard and left the perpetrators of the coup practically untouched.

Phase II lasted from September 1994 until February 1996. It was characterized by the successful deployment of the Multinational Force (MNF) and the UN Mission in Haiti (UNMIH), the removal of the military junta in September 1994, and the return of Aristide to power in October 1994. To bring these developments about, the international community had authorized the use of military force in Haiti and committed overwhelming resources to an intervention force capable of crushing the Haitian military if necessary. In the end, the mere threat to use military force proved to be sufficient: the junta gave up power and politically inspired violence was deterred. Some 21,000 U.S. troops were involved in the first two weeks of the international effort—Operation Uphold Democracy. In March 1995, the MNF transferred responsibility for the Haitian operation to UNMIH. With 6,000 troops, it maintained a secure and stable environment in Haiti, and permitted the conduct of democratic elections and the peaceful transition of power in February 1996 between Aristide and René Préval, the new Haitian president who had been elected in December 1995.

Phase III started in February 1996 and was continuing as this chapter went to press. It is characterized by a weakening international and U.S. commitment to help the Haitian government sustain civil order, rebuild the economy, and consolidate the gains made toward democratic governance. Economic assistance has been slow to arrive. U.S. military disengagement and a sharply reduced international military presence—the UN Support Mission in Haiti (UNSMIH) established in July 1996 had a strength of 1,300 soldiers—has led to increased political violence and raised doubts regarding the success of Operation Uphold Democracy.

The first part of this chapter examines the origins of the Haitian crisis and the process that led to the decision to use military force. The second part of this chapter focuses on phase II of the international effort and in particular on the U.S.-led MNF that landed in Haiti on 19 September 1994. Indeed, the MNF was the only international operation with respect to Haiti authorized to use military force. When the MNF transferred responsibilities to the UN-led force—UNMIH—many predicted the collapse of Operation Uphold Democracy. This chapter explains why this did not happen and examines the successful transition of command.

HAITI AND OUTSIDE POWERS: AN UNEASY RELATIONSHIP

Ever since winning its independence from France in 1804, Haiti has struggled with domestic despots and outside powers. Situated in the Caribbean, it has suffered from both U.S. intervention and U.S. neglect. The United States ignored the Haitian Republic for the first fifty-eight years of its existence.[2] Once recognized by the United States in 1862, Haiti's independence was treated in a cavalier manner by Washington. Indeed, in 1915 Haiti was invaded by the United States. The invasion, while defended as a humanitarian mission—political and mob violence was rampant[3]—also had strong economic motives—making Haiti safe for U.S. investment. Lastly, the United States had a strategic interest in Haiti—preventing Germany from establishing a naval base that could threaten the freedom of navigation in the Caribbean and entry to the Panama Canal.[4]

The American occupation lasted until 1934 and was reviled not only by Haitian peasants and the emergent black elite but also by the traditional mulatto business class. In 1934, with the foreign threat to Haiti having disappeared and the economic depression hitting the United States hard, President Franklin Roosevelt, as part of his "good neighbor" policy, decided to bring the U.S. Marines in Haiti back home. The occupation had accomplished little, the most lasting legacy being the creation of the Haitian armed forces (later known as the Forces Armées d'Haiti [FAdH]). After the U.S. departure, the mulatto elite briefly regained political control of the country under the watchful eyes of the U.S.-trained Haitian army. However, the emergence of black nationalist forces and the election in 1957 of François "Papa Doc" Duvalier pushed them out of political office.[5]

Duvalier proved to be a ruthless leader. Recognizing the potential of the FAdH, he set out to bring it under his control by replacing the largely mulatto officer corps with black Duvalier loyalists and by creating the *tontons macoutes*—a corps of paramilitary forces that acted as a countervailing force to the army and as an internal security force that kept the civilian population terrorized.[6] The mulatto business elite was left alone as long as it stayed out of politics.[7] Moreover, by nationalizing many utilities and creating state-controlled import-substituting manufacturing enterprises, Duvalier created his own economic power base.[8]

For most Haitians, the Duvalier reign was synonymous with economic extortion, brutal intimidation, and political assassination. The blatant human rights abuses perpetrated by the Duvalier regime prompted many countries to curtail economic assistance to Haiti. The United States closed its economic assistance mission to Haiti in 1964 and excluded Haiti from the Alliance for Progress.[9] Once more, Haiti was rejected and neglected by its powerful neighbor.

Haiti's relations with the United States improved in the 1970s. In April 1971, Papa Doc died and the Haitian presidency passed to his son, Jean-Claude—"Baby Doc." During Jean-Claude's rule, modest political reforms and economic development programs were introduced. Tourism

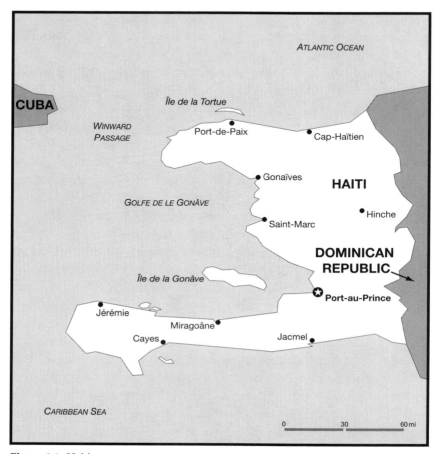

Figure 6-1. Haiti

picked up, as did foreign assistance and the economy, in general.[10] The 1976 U.S. presidential election, which brought Jimmy Carter to power, did not go unnoticed in Haiti. Carter's linkage of human rights issues to U.S. foreign aid prompted a wave of political liberalization measures. However, the tide of freedom was as short-lived as Carter's presidency. Indeed, things took a turn for the worse at the end of the 1970s.[11] Political repression regained momentum and corruption as a way of government reached new heights. Large amounts of money were skimmed off from the national budget for the personal benefit of the ruling elites, including the handful of

Haitian families who controlled the Haitian economy. The prices of utilities and essential commodities such as sugar and flour rose to unprecedented levels. To escape the political repression and economic misery, a growing number of Haitians sought to migrate to the United States. The number of Haitian boat people increased from fewer than 1,000 per year in 1972–78 to 2,500 in 1979 and 25,000 in 1980.[12]

To stop the influx of poor Haitians, the United States signed an agreement with the Haitian government in 1981, whereby the U.S. Coast Guard would bar and return all Haitians encountered on the high seas who were believed to be attempting to migrate to the United States. The number of illegal Haitians intercepted at sea consequently dropped from 8,000 in 1981 to 134 in 1982.[13] Forced to remain in Haiti, the growing urban workforce —led by a politically literate black middle class—became increasingly militant. The threat of a popular uprising prompted the Haitian army, with the blessing of the United States, to force Baby Doc from power on 6 February 1986.[14]

From 1986 to 1991, Haiti experienced a succession of sabotaged and rigged elections (in November 1987 and January 1988), military coups (in June and September 1988), and forced resignations (in March 1990). With the Duvaliers gone and the *tontons macoutes* disbanded, the army, as one of the few functioning organizations in Haiti, ran the country. Under Baby Doc, the army had suffered from declining military expenditures. To compensate, the army had expanded its interests in Haitian state enterprises, and it took over these businesses once Duvalier was deposed.[15] The army also took over part of the lucrative drug trade.

That said, the end of the Cold War and the growth and consolidation of democratic forms of governance throughout much of Central and South America did not leave Haiti untouched.[16] Pressured by the United States, the Haitian military committed itself to free and fair elections. An OAS electoral assistance mission was invited to Haiti in February 1990, and in October 1990 a United Nations Observer Group for the Verification of Elections in Haiti (ONUVEH) was deployed to help monitor the presidential December 1990 elections.[17]

When Aristide won two-thirds of the vote and defeated the candidate backed by both the United States and the Haitian military—Marc Bazin— the election results were difficult to contest. The OAS and UN observer missions validated those results. However, Aristide's position was weak.

Indeed, the forces that had propelled Aristide to power did not turn out for subsequent rounds of municipal and legislative elections held in January and February 1991. Consequently Aristide's Front National pour le Changement et la Démocratie (FNDC) failed to win a majority in parliament. Moreover, the FNDC was divided and internal political struggles soon broke out.[18] In addition, Aristide's wars on corruption and drugs were very unpopular with the security forces who thrived on both. Finally, his economic plans and leftist revolutionary rhetoric sent shudders through the ranks of the army and the business elite. On 30 September 1991, with support of the latter, the army, led by General Raoul Cédras, seized power.[19]

The Refugee Crisis I

Many Aristide supporters were killed and persecuted immediately following the coup. Others took to the sea in an attempt to seek refuge in the United States. The U.S. Coast Guard, unable to handle this sudden influx, transferred them to the U.S. military base at Guantanamo Bay in Cuba for processing. By May 1992, the base was overloaded—thirteen thousand Haitians awaited screening for political asylum. To turn this tide, on 24 May 1992 President George Bush ordered that all Haitians found on the high seas were to be returned directly to Haiti without prior screening for refugee status.

Bush's executive order provoked a public outcry. It disavowed an essential commitment of the 1981 bilateral interdiction agreement with Haiti, whereby refugees would be screened so that no person who was escaping political persecution would be returned to Haiti without his or her consent. It also ran counter to the 1951 Convention Relating to the Status of Refugees, which provides that no state "shall expel or return a refugee . . . to the frontiers of territories where his life or freedom would be threatened on account of his race, religion, nationality, membership of a particular social group or political opinion."[20]

U.S. presidential candidate Bill Clinton was quick to denounce Bush's policy as "a blow to America's moral authority in defending the rights of refugees."[21] However, on 15 January 1993, five days before his inauguration, Clinton announced that he would continue Bush's policy and return Haitians to Haiti without screening. Indeed, following Clinton's campaign remarks, boat building had boomed in Haiti—American officials estimated that 150,000 Haitians were ready to go to sea on a flotilla of 1,600 boats, when Clinton assumed office.[22]

UN Peacekeepers Rebuffed: The USS *Harlan County* Incident

On the diplomatic front, the military coup was immediately condemned by the OAS, which called for the reinstatement of Aristide and recommended that all member states suspend economic and commercial relations with Haiti. Since the end of the Cold War, the United States had actively supported democracy as an alternative to military dictatorship in Latin America. A historic resolution of the OAS, adopted barely four months before the Haitian coup, had committed all of the organization's members to common action in the event of "any sudden or irregular interruption of the democratic political institutional process or the legitimate exercise of power by the democratically elected government in any member state."[23] Hence, the overthrow of Aristide could not be ignored, even if his leftist and populist views were anathema to the United States. However, unlike the United Nations, the OAS cannot impose formal sanctions on its members. The OAS action, therefore, was limited.

The initial reaction of the United Nations to the coup was reserved. The UN General Assembly, which had been involved in the monitoring of the elections, expressed general indignation,[24] but it was only in 1992 that it requested the UN secretary-general to get involved in efforts to find a solution to the Haitian crisis.[25] The Security Council discussed the Haitian problem in its meeting of 3 October 1991, but did not define the situation as a threat to international peace and security, as requested by the Haitian representative.[26] Hence, no action was taken. It was not until June 1993 that the Security Council became actively involved in the search for a solution to the Haitian crisis. UN engagement signaled the failure of American attempts to solve the Haitian crisis through the OAS, and success for Aristide, who from the start had sought UN action with respect to the coup.[27]

Initial efforts by the UN secretary-general's special envoy to Haiti, Dante Caputo, to bring about Aristide's return to power were unsuccessful. In February 1993, the military junta had agreed to the deployment of a joint OAS-UN International Civilian Mission in Haiti (MICVIH) to verify the respect of human rights and to open a dialogue with Aristide.[28] However, while the civilian mission arrived in Haiti in February, the dialogue went nowhere. To increase international pressure on the military, Aristide requested the Security Council to make the OAS sanctions mandatory, particularly those measures prohibiting the supply of oil and arms to Haiti. Such a resolution was adopted by the Security Council on 16 June 1993.[29] The United States had finally come to recognize that coercion was needed to get the Haitian military to the negotiating table. On 21 June, two days before the sanctions were to enter into force, General Cédras agreed to meet Aristide.

The meetings, which were chaired and orchestrated by Caputo, took place on Governors Island in New York and resulted in an agreement signed by Aristide and Cédras on 3 July 1993. The Governors Island Agreement provided for the return of Aristide to Haiti on 30 October 1993 and the appointment of a prime minister by Aristide. The agreement, and the subsequent New York Pact, signed on 16 July 1993, called on the United Nations and the OAS to verify the implementation of the agreements. It also envisaged that UN personnel would assist the Haitian government in modernizing the country's armed forces and creating a new police force. To this effect a peacekeeping mission was established.[30] The mission was to be composed of 567 civilian police monitors, 60 military trainers, and a 700-strong military construction unit. The United States had pledged to contribute 500 troops to the UN force. An advance team of UNMIH was deployed in September and October 1993. Robert Malval's appointment as prime minister–designate was ratified by the Haitian parliament on 25 August 1993. UN sanctions were suspended on 27 August 1993,[31] and the United States, France, and Canada—Haiti's most important foreign aid donors— along with the major international financial organizations, were ready to resume aid and financial support.

However, when the USS *Harlan County*, carrying the first batch of UNMIH peacekeepers, including 220 U.S. troops, sailed into the harbor of the Haitian capital on 11 October 1993, some one hundred armed civilians —also known as *attachés*—staged an unfriendly reception in the dock area. Armed with banners warning that the deployment of UN troops would result in "another Somalia"—where barely one week before eighteen American soldiers had been killed—the mob prevented the ship from docking.[32] The military junta and chief of police did not intervene; on the contrary, they had allowed the demonstrators into the dock area.[33]

With the debacle of Somalia still fresh in the minds of U.S. policymakers, Clinton ordered the ship to return to the United States. The risks associated with deploying lightly armed American servicemen in Haiti were believed to be too great. However, the image of the U.S. ship fleeing from a bunch of armed thugs was to haunt the Clinton administration—it made Clinton and the United States appear weak. Moreover, it sounded the death knell for the Governors Island Agreement[34] and emboldened the junta. Political violence and terror had increased following the signing of the Governors Island Agreement. Most cabinet ministers had gone into hiding and feared for their lives. Even Malval was afraid to leave his heavily guarded home. A few days after the *Harlan County* sailed away, and hours after Clinton had reasserted Washington's commitment to Aristide's return, Aristide's minister of justice, Guy Malary, was murdered. The military junta was widely believed to be responsible.

With the Haitian military clearly signaling its unwillingness to cooperate with international efforts restoring Aristide to power and with the United States in retreat, the UN secretary-general had no choice but to recall the advance team of the UNMIH peacekeeping mission as well as the bulk of the civilian mission, MICVIH.[35] The international community seemed to have abandoned Haiti.

This sentiment was reinforced by a rudderless U.S. foreign policy: the retreat of the *Harlan County* mirrored U.S. hesitation with regard to the use of force in Bosnia and Somalia. Moreover, U.S. congressional support for Aristide was at an all-time low. Responding to and reinforcing the anti-interventionist mood in Congress, the CIA distributed highly controversial and unflattering reports that portrayed Aristide as mentally unstable and asserted that many human rights abuses had been committed during his presidency.[36]

The UN Security Council promptly reimposed the oil and arms embargo on Haiti and authorized member states to enforce it through a naval blockade, but this had little effect on the Haitian military and its supporters.[37] They had stockpiled enough oil to weather the storm. Moreover, contraband coming through the Dominican border and a booming drug-trafficking business kept the military financially afloat.

Lawrence Pezullo, the U.S. special envoy for Haiti, and Caputo continued to negotiate with the junta and Aristide. However, their leverage on the junta was close to nil. Moreover, Malval and Aristide disagreed about what should be done. Malval believed in a negotiated solution to the crisis. Supported by the United States and France, he advocated the convening of a national conference. Aristide, on the other hand, believed that his return was a prerequisite for the reestablishment of democracy and national reconciliation. Unable to bridge their differences, Malval resigned in December 1993. In January 1994 Aristide found himself being pressured again by the United States. Washington wanted Aristide to appoint a new prime minister, create a government of national unity, and grant amnesty to the Haitian military. Once the junta had surrendered power, the new prime minister and Aristide would negotiate Aristide's return. Aristide, however, insisted on the military's resignation before the adoption of an amnesty law and the appointment of a prime minister.

The deadlock in the negotiations and reports that several members of the junta had been paid CIA informants before the coup brought disagreements to the surface between and among the United States, France, Canada, and Venezuela—the countries most closely involved in finding a solution to the Haitian crisis. France called for expanded sanctions, but this was opposed by the United States. Threats that a comprehensive embargo on all Haitian commercial goods would be imposed were issued by members of the Security Council, but none was carried out. The United States favored selective sanctions that would target specific individuals rather than the Haitian people—its fear of vast numbers of Haitian refugees had not subsided. Meanwhile, the level of terror in Haiti increased. The Front pour l'Avancement et le Progrès Haitien (FRAPH), an organization with close ties to the military and composed of soldiers, paramilitary *attachés*, and former *tontons macoutes*, systematically targeted Aristide supporters and used intimidation, torture, and violence to suppress opposition to the military regime. Many were left terrorized, mutilated, or dead.

The Refugee Crisis II

The rise of violence in Haiti led to an increase in the number of Haitian boat people. However, to evade the naval blockade, those who risked the high seas had to stay longer afloat and run greater risks in their efforts to reach the Florida coast unseen. Many perished in the endeavor.[38] Images of shipwrecked and drowned Haitians led the U.S. congressional Black Caucus and other Democratic interests groups in Washington to mobilize on their behalf.[39]

Bowing to this pressure, Clinton announced in May 1994 that screening procedures for Haitian refugees would be reintroduced in June. Reservations about Aristide were set aside and a new policy aimed at ousting the junta, forcefully if necessary, was put into place. Pezullo, who had resigned in April, was replaced on 8 May 1994 by William H. Gray III, a former chairman of the congressional Black Caucus. Gray was known for favoring a more aggressive policy toward the Haitian military, and the Clinton administration hoped that his appointment would neutralize U.S. domestic opposition to its Haitian policy. To deal with the refugees themselves, assistance was sought from the UN High Commissioner for Refugees (UNHCR). UNHCR's involvement lent an aura of international respectability to the U.S. refugee policy.[40]

Simultaneously, a comprehensive set of sanctions against Haiti was finally voted on by the Security Council on 6 May 1994. The council also decided that all officers of the Haitian military and police, including their immediate families, would be prohibited from entering any UN member state. It urged all states to freeze the financial assets of these Haitians.[41] Moreover, it decided that sanctions would not be lifted until UNMIH could be safely deployed; Cédras, the commander-in-chief of the armed forces had retired; and Michel François and Philippe Biamby—respectively, the chief of police of Haiti's capital, Port-au-Prince, and the chief of staff of the Haitian armed forces—had resigned or departed.[42] To make the embargo more effective, the United States sent two additional navy vessels off the coast of Haiti, where they joined six other U.S. ships, one Canadian ship, one Argentine ship, and one Dutch ship. In addition, under auspices of the United Nations, a team of technical experts was dispatched to the Dominican Republic to assess the situation on the Haitian-Dominican border and to examine how to stop the contraband.

In Haiti, word of the new U.S. refugee policy and UN sanctions spread quickly. By July 1994 refugee levels rivaled those of September 1991: between 5,000 and 14,000 people fled weekly on frail and overloaded boats.[43] U.S. Coast Guard cutters were swamped by Haitian refugees. As one villager put it: "We know that if we take to the boats it will help Aristide. . . . No one told us this, we just know it is true. We are not afraid to die in the sea if it helps to return Aristide. . . . The only way to fight is to get the Americans to keep their promises. The only way to do that is to do what they fear most."[44]

In early July, U.S. officials considered reintroducing summary repatriation, but in the end this was ruled out because of its potentially disastrous political repercussions. Instead, the United States asked other countries to provide "safe havens" for those picked up at sea. The response was dismal. In the region only Dominica, Grenada, and Antigua were willing to take in refugees; Panama, which the United States had invaded in December 1989 to overthrow Manuel Noriega, reneged on its initial offer to take in 10,000 Haitian refugees.[45] Rumors spread that an American invasion of Haiti was imminent. These rumors were sustained by highly publicized maneuvers off the coast of Florida and the dispatch of 2,000 combat-ready marines off the coast of Haiti.

OPERATIONS RESTORE DEMOCRACY AND UPHOLD DEMOCRACY

The MNF, September 1994–March 1995

Following the *Harlan County* incident, the U.S. Atlantic Command established a small planning cell to prepare for a forceful imposition of the Governors Island Agreement, even though the Pentagon was adamantly opposed to sending U.S. troops to Haiti. The idea of a military invasion gained momentum in the spring of 1994.

When Clinton reversed his refugee policy in May 1994, he also pledged to make a more aggressive effort to restore Aristide to power. He declared that the use of military force had not been ruled out.[46] At the same time, the U.S. Army Special Operations Command was instructed to develop a comprehensive plan to depose the junta and bring about a secure environment that would enable Aristide to return to Haiti.[47]

Clinton's remarks triggered a host of rumors about an imminent U.S. invasion, but Haitian military leaders were impressed neither by the tighter economic sanctions decided on by the Security Council nor by the rumors of an invasion. On the contrary, on 11 May 1994, the junta-controlled Haitian Senate proclaimed Emile Jonassaint, the head of the Haitian Supreme Court, provisional president of Haiti.[48] Two months later, on 11 July 1994, international human rights observers, who had remained in Haiti after the October 1993 withdrawal, were given forty-eight hours to leave Haiti.

The defiant pose of the Haitian military helped the United States persuade the other Security Council members to support a military intervention of Haiti. Under the terms of the Security Council resolution adopted on 31 July 1994, the U.S.-led Multinational Force (MNF) would enter

Haiti first and establish a secure and stable environment.[49] The United Nations would take over once such an environment had been created and once the UN-led peacekeeping force had the capacity to do so. This two-stage operation, which had been proposed by the secretary-general,[50] took into account the insistence of the U.S. military that any action that might involve the use of force—and thus the risk of U.S. casualties—had to be under U.S. command. Moreover, it shielded the United Nations from finding itself in a situation where it could not carry out its mandate due to a lack of resources.[51]

As it turned out, the MNF did not have to fight its way into Haiti. Just before the MNF landed in Haiti on 19 September 1994, the Haitian military leaders agreed to relinquish power and accept the deployment of the MNF. This agreement had been obtained in a last-ditch U.S. diplomatic effort led by former President Jimmy Carter, former Chairman of the Joint Chiefs of Staff Colin Powell, and Senator Sam Nunn.

The U.S.-led force, therefore, landed in Haiti with the grudging consent of the local parties, and the invasion plan, which had envisioned a forceful ousting of the junta, was quickly changed into a permissive entry plan.[52] The main problem with the new plan was that it had not anticipated the complete collapse of the Haitian security and police forces while their leaders were still in the country and retained nominal control.[53] This led to confusion regarding the tasks and rules of engagement of the MNF.

MNF's Rules of Engagement

Rules of engagement (ROE) define how military forces are to respond to different situations and when they can use force. In traditional peace-keeping operations, the use of force is authorized in self-defense and in response to rogue elements who are impeding the mission. In his July 1994 report to the Security Council, the UN secretary-general had assumed that even after a voluntary departure of the Haitian military, the environment in Haiti would be volatile and possibly hostile. This could easily translate into violent actions against the international force or into intra-Haitian violence. Therefore, the secretary-general had warned that the international force might have to use coercive means to fulfill its mandate. He had recommended that it be provided with the authority to use force under Chapter VII of the UN Charter.[54] Although invested with such authority, U.S. troops in Haiti had been instructed by their military commanders not to become involved in law-and-order issues and to hold their fire in such cases—that is, in intra-Haitian violence.

This, however, led to unacceptable situations in which U.S. troops found themselves unable to respond when Haitian army and police personnel beat up civilians who had poured out of the slums of Port-au-Prince to cheer the arrival of the American soldiers. These incidents, widely reported in the international press, led to a quick reversal of the ROE.[55] On 21 September 1994, a U.S. military spokesman told the press, "The presence of U.S. troops is intended to be an intimidating, deterring factor. Nobody is going to sit on a seawall any more and just watch violence proceed."[56] Henceforth, the use of force was recommended to prevent serious criminal acts, such as rape, murder, and robbery.[57]

Three days later, U.S. Marines engaged Haitian security forces suspected of abusing civilians in a shoot-out in Cap-Haïtien. Ten Haitian army and police officers were killed. The incident led almost overnight to the disappearance of the army and the police in large parts of the country. Faced with this security vacuum, the U.S. military at first hesitated, but soon realized that it had no choice but to step in. The U.S. military was nonetheless extremely nervous about this development and the possibility of mission creep. The size of the force was increased. Counting the troops at sea, a total of 28,800 soldiers were engaged in the Haitian intervention, 21,000 of whom were deployed on the ground in Haiti.[58] With the departure of Cédras and Biamby, the U.S. military commander, Lieutenant General Hugh Shelton, became the de facto ruler of Haiti.[59] The situation rapidly stabilized and U.S. forces became engaged in tasks ranging from the maintenance of public order to organizing town meetings and restoring electricity.

The 7,500 Haitian soldiers and the 1,000 or so members of Haitian paramilitary organizations were no match for the 21,000-strong MNF. Once the authority of the latter was established, the number of violent incidents in Haiti diminished quickly. In the third week of its operation, the MNF started to reduce force levels. The third week also saw the arrival of the first non-U.S. troop contingents,[60] as well as the arrival of a 60-person UNMIH advance team, the UN-led force that was to take over from the MNF once a secure and stable environment had been created. Shortly after Aristide's return to Haiti on 15 October 1994, the number of MNF troops was reduced further to 16,750.[61] From mid-December 1994 to March 1995, the level of MNF forces averaged 8,000 troops including 700 police monitors.[62] The majority of MNF's operations were centered in the capital, Port-au-Prince, although small special forces units regularly visited other towns and regions throughout the country.

The Challenge: Sustaining a Stable and Secure Environment

Although the immediate threat posed by Haitian armed forces and para-military units was neutralized quickly and efficiently, the longer-term problem of keeping these forces from becoming rogue elements was not as easy to solve. The initial international response to the security void in Haiti was to create an Interim Public Security Force (IPSF).[63] This force was composed of 3,000 former Haitian soldiers, who were given a one-week training course; 900 Haitian refugees recruited at the U.S. Guantanamo base in Cuba, who had received a three-week training course; and 100 Haitians, who had graduated from a three-month police course in Canada. The IPSF was given the job of dealing with intra-Haitian law enforcement problems. It soon became clear that the IPSF was not up to the task. Its personnel were inexperienced, they lacked basic equipment, and they were mistrusted by the population. Moreover, members of the IPSF often lacked the motivation and incentives to act as responsible policemen. Indeed, their tours of duty were only temporary and their chances of joining the new Haitian National Police were slim.[64] Finally, the absence of a working penitentiary and justice system made law enforcement extremely difficult. Law and order therefore remained heavily dependent on the MNF. The MNF's display of force early on was of great importance in establishing the credibility of the force; it helped contain political violence and civil disorder in a time of turmoil.

In addition to organizing the establishment of a police force, the U.S. military was instructed to confiscate the heavy weapons of the Haitian armed forces and screen its personnel for troublemakers and gross human rights abusers. Indeed, the U.S. view was that the military should be retrained, but Aristide favored disbanding the FAdH. Not wanting to antagonize the United States head-on, Aristide, once back in Haiti, demobilized the army by bits and pieces. He simultaneously created several specialized security forces and staffed some of these units with former military.[65] Even so, most army personnel found themselves in a state of limbo, and they therefore constituted a potential source of unrest. Attempts to compensate or resettle de-mobilized military personnel met with opposition from the impoverished population, which saw the FAdH as a group of oppressors and murderers.[66] The issue of the status of the Haitian army was not resolved until January 1995, when the FAdH was disbanded by presidential decree.[67] To deal with demobilized soldiers, not retained for service in the IPSF, the U.S. Agency for International Development funded a six-month vocational training program. However, in September 1996, the UN secretary-general estimated that of the 5,000 soldiers who had followed the program, over 80 percent had not been able to get a job.[68] Throughout 1996 the problem of unemployed former soldiers continued to haunt the Haitian government, particularly since the disarmament program had not been very successful and many soldiers had retained their weaponry.[69]

Finally, the U.S. military was given the task of neutralizing paramilitary organizations and disarming its members. Raids on FRAPH headquarters in Port-au-Prince and Cap-Haïtien in October 1994 led to a pledge by the FRAPH leader, Emmanuel Constant, that he would cooperate with Aristide and renounce the use of violence.[70] His subsequent disappearance from Haiti gave the impression that FRAPH had, indeed, been neutralized.[71] However, most Haitians, and the secretary-general believed that most FRAPH members had simply gone underground.[72]

U.S. attempts to disarm the paramilitaries were, similarly, not very successful. In 1993, FAdH had issued arms permits to tens of thousands of civilians and large numbers of weapons had been distributed.[73] The Office of the U.S. Secretary of Defense estimated that in 1994 a total of 175,000 guns were in circulation.[74] The weapon buy-back program, which offered U.S. dollars for weapons ($50 for handguns, $100 for semiautomatic weapons, and $300 for heavy weapons), in a country where the annual per capita income did not exceed $250, had by 19 March 1995 collected only 13,281 weapons, or less than 8 percent of the total number of weapons thought to be in circulation.[75]

Most of the weapons collected by the MNF were seized or confiscated. Early on, the MNF had issued a public warning that weapons carried in public would be seized. It set up some roadblocks, but refused to actively engage in weapon searches.[76] Aristide blamed the lack of success of the disarmament program on halfhearted U.S. efforts.[77] A more aggressive disarmament campaign, however, might have entailed U.S. casualties, a risk Clinton was not willing to take. Moreover, from the U.S. perspective the disarmament program had been designed primarily as a U.S. force protection measure, and not as a measure aimed at the demilitarization of Haitian society. As a result tens of thousands of weapons remained in circulation in Haiti.[78]

That said, the first phase of Operation Uphold Democracy was a great success. It involved over 28,000 troops, but suffered only one casualty. Aristide was returned to power, and dates for municipal and legislative elections were set. Though still fragile, the security situation had improved, and no serious threat to the government existed.[79]

Transfer to the United Nations

If domestic political pressure persuaded Clinton to engage U.S. forces in Haiti, domestic politics also pressed for disengagement at the earliest possible date. Before adjourning for the November 1994 elections, the U.S. Congress adopted a resolution that called for the "prompt and early withdrawal" of U.S. troops from Haiti.[80] The November 1994 elections gave control of both houses of Congress to the Republicans, and the Clinton administration was more keen than ever to transfer responsibility for the Haiti operation to the United Nations as quickly as possible.

UNMIH: March 1995–June 1996. On 31 March 1995, six months after the first American troops had been deployed in Haiti and three months before municipal and legislative elections were to take place, the MNF handed off responsibility for Haiti to UNMIH. UNMIH was to assist the Haitian government in sustaining a secure and stable environment, professionalizing and creating a new Haitian police force, and establishing an environment conducive to the conduct of free and fair elections.[81]

UNMIH was authorized to deploy 6,000 troops and 900 civilian police. At the time of the handover from the MNF, 5,500 UNMIH troops were already in Haiti and two-thirds of its forces came from MNF contingents.[82] The United States contributed 2,400 troops to UNMIH, including its commander, Major General Joseph Kinzer, who had arrived in Haiti one month before the transfer of authority.

UNMIH did not operate under the same rules of engagement as the MNF. Indeed, the MNF had acted under Chapter VII of the UN Charter because the situation in Haiti had been defined as a threat to international peace and security. The MNF therefore had enforcement authority—permission to use military force—to bring about an end to the illegal regime in Haiti and to create a secure and stable environment for Aristide's return. UNMIH was deployed only after these conditions had been created and the threat to international peace and security no longer existed. UNMIH therefore functioned as a traditional peacekeeping force under Chapter VI of the UN Charter.[83]

Even so, UNMIH's military commander received assertive rules of engagement and proactive operational guidelines.[84] Military force could be used to sustain a secure and stable environment. The use of force would be decided upon by the UN special representative in consultation with Kinzer, and in close cooperation with the Haitian president and his government. It was made clear, however, that UNMIH's mandate to assist the Haitian government in sustaining public order did not extend to such law-and-order activities as the arrest, detention, and prosecution of individuals, or the seizure of illegally detained weapons. Anyone who directly attacked members of UNMIH or tried to keep it from carrying out its mandate could be arrested and detained only for a brief period, until they could be handed over to the Haitian authorities.[85]

Initial concerns that the lack of enforcement authority might jeopardize the success of UNMIH proved unfounded.[86] The fact that 70 percent of the UNMIH force came directly from the MNF, and that the total number of military remained virtually unchanged, meant that there were few visible changes on the ground. The subtle differences between Chapter VII and Chapter VI operations were ignored by the average Haitian. However, what was not ignored was the fact that the U.S. contingent in Haiti remained strong. It signaled political resolve.

UNMIH's main security problem was the absence of an efficient Haitian police force. Although no widespread political violence occurred and the number of vigilante killings declined over time, crime remained a big problem.[87] The good news was that former military and paramilitary forces continued to be intimidated by the foreign troops and hence did not pose any major law-and-order problems. Like the MNF, UNMIH could call on an all-American Quick Reaction Force, which could be deployed anywhere in the country within four hours. Finally, Kinzer could request help from a separate U.S. Support Group in Haiti. This force under U.S. operational control had as its task "to protect U.S. military personnel and property, and to provide operational control to non-UNMIH U.S. forces operating in Haiti."[88]

However, the political situation in Haiti remained fragile. The municipal and legislative elections of June and July 1995 passed without significant violence. That said, the June elections were marred by irregularities that led to reruns and a boycott by many parties of the second round of the legislative elections. Moreover, at the end of 1995 relations between the United States and Aristide were again deteriorating. Aristide's ambiguous statements, which led many to believe he might cancel the presidential elections scheduled for December 1995, and his refusal to go forward with an economic reform plan that would have privatized many state-owned enterprises, brought a halt to U.S. and foreign aid.[89] In the end, presidential elections were held in December and, despite a low voter turnout (around 28 percent), irregularities were few and the presidency was handed over to Préval on 7 February 1996.[90]

The handover was to have signaled the end of UNMIH's deployment. Some 5,000 new Haitian policemen had been deployed by that time. The security situation nonetheless remained tense and the Haitian police force, while motivated, was inexperienced and lacking in leadership. Therefore, UNMIH's deployment was extended for a final four months, albeit at reduced troop levels.[91]

The extension of UNMIH did not receive unanimous support in the Security Council, and the length and level of UNMIH deployment were the result of a compromise. The UN secretary-general had suggested that UNMIH be extended for six months at a reduced strength of 1,900 troops.[92] However, the council authorized the extension of UNMIH for only four months and at a troop level of 1,200 soldiers. China was the main reason why the council did not follow the secretary-general's recommendations.[93] Irritated with the Haitian government for inviting Taiwanese vice-president Li Yuan-zu to the inauguration of Préval on 7 February 1996, China threatened to veto UNMIH extension.[94] Once China's concerns were acknowledged, a compromise was quickly reached, and Canada, which had offered to take the lead in Haiti, pledged an 700 additional soldiers at its own cost.[95]

That said, a more fundamental problem plagued the UN operation in Haiti—U.S. disengagement. The Clinton administration, under intense domestic pressure to reduce its troops abroad, had promised Congress that U.S. troops would pull out of Haiti once a new Haitian government had taken office. Although the United States supported the extension of UNMIH, it was no longer prepared to contribute troops.[96] The United

States believed that this final phase of UNMIH could be carried out at much reduced troop levels and was prepared to hand over its leadership role in Haiti to Canada.[97] However, without active U.S. engagement, the willingness of other Security Council members to support international efforts in Haiti quickly diminished.

UNSMIH and UNTMIH: July 1996–November 1997. As it turned out, four months was not enough time to make the Haitian police and security forces fully operational. Indeed, an increase in political violence in Haiti made a continuing outside military presence indispensable. On 28 June 1996, the Security Council launched the United Nations Support Mission in Haiti.[98] UNSMIH's mission was to assist Haitian authorities in training the new police force and to maintain a secure and stable environment in Haiti. It was also to coordinate UN institution-building efforts and national reconciliation and economic rehabilitation activities. UNSMIH was composed of 1,200 troops, mainly Canadian and Pakistani, and 300 police officers.[99] The military element of UNSMIH was concentrated in Port-au-Prince. In addition to UNSMIH, a bilateral agreement between Haiti and the United States provided for the deployment of 250 troops from the 82nd Airborne Division and a small detachment of U.S. Marines in the summer of 1996. These U.S. troops strengthened the 500-member U.S. military support group, composed of engineers and medical specialists, which had never left Haiti.[100] None of these U.S. troops were under UN command. The dispatch of U.S. troops had gone largely unnoticed in the United States and hence did not become an issue in the 1996 U.S. presidential campaign. However, in Haiti the U.S. presence was far from discreet. U.S. military personnel began patrolling the streets of Port-au-Prince as soon as they arrived.

As 1996 drew to an end, it became clear that the Haitian National Police, although fully deployed in 174 locations throughout the country and totaling 6,000 members, was in no position to maintain a secure and stable environment and that the international community, including the United States, would need to continue to maintain public order in Haiti for an indefinite period. However, instead of trying to define the length of that period, the Security Council continued to treat the Haiti case as a short-term problem and authorized mission extensions on a monthly rather than an annual or semiannual basis. This impeded long-term planning and injected an amount of uncertainty that was deftly exploited by former FAdH and FRAPH members.[101]

It also became clear that unless progress was made in the economic field, the political situation would continue to remain volatile. International economic assistance was badly needed, but not always forthcoming. The $1.8 billion pledged by international donors over a five-year period was too slowly disbursed.[102] Moreover, the United States had reduced aid to Haiti for 1996 by more than half, from $235 million in 1995 to $115 million in 1996. Throughout 1995 the deadlock over privatization persisted, which resulted in $200 million of foreign aid being withheld.[103] In 1996, the situation improved somewhat. The secretary-general believed that economic development had been lagging behind mainly because of administrative inertia and not because of a lack of financial resources. He pointed to the lack of qualified personnel in the Haitian administration to formulate and execute economic and social programs.[104]

Préval was faced with difficult political and economic decisions that even under the best of circumstances were bound to increase the pressures on the poor. As a result, violence, both criminal and politically motivated, was likely to increase. Lacking the charismatic appeal of his predecessor and sufficient resources to pay his police forces, Préval remained dependent on the support of outside military forces, even for his own safety.[105]

In July 1997, the Security Council decided to extend UNSMIH for an additional four months. Known under its new name the United Nations Transition Mission in Haiti (UNTMIH), it operated with basically the same forces as UNSMIH.[106] UN peacekeepers were replaced in December 1997 by the United Nations Civilian Police Mission in Haiti (MIPONUH), which consisted of 150 police officers who were to assist the Haitian government in the professionalization of the Haitian national police. An additional 120 police officers were deployed to protect the UN mission and its personnel.[107] MIPONUH was to stay in Haiti for one year and depart only after the November 1998 legislative elections.

CONCLUDING REMARKS

The international community's involvement in Haiti has been and continues to be dependent on U.S. engagement in Haiti. When U.S. engagement is lacking, international action will remain restricted to hortatory resolutions and limited humanitarian assistance—as it did from 1991 to 1994.

When the United States is committed, success is ensured, even if command is in the hands of the United Nations. Indeed, UNMIH was very successful in sustaining a secure and stable environment during the first year of its deployment, and this despite the fact that it had no enforcement authority. The use of military force by U.S. troops during the MNF operation symbolized political will and showed the parties on the ground that the United States was determined to see the operation through. The credibility of the U.S. troops was not affected by the formal change in command and the more restrictive rules of engagement.

The credibility of the military forces in Haiti started to weaken only in February 1996, after its troops had been sharply reduced—by two-thirds —and after they had been replaced by untested, non-U.S. troops. Both actions signaled the disappearance of purpose and political will. It resulted in increased political violence in Haiti, which was stopped only by a reintroduction of a limited number of U.S. troops in Haiti. Time will tell whether this will be sufficient.

With the exception of the Dominican Republic, the United States is the only outside power with an immediate interest in Haiti. Yet that interest needs to be more clearly defined. The junta was removed from Haiti, Aristide was returned, and a peaceful transfer of power from Aristide to Préval took place. However, democracy has not taken root—Préval was elected by only 28 percent of Haitian voters—the Haitian economy is still in shambles, and internal security remains dependent on UN and U.S. troops.

Although Haitian democracy can be built only by Haitians, the United States should not be indifferent to what happens in Haiti. With a population of 7 million in 1995 and an expected population of 13 million by 2025, Haiti is, along with the Dominican Republic and Cuba, one of the three largest countries in the Caribbean.[108] Political unrest and economic misery in Haiti will increase migration pressures, as was demonstrated in 1991–94. Migration affects U.S. national interests and domestic politics. Ultimately, though, the U.S. response to these challenges must be defined in broader and more constructive terms than military engagement. Haiti must be made part of a larger and more interdependent regional economy and it must become a member of an expanded North American Free Trade Agreement. Preparing the Caribbean Basin for such integration requires efforts not just at the economic and bilateral level, but also at the political and regional level.

7

OPERATIONAL GUIDELINES

Chapter 1 summarized seven traditional peacekeeping principles that UN officials see as having arisen during the first forty years of the organization. Chapter 2 developed a parallel set of principles for an activity that relies on military force that goes beyond traditional peacekeeping and that Secretary-General Kofi Annan has labeled "coercive inducement." The case studies presented in chapters 3 through 6 constituted windows into the realities of peace support that proved useful for developing guidelines to facilitate implementation by planners and operators of the coercive inducement principles. Containing as they do instances of near-term success and failure in the same geographic and political settings (see table 7-1), the cases lend themselves to the development of operational guidelines. This chapter presents those guidelines principle by principle; they are summarized in table 7-2 (pages 186–187).

Principle One. *Inducement contingents function under the aegis of a leading state or coalition in operations endorsed by the United Nations.*

The case studies well illustrate how a dangerous mission can test the determination of peace support contributors and how coercive inducement seems to require one state or one organization, such as NATO, to come forward and take charge of implementation. Command and control generally cannot rest with the secretary-general in such instances because he is too easily buffeted by the Security Council, whose servant he is, and by force contributors that, concerned about the dangers, exercise their sovereign right to put limits on the use and continued availability of their soldiers. In addition, the secretary-general is incapable of engaging in the logrolling

Table 7-1. Near-Term Success and Failure of UN-Authorized Military Interventions

	Near-Term Success	Failure
Bosnia	August 1995, Operation Deliberate Force December 1995–December 1996, IFOR December 1996–present, SFOR	1992–August 1995, UNPROFOR
Somalia	December 1992–March 1993, UNITAF	1992, UNOSOM I June 1993–March 1995, UNOSOM II
Rwanda	June–August 1994, Operation Turquoise	1993, April–June 1994 (genocide), UNAMIR I July 1994–April 1996, UNAMIR II
Haiti	September 1994–March 1995, MNF March 1995–June 1996, UNMIH July 1996–July 1997, UNSMIH	October 1993, UNMIH

that solidifies the cooperative participation of member states, not the least of which involves providing guarantees. He also will never be given unfettered access to the kind of military power available for use in UNITAF, IFOR, the MNF, and Turquoise.

The dangers inherent in a coercive inducement operation dictate that *members of an inducement force should not violate a fundamental principle of command and control, that of unity of command.* Absent one chain of authority recognized and accepted by all military personnel working toward the same ends, there is a risk that they may work at cross-purposes with one another. The possibility that this could happen is higher in a UN-controlled mission since national contributors make independent decisions to protect their own troops or simply to do things their own way. The refusal of some UNOSOM II contingents to engage in Chapter VII–type activities and the unilateral U.S. decision to launch Rangers in a daylight raid to capture Aideed without coordinating with the UN mission, resulting in the loss of twenty-four soldiers, are archetypal of what should *not* happen if coercive inducement is to succeed.

If parallel command structures must exist, dual-key arrangements can provide for checks and balances that would prevent the two commands from acting at cross-purposes; specifically, each must "turn its key" before the other can act coercively, thereby ensuring that one knows and approves of what the other intends to do. While a dual-key system can mean the loss of some near-term coercive potential for the peace support effort, it also can prevent major political and military embarrassment that can be far more corrosive in the long run. In Somalia the 1,300-man U.S. Quick Reaction Force (QRF) was there to provide protection to the UNOSOM II contingent, but it remained under the control of the American Central Command in Florida. General Bir, the UNOSOM II commander, had no effective prior knowledge of or say in how it was used. That situation contributed not only to confusion—when QRF operations ran counter to UNOSOM II's activities, and vice versa—but also to disastrous humiliation. Bir's inability to engage in contingency planning to support or shape the conduct of QRF operations proved fatal on 3 October 1993 when the United States, on its own initiative and with no effective advance notification to the UN Command, launched its Ranger raid to capture Aideed. The resulting debacle was the catalyst for U.S. and UN withdrawal from Somalia altogether, yet it might have been prevented had there been either a unitary chain of command for all the peace support forces or, in its absence, a dual-key arrangement that would have allowed for their proper coordination.

As the Bosnia case illustrates, a dual-key system is not foolproof and will almost certainly not be a happy experience for the participants. The very fact that it is instituted probably means that they have different objectives. It almost certainly means that they do not trust each other's political or military judgments or proficiency enough to be willing to place themselves at the other's disposal. In Bosnia the United Nations and NATO commanders both had to agree on whether and when air strikes would take place and against what targets. The sharing of responsibility was a continual source of friction as each side approached the decision process with sharply differing perspectives except for a like determination not to be seen as in the other's pocket. The Americans and others who wished to send a violent message to the Bosnian Serbs had to contend with UNPROFOR commanders who feared, among other things, that, as long as their soldiers were vulnerable, repercussions would be taken against them. The Bosnian Serbs did indeed seize UNPROFOR troops and made them hostage at least three times in response to air strikes, leading NATO as well as the United Nations to back down and suffer public embarrassment —a development that only emboldened the very parties that air strike proponents had wanted to impress. In short, the dual-key system did not prevent problems in those instances, but, in hindsight, had air strike opponents not "turned on their key" in the face of political pressure, the entire Bosnia operation might have been the better for it. In short, though dual-key arrangements are no panacea and may occasion unhappy political friction, they may be the best alternative to ensure proper coordination if all peace support elements are not under unitary command.

Along the same lines, *a coercive inducement contingent should coordinate as quickly as possible its activities with the peacemakers, nation-builders, and humanitarian organizations with which it will interact with a determination to achieve speedy synergy.* Coordination would involve recurring cooperative dialogue with the special representative of the secretary-general or whoever is locally charged with mediating the differences between the local parties. It would also entail forming a Civil-Military Operations Center (or CMOC as in Somalia) or a Civil-Military Coordination Organization (or CIMIC as in Bosnia) and holding daily meetings to exchange intelligence, inform each other about upcoming intentions, and, if relevant, open discussion on joint or complementary activities.

As the case studies show, a coercive inducement force can sometimes expect to be replaced by a UN-controlled peace support contingent. *The handover to the follow-on group should be as seamless as possible and designed to sustain the image of unity and strength established by the coalition force.* This would involve beginning the preparation to transfer control as soon as the coalition is in place. Its members, especially the leader(s), should facilitate the secretary-general's efforts to assemble the follow-on contingent by pledging their own troops and helping to obtain others. In particular, they should make clear that a transfer of control means, not a lessening of commitment, but rather a judgment that enough progress has been made to justify the shift. A classic example may be the transfer from the U.S.-controlled MNF to UNMIH. The latter, building on substantial U.S. support and participation, had an advance team in Haiti three weeks after the MNF forces landed and five months before it took over from them. Even though UNMIH did not have Chapter VII enforcement authority, it managed early on to limit violence in Haiti and to extend the length of time available to institute positive changes in the country. Nevertheless, the Haitian experience also confirms the need for the long view, for as UNMIH reduced its own numbers and the United States increasingly disengaged, violence increased enough to cause a reintroduction of U.S. troops to signal international resolve.

Principle Two. *Coercive inducement personnel represent both moral authority and credible force.*

To possess moral authority means being able to get people to do one's bidding because one is recognized as representing an accepted system of transcendent values such as those contained in the UN Charter. In a consensual operation where the parties are genuinely interested in a cessation of hostilities and concerned about their international public image, the moral weight of an internationally appointed peace-facilitation group can be significant. The purpose of engaging in coercive inducement, however, is that moral authority, while necessary, may not always suffice.

UN endorsement of a coercive inducement mission means that it arrives with a presumption of moral as well as legal authority, but the contrasts between UNOSOM I and UNITAF, UNPROFOR and IFOR, UNAMIR and Turquoise, and the early UNMIH and the MNF make clear that *it is a force's credibility, usually linked with other factors, and not its moral authority, which initially catches the attention of recalcitrant parties.* None of the cases suggests that moral conversions caused any moderation in violence or willingness to accede to what the international community desired. When Aideed, Mahdi, Karadjic, Mladic, or Cédras decided to cooperate, it was not because they were struck down on their way to Damascus. Rather, the deployments of UNITAF, IFOR, and the MNF (including the latter's threat of forceful entry) were instrumental in bringing at least temporary peace because of the coercive power each represented.

At the end of the day, however, *moral authority has greater long-term importance* because of its potential to bring about the changes of heart necessary for reconciliation. Credible force can buy time for mediators and people of goodwill, allow short-term emergency relief to be delivered, and even allow for elections, but it does not change attitudes. UNITAF and Turquoise were immediate successes, but their lasting impact seems negligible. The juries are still out on the long-term effects of coercive inducement in

Bosnia and Haiti, but the agents of instability in each region probably have greater staying power than do the contributors to peace support missions. Thus, the prospects are not optimistic, especially if the average citizen sees little sustained improvement in daily life.

The long-term significance of potentially credible force may be its impact on the general willingness to accept the UN mission as authoritative and thus worthy of serving as an agent of positive change. Specifically, the authority of an inducing force is buttressed when it is seen as doing good and preventing evil, and it is degraded when it is viewed as doing too little or going too far. Turquoise is a most interesting illustration. The widespread skepticism that initially greeted its deployment significantly abated after the French were judged by most people in the area (including some Tutsis but not the RPF government) to be acting as stabilizers. That initial skepticism is ironic since, when Turquoise was terminated, the skeptics then felt abandoned and berated the departure of the French. As for doing too little once in place, the MNF's early failure to prevent street violence directed against those who had cheered its arrival made it a symbol of ridicule and not of authority. Conversely, when the Quick Reaction Force supporting UNOSOM II attacked Aideed's headquarters in the summer of 1992, dozens of people were killed. A result was an increase in Aideed's popularity at the expense of that of the United Nations.

The case studies suggest that, as a rule, *a peace support force augments its perceived authority by being reactive in its use of violence but proactive otherwise.* There are differing dimensions to reactive violence. One, of course, is the use of force in self-defense. A second is the use of force after warning that force may be used if recalcitrant behavior persists. Such use could be limited to a specific incident (such as when the U.S. Marines after repeated warnings destroyed a weapons storage compound from which Aideed's men had fired on its patrols), or it could entail a sustained campaign (such as Deliberate Force). There are many dimensions as well to being proactive, including supporting the provision of basic social services, sustaining political dialogue with and between the factions, and keeping all informed on its impartiality toward the mandate. The widespread anxiety that arose at the prospect of the termination of both the Turquoise and UNITAF operations testifies to the regard in which they had come to be held among the populations and NGOs. Similar to what was noted about Turquoise in the above paragraph, for example, UNITAF initiated violence only reactively. It was also visibly instrumental in delivering aid and reducing instability so that an average citizen could try to get on with life. At the same time the mission's political leader, Robert Oakley, recurringly consulted with the factions and sought with some success to mediate differences between them.

Oakley's attempts at mediation were not facilitated by rumors that Aideed spread that he had a special relationship with UNITAF. The impact of such a perception of favoritism on the other factional leaders needs no elaboration, but it does underscore the need for a mission to strive through all available channels to make the facts clear on such an issue. In other words, *a mission* must not only act impartially—an issue discussed further below—it *must also make certain that it is perceived as impartial, as being guided by the mandate, so as to retain its moral authority.*

Principle Three. *While aspiring for as much universality as possible, inducement contingents primarily reflect the capabilities that make for an immediately effective crisis response.*

It is axiomatic that the greater the number of states that endorse or participate in a peace support operation, the easier it is for the participants to convince their own publics, other nations, and the peoples in the crisis region of its legitimacy. Assembling a coalition and coordinating the respective inputs, roles, and requirements takes weeks to months, with time increasing as a function of the size of the coalition and the demands of the mission. Thus, the more universal the initial participation, the longer it takes to get on with doing what needs to be done. The problem is that speed is consequential since the faster the response, the better the chance of heading off any incident or development that could derail the stabilization process to which the parties had consented. As all the case studies in this volume amply show, potentially derailing incidents almost always arise early on in missions where consent is doubtful. Often as not they reflect a local party's ready willingness to test how much it can get away with before the newly deployed inducement contingent reacts with firmness; thus, compared with traditional peacekeeping, an immediately effective response becomes that much more urgent and overshadows the need for universality.

The case studies suggest two guidelines, with the first seeming to run against the grain of the principle and the second resolving the apparent problem. The first accepts that local elements will indeed look for exploitable vulnerabilities in an arriving contingent; thus prudence dictates that *it not be deployed before it is ready to deal with challenges it might confront.* It must first be properly led, equipped, and prepared to react to contingencies. This can be a difficult rule to follow once a mission has been decided because people in need, relief agencies, and contributor state publics are impatient to see results, especially when civilian lives are in the balance. For instance, the pressure on the UNITAF commander to speed up the deployment of his troops in the Somalian countryside to provide for the secure delivery of food is understandable; so too was his decision to move only when local conditions and the forces available to him made the risks to his soldiers acceptable.

The requirement for prudence does not negate the need for a speedily effective response. The way to reconcile the competing demands is to conduct *detailed advanced planning and preparation.* While not sufficient by themselves, they *are essential to guarantee success.* That they were well primed for execution contributed significantly to the accomplishments of UNITAF, Turquoise, MNF, IFOR, and the revived UNMIH. For the first three, planning and execution were facilitated by the fact that most or all of the initial operational activities involved only the United States or France, essentially obviating international coordination problems. Though IFOR was a multinational coalition operation from the start, it benefited from the fact that the NATO elements, accustomed to planning together, had been preparing for several months before execution in anticipation of being sent to Bosnia. That experience contrasts sharply with that of UNITAF's follow-on, UNOSOM II. Though it had a more ambitious mandate than UNITAF, it arrived more poorly equipped, was inadequately staffed, was given little guidance on how it ought to proceed, and, though given Chapter VII authority, it lacked rules of engagement agreed to by all. Not surprisingly, Somali leaders quickly concluded that it could be pushed around. It never really recovered from its poor first impression.

Principle Four. *Deployed personnel assume no better than provisional consent and act to impose the will of the international community on recalcitrant parties.*

The case studies underscore the relevance of coercive inducement when the international community, as represented by the United Nations, concludes it must (continue to) intervene in situations where strategic consent and pledges of cooperation range from provisional to illusory. Bosnian and Somalian factions regularly violated agreements within days if not hours with little evident concern about the reaction of the UNPROFOR and UNOSOM contingents on the ground. The initiators of violence in Rwanda were not concerned with the provisions of the Arusha Agreement or by the presence of UNAMIR. The extensive attention that the United States and other countries gave to brokering the Governors Island Agreement did not stop the Cédras government from reneging on its commitment to allow a UN peacekeeping force in Haiti.

The case studies suggest several guidelines in this regard. One is that *the arriving inducement contingent should rapidly build up visible combat power and boldly take the initiative, making clear to all concerned that it fully intends to exercise the authority granted it.* This may even mean that, for some initial period but without initiating violence, it should "push its weight around" so as to forestall planned attempts to put it to the test. Both the Turquoise and IFOR contingents, for example, quickly moved to confront and overturn factional control of roadblocks and checkpoints. Immediately before UNITAF's arrival, Oakley reminded the Somali leaders of the firepower the United States had used in Desert Storm, a factor that undoubtedly contributed to the lack of tactical opposition to the U.S. deployment and to ready acquiescence to the demand that "technicals" be removed from the streets of Mogadishu. Such actions made it clear to local leaders and rank and file in Rwanda, Bosnia, and Somalia that the arriving force was not to be trifled with. Conversely, the MNF contingent in Port-au-Prince quickly had to adapt after initially standing aside when Haitian army and police beat up civilians who had poured out to cheer its arrival. It modified its rules of engagement in order to guarantee the deterrence effect intended by its deployment. Once an inducement force has made its point, it can then consider when any slacking off is appropriate. Within three weeks of the MNF's arrival, enough stability had returned to Haiti, for instance, to allow the force to begin a gradual downsizing.

It is very costly to assemble, train, equip, and deploy military forces in sufficient number to achieve a deterrent effect; thus it is understandable if those nations that have to bear those burdens—including the possibility of casualties—often look to combat air power as a substitute for troops on the ground. Nevertheless, the conclusion seems inescapable that *deploying well-equipped and trained soldiers in ample number to a crisis area is far more effective than (the threat of) air attack for securing the cooperation of local parties.* Ground troops symbolize a seriousness of purpose, a willingness to immerse oneself in helping solve a problem, that air strikes alone cannot match since they are more episodic and usually staged from distant bases. If the Bosnian "safe areas" had been adequately garrisoned, the air campaign might not have been needed. The unwillingness of contributors to take on the very heavy troop burden to secure the safe areas— estimated at 35,000 by the Secretariat on top of the over 30,000 already in UNPROFOR—is understandable, however, and it is fortunate that fewer troops overall were required to allow UNITAF (with an upper strength of 38,000), Turquoise (3,000), and the MNF (21,000) to bring stability to Somalia, Rwanda, and Haiti.

If the use of violence is justified, it should be robust enough to bring about a positive change in behavior. *Half-measures*—such as NATO's anemic or "pinprick" air attacks against Serb targets—*backfire and thus must be avoided; they send a message that the United Nations and those who act in its name lack resolve and are not serious after all.* Indeed, such a reputation can spill over from one operation to another. The people who turned back the *Harlan County* loudly proclaimed their intent to face the United States with "another Somalia" should it land a peacekeeping force.

Although it contributed to modification of Serb behavior, Deliberate Force was almost certainly inadequate by itself to achieve that end. It thus underscores that credible coercive power is not solely instrumental in each case. Its relative impact varies depending on circumstances. The prospect of a forceful takeover was enough in Haiti, but in Bosnia the Serbs were reacting to several factors when they ceased fighting. These included political pressure from past friends or allies (Milosevic and the Russians) and worrisome military losses to the Muslims and Croats, who had decided to coordinate their activities. This example suggests then that, *where relevant, the threat or use of inducing force should be timed to take advantage and reinforce the impact of other influences on the local parties.*

In addition, *an inducement force* must itself do more than generate fear among those who would otherwise transgress community norms and mandates. It *must also co-opt local elements, that is, augment whatever consent exists, by inspiring both confidence and gratitude.* This can involve several kinds of activities. One consists of the traditional monitoring and interposition tasks, which can encourage parties to abide by cease-fire or other agreements and can reassure them that violations are not occurring. A second is visibly circulating among the people so that the average citizen (and relief worker) feels personally more secure as he or she moves about. A third is assisting the performance of or temporarily taking over basic police functions until a system for public order is reestablished. A fourth and no less important set is facilitating the provision of basic needs such as food, water, electricity, medical care, and public works (roads, bridges, public transport, and the like).

Some of the above tasks may already be provided for in the mandate under which the forces are operating, but if not, the case studies suggest that they will probably have to be done anyway in civil conflicts where the international community feels it must intervene,[1] unless the intervention is strictly a tourniquet operation as occurred with U.S. efforts to provide potable water to the Rwandan refugees. As noted in the Rwandan analysis, the United States was so determined to avoid mission creep there that it engaged instead in mission shrink. Although that may or may not have been a sensible policy in the circumstances, other cases may not always be as permissive, so to speak. Specifically, the conditions IFOR faced in Bosnia and those the MNF faced in Haiti required that they take on tasks that went beyond a narrow and military-centered conception of the missions assigned them. The total collapse of the Haitian police left a public order vacuum, for instance, that only the MNF could fill at the time. In Bosnia IFOR's efforts to facilitate elections and to restore basic services (such as water, power, and telecommunications) were not part of the military tasks assigned it in the Dayton Peace Accords. Nevertheless, they contributed to fulfillment of its mission to build confidence in a lasting peace. In short, a corollary of the previous guideline is that *some tasks sometimes labeled "mission creep" may actually be mission supportive (if not mission essential) and should be planned for as such.* Which tasks and for how long are situation dependent. In sum, although soldiers are neither Peace Corps volunteers nor cops-on-the-beat, there may be times when they and only they can and should do what a volunteer or law enforcement official would do if he or she were present.

Whatever else *a peace support force* does to augment consent, it *must additionally undertake a media campaign with special concern to counter untruthful or inflammatory messages put forth by local elements.* Aideed, for example, was a master at spreading rumors and aggressively utilized the airwaves for scathing attacks against the United Nations and the intervention force when it served his purposes. Far more profound consequences flowed from the broadcasts of Radio Télévision Libre des Milles Collines. It raised fears among the Hutus and instigated them to lash out unmercifully against the Tutsis. It also complicated the French intervention by broadcasting that Turquoise was pro-Hutu and by encouraging refugees to flee to Zaire. The French shut it down and pressed to put out what General Lafourcade termed "positive information" instead. After Turquoise left, UNAMIR II did deploy an FM broadcasting capability.

Finally, the case studies also underscore that a coercive inducement operation can accomplish only as much as the leader is willing to take on and that its aims may tend to be relatively narrow and short term: that is, within a prespecified period, to stop violence, ensure the delivery of humanitarian goods, help provide basic services, possibly facilitate elections, and then either turn the operation over to a follow-on force under UN control or get out altogether. (When the United States leads, the last alternative can trump all others should its soldiers suffer headline-grabbing casualties.) Under those circumstances, an inducement operation may well not allow peacemakers and local peoples of goodwill enough time to put in place a firm foundation for sustained positive change. *In particular, an exit strategy based on a preset date driven by the leader's domestic agenda*—something seen in all of our cases—*simply encourages local extremists to lay low until the coercive inducement force leaves and puts the long-term success of the operation in doubt.*

Principle Five. *While not intending to harm anyone's interests, an inducement force must implement mandates even when doing so prejudices the interests of one or more of the sides.*

Factions in a power struggle are hypersensitive to the possibility of bias, making it foremost among the factors that can derail any peace support operation.[2] In particular, it is often the reason a party gives to explain why it will no longer abide by an agreement to which it had consented.

Because it is natural for a local party to feel aggrieved when mandate enforcement runs counter to what it considers its interests,[3] *it is imperative that the actions of an inducement force be transparent, predictable, and grounded in the terms of the mandate.* There should be no surprises.

Through as many channels of communication as possible, the force should make clear to faction leaders, rank and file, and the general populace what it will do and when. It must specify what it believes the mandate requires as well as how it will react if one or another party chooses not to abide by it. For example, Ambassador Oakley in one-on-one meetings and his military commanders in the Joint Security Committee sessions consistently informed the Somali groups (and through the Civil-Military Operations Center, the humanitarian agencies as well) what UNITAF forces were about and what they expected or desired from the Somalis. UNITAF personnel also made it a point to meet with a faction after any altercation to explain what happened and why. The same type of activity occurred as well with IFOR, the MNF, and Turquoise, with this last involving, among other things, the UNAMIR commander, General Roméo Dallaire, shuttling among the French force, the former Rwandan Army chief-of-staff, and RPF commanders.

There may, of course, be some give-and-take between the United Nations and factional representatives to establish how the mandate should be interpreted and implemented. As the Bosnia case study concluded, however, *what must be avoided is a never-ending series of negotiations on issues.* Through negotiations, UNPROFOR commanders sought to prove their impartiality toward the parties in the hope thereby of winning their cooperation on humanitarian matters, but at the end of the day, they came across as weak and vulnerable to manipulation. At some point, the inducement force must either stand its ground on what the mandate requires or recommend either a change in the mandate or its own withdrawal.

Maintaining an image of impartiality becomes especially difficult (if not impossible, as will be discussed in our final chapter) if coercive actions are directed mostly against one faction. In such circumstances *the inducement force should seek out opportunities to mirror its activities benefiting or harming one faction with similar activities, if warranted, vis-à-vis the others.* Ambassador Oakley was sensitive to questions of perceived favoritism and acted to ensure that UNITAF balance its raids on Aideed's weapons caches with similar raids against those of Mahdi and the other factions in the Mogadishu area. Similarly, though considered pro-Hutu, the French made clear to all they would protect Tutsi refugees as well. In contrast, UNOSOM II doomed itself to failure with the issuance of an arrest warrant against Aideed, and UNPROFOR, though operating under mandates that could certainly be interpreted as anti-Serb, nevertheless passed on opportunities to act against the Bosnian Muslim and Croats when they ignored mandates. The "safe areas" mandates were intended to protect the civilian population living in Bosnian Muslim towns. The Bosnian Serbs were neither to launch attacks against the towns nor to place heavy weapons within twenty kilometers of them. For their part, the Muslims were to demilitarize the areas and, thus, not allow their armed forces to use them either as sanctuaries or as staging points for offensives. In the end, there was ample blame to place on both sides, but basically it was only the Bosnian Serbs who were roundly condemned for violating the "safe areas." Similarly, the Croatian air force blatantly transgressed the Bosnia no-fly zone in August 1995 when it bombed Serbian sites in the Krajina, but NATO, the United Nations' agent, did nothing. Its failure to do so, coupled with its attacks against Serb anti–air missile systems near Knin and Ubdina, could only serve to further convince the Bosnian Serbs that both the mandates and their implementation were biased.

Principle Six. *If necessary, force may be used for other than self-defense, but any use should not exceed the minimum required to bring about the desired behavior.*

As noted in chapter 2, the right of self-defense accorded traditional peacekeepers "theoretically" allows them to use force in "mandate defense." The option has rarely been exercised, however, and a major reason was that peacekeepers usually did not have sufficient firepower. If one assumes the requisite firepower, as should be the case if coercive inducement is to be practiced, then the issue of limits on its use comes to the fore.

Some limits have already been mentioned earlier, particularly in the discussion under Principle Two dealing with a contingent's moral authority, and they need not be repeated. What bears emphasis here is that *violence should be initiated only in response to recalcitrant behavior.* The parties must be given the benefit of the doubt. Until the evidence is clear that they are being recalcitrant, violence must remain a threat, not a fact. Even though UNITAF, Turquoise, and IFOR did throw their weight around early on, they wisely remained reactive when resorting to violence. Their aim was to establish their authority; it was not to create enemies.

Beyond the question of whether violence is used are issues concerning its magnitude and duration. It was offered under Principle Four that violence should be sufficiently robust to bring about a positive change in recalcitrant behavior and that half measures would probably backfire, but there is no rule of thumb to establish what constitutes the right measure. Theories of self-defense usually focus on proportionality understood in terms of the minimum use of force necessary to eliminate the immediate threat. This is the standard applied by any peace support force coming under fire or facing imminent attack. *Compared with the self-defense standard, however, that for coercive inducement must be broader if violence is to succeed in bringing an end to a pattern or prolonged period of recalcitrant behavior, but that violence must end as soon as there is verifiable evidence that behavior is changing.* The catalyst for Operation Deliberate Force was a mortar attack on a Sarajevo marketplace. Involving 750 attack missions against 56 ground targets, it certainly exceeded any narrow interpretation of proportionality. Consistent with the wider interpretation, the campaign was sustained until Bosnian Serb leaders acquiesced to demands that they withdraw the heavy weapons surrounding Sarajevo. It then ceased as soon as they indicated that they would comply.

The point has already been made that Deliberate Force was almost certainly inadequate by itself to achieve that end. At best, it was a contributory factor. Even if it had been uniquely instrumental, however, such an operation should be an exception, for *to the utmost degree possible, violence should remain not only defensive but also tactical in nature.* By the latter is meant that it should be limited to responding to individual incidents one by one as they come up and directed only against the specific on-scene provocateurs. Doing so allows the commanders of the intervening force to maintain a dialogue with factional leaders who could, as Aideed did, for example, claim that the provocations were the responsibility of presumably misguided followers. Of course, if a provocation is too great or if provocations recur so often as to suggest a centrally directed policy favoring them, then the response may have to be a sustained campaign of violence directed at having factional commanders correct the situation, but such a campaign may not be necessary if individual incidents are consistently and robustly dealt with as they arise. Both Deliberate Force and the hunt for Aideed might have been avoidable if UNOSOM II and UNPROFOR had

had the capability (and, of course, the will) to bring individual recalcitrants to heel on the spot.

Principle Seven. *Anticipating risks, inducement contingents must plan to minimize casualties while preparing for the worst.*

The case studies repeatedly remind us that (prospective) personnel losses in a peace support operation can devastatingly affect a country's willingness to initiate or continue participation in it. This reality can be a particular problem for coercive inducement since it is risky by nature. Factional elements that perceive mandate implementation as harming their interests may well respond violently at the time or retaliate later if given the opportunity. Hence, among the most critical variables in readying for the worst may be *preparing the public to accept casualties should they occur.* Before the Gulf War, publics of the various coalition partners were told to anticipate fatalities (and lots of them), and, for the most part, they responded favorably. No such preparation was made prior to the Somalia mission because it was advertised as a humanitarian operation. It can be argued that the United States has prepared its public for casualties in any future confrontations with either Iran or Iraq by repeatedly stressing the dangers these states pose to international peace and security. If public support is not generated, future interventions could resemble "nothing more than the moon landings, with the principal objective being to send men far away and bring them back safely."[4] As this principle states, however, in addition to preparing for the worst there must be plans to minimize casualties.

The obvious implication that inducement personnel be given the wherewithal to defend themselves has already been subsumed under earlier guidelines and needs no elaboration. A second implication, borne out in particular by contrasting Deliberate Force with earlier NATO air strikes, concerns the opportunities open to factional elements to strike back at a peace support force. That Deliberate Force involved 750 missions sustained over two weeks differs sharply from previous (proposed) bombing campaigns that either were never initiated after all or were terminated almost as soon as they began. The reason why the United Nations forewent or quickly ceased its use of NATO air power is simple: its personnel were highly vulnerable to retaliation. Possibly the most agonizing moment in UNPROFOR's history took place when captured peacekeepers were chained to targets that NATO might otherwise have attacked. In short, instead of deterring or reversing unacceptable behavior by local elements, the United Nations was self-deterred from calling for NATO air power. Among the things that the command did after its soldiers were released was to quietly redeploy vulnerable personnel to protected positions, thereby illustrating the *necessity to limit the violent response or retaliation options open to the factions subjected to coercive inducement.*

In an ideal world, a variant of this guideline would be that factions should be fully disarmed to foreclose their ability to use violence to hinder mandate implementation. The case studies suggest that this is a will-o'-the-wisp. In a limited way the Turquoise force probably came closest when it disarmed people entering its security zone, but it did not aggressively pursue weapons control outside the zone. During the Somalia interventions, Boutros-Ghali urged that UNITAF and UNOSOM II comprehensively disarm the factions, but UNITAF adopted a more modest approach, insisting on the cantonment of artillery and "technicals," destroying the weapons depots of those elements attacking UNITAF's soldiers, confiscating the arms caches of bandits, and seizing guns from those who brandished them in the vicinity of UNITAF personnel. Somalis who kept their guns out of sight, however, got to hang on to them. In contrast, the less capable UNOSOM II implemented a more systematic disarmament campaign in accordance with its ambitious mandate, only to catalyze Somali violence and lose numerous soldiers in the process. In short, what made sense in the abstract was less sensible in hindsight.

A complication affecting any decision to disarm is the number of weapons extant, especially of the personal variety. Even in Haiti, a poor country with a small army and police force, there were an estimated 175,000 guns in circulation in 1994. A second complication is that incentive schemes for encouraging the voluntary turnover of weapons have only a limited success record. The Haitian gun-for-cash program garnered less than 10 percent of the arms. This is not surprising in view of a third factor: guns are usually considered essential to factional and personal survival during and in the immediate aftermath of a civil conflict when distrust remains high, bandits and armed irregulars are still about, and the police and armed forces are seen by many as ineffective or hostile. In short, the incentives to retain guns can be as great for people of goodwill as for those with evil intent.

Table 7-2. Coercive Inducement Principles and Operational Guidelines

Principles	Guidelines
1. Inducement contingents function under the aegis of a leading state or coalition in operations endorsed by the United Nations.	Do not violate the fundamental principle of command and control—unity of command. If parallel command structures must exist, dual-key arrangements can provide checks and balances that prevent the two commands from acting at cross-purposes. Coordinate activities, as quickly as possible, with peacemakers, nation builders, and humanitarian organizations in order to achieve synergy. Ensure that the handover to follow-on organizations is as seamless as possible and designed to sustain the image of unity and strength established by the coalition force.
2. Coercive inducement personnel represent both moral authority and credible force.	Deploy with sufficient force. A force's credibility, and not its moral authority, initially catches the attention of recalcitrant parties. Operate under UN sanction. Moral authority has significant long-term importance. Keep in mind that how force is applied affects the willingness of the parties to accept the UN mission as authoritative. Use violence reactively, but be proactive otherwise. The mission's mandate should guide impartiality.
3. While aspiring for as much universality as possible, inducement contingents primarily reflect the capabilities that make for an immediately effective crisis response.	Do not deploy before the operation is ready to deal with challenges it might confront. Foster success by conducting detailed planning and preparation.
4. Deployed personnel assume no better than provisional consent and act to impose the will of the international community on recalcitrant parties.	Rapidly build up visible combat power and boldly take the initiative, making it clear that the mission intends to exercise the authority granted it.

- Deploy well-equipped and trained ground troops in ample numbers rather than rely on air power alone.
- Avoid half measures.
- Time the threat or use of force to take advantage and reinforce the impact of other influences on local parties.
- Co-opt local elements in order to augment consent and inspire confidence and gratitude.
- Plan to execute nonmilitary tasks that are both mission supportive and essential.
- Undertake a media campaign to counter false or inflammatory messages.
- Base the exit strategy on measurable progress, not a preset date.

5. While not intending to harm anyone's interests, an inducement force must implement mandates even when doing so prejudices the interests of one or more of the sides.

- Avoid surprises. The actions of an inducement force must be transparent, predictable, and grounded in the terms of the mandate.
- Allowing for some give-and-take, avoid a never-ending series of negotiations on issues.
- If warranted, seek opportunities to mirror activities benefiting or harming the factions.

6. If necessary, force may be used for other than self-defense, but any use should not exceed the minimum required to bring about the desired behavior.

- Violence should be initiated only in response to recalcitrant behavior.
- The use of violence can be broader than for self-defense, but should cease when behavior changes as desired.
- Violence should, to the utmost degree possible, remain defensive and tactical.

7. Anticipating risks, inducement contingents must plan to minimize casualties while preparing for the worst.

- Prepare the public to expect and accept casualties.
- Limit the opportunities for retaliation against or violent response to mission operations.
- Pursue limited arms control programs, but resist large-scale coercive disarmament and be prepared to fill any resulting security vacuum.

At the end of the day, then, *an inducement force should discharge any assigned responsibilities to oversee or facilitate agreed-upon arms reductions* by providing inspection teams, manning and guarding weapons collection points, and the like, *but unless overwhelmingly powerful, it should only selectively engage in coercive disarmament* lest it embroil itself, as Ambassador Oakley predicted, in recurring clashes. Its fundamental incentives in such cases should be to ensure the safety of its own personnel. It can then carry out its larger duties to the benefit of the local parties while also assuaging the anxieties of the governments and nations contributing personnel to the peace support force. Additionally, *where arms control does take place, the inducement contingent must make clear to local peoples that it will fill any resulting security vacuum* so as to forestall violent resistance by those who see their weapons as necessary to their own survival.

8

FINAL THOUGHTS

Our basic assumption is that a policy choice must be labeled before it can be fully considered, and our basic argument is that there is indeed a choice, herein termed "coercive inducement," that straddles the continuum between classical peacekeeping and simple enforcement. This argument runs counter to the possibly predominant view that any middle option does not constitute a course of action worthy of separate recognition. To some in particular, the differences between enforcement and coercive inducement are insufficient to justify regarding the latter as a distinct category. As we see it, enforcement is directed against a designated malefactor whose behavior is deemed so offensive or destabilizing that the Security Council cannot remain impartial vis-à-vis that actor and authorizes military operations in response to its unwillingness (that is, its determination not to consent) to remedy the situation. High-end enforcement (such as the Desert Storm operation) is synonymous with war—the use of sustained and widespread violence—and, consistent with the principles of combat, it usually involves resort to stealth, deception, and surprise. Low-end enforcement (such as in the Kurdish relief operation in northern Iraq) need not involve intense or sustained violence, but there is no intrinsic concern about augmenting consent or about acting only against one side if violence is employed. Persuasion and negotiation would not necessarily play an important role in enforcement. In contrast, coercive inducement obtains when competing entities might or do threaten to overturn a truce, a cease-fire, or to otherwise so heighten the undesired consequences of a crisis as to cause the international community to intervene. The role of coercive inducement forces is to hold the parties to what they agreed to or otherwise help keep them in line. Like a policeman on the beat, coercive inducement forces remain visible to all and hope to induce compliance by virtue of their very presence and their potential for violence. They actively avoid surprise, and if they resort to violence, they do so only reactively and with great restraint. The violence is tightly focused, highly restricted, and ends at the first sign of compliance. It aims to augment consent and is intended to deliver a message. It is the demonstrative part of a campaign of continued dialogue that keeps all parties apprised of what to expect and why (both before and after violence has been employed).

That said, ambiguities remain on how best to implement coercive inducement. The middle ground it occupies is often characterized as a "gray area" between peacekeeping and enforcement,[1] and the characterization is apt because it implies an activity domain that can be murky when deciding exactly what to do on the day. The principles and guidelines presented in this analysis are not chiseled in stone. They remain subject to further refinement and are not intended to preempt judgment. Circumstances will determine not only when, how, and how much they should be applied but also whether they can be. Directives about unitary and coordinated command systems cannot help much if political differences or lack of trust inevitably dictate that peace support contributors remain at cross-purposes with one another. Prescriptions about impartiality can be unimplementable if mandates are inherently partial; so too can prescriptions about co-opting indigenous elements if the locals are consumed by uncompromising hate, revanchism, or desire for absolute control. Such problems, if intractable, can negate the practicality of almost any measure to advance peace and stability.

There is no guarantee, of course, that an international collective would go forward with coercive inducement even if judged implementable. The present reluctance of UN members to take responsibility for hazardous operations is understandable. There will always be more conflict and suffering than they can handle with peace support forces, and practical dilemmas can always overwhelm moral qualms and suppress consequent guilt. To act in one case, furthermore, raises the presumption of acting in the next and then the next after that. One breaks the cycle by not acting at all.

Nonetheless, we believe the international community has a responsibility to respond if all the following criteria obtain:

- Failure to intervene will abet genocide or other widespread humanitarian disaster.
- Strictly noncoercive measures have been exhausted and are not sufficient to contain the problem.
- The international community has readily available the assets required to undertake coercive inducement (as opposed to their already being tied down in deterrence, warfighting, enforcement, or other coercive inducement missions).
- Coercive inducement constitutes a timely and practical option to contain the problem—that is, keep it from worsening—while providing scope for humanitarian agents and/or peacemakers to try to make things better.[2]

How long the coercive inducement forces should remain and how much they should actively engage in or support nation building—the reestablishment of an economic infrastructure and of basic social and governmental services—is a follow-on decision. Ideally, the nations that call for, vote in favor of, and undertake coercive inducement should strive to ensure that the situation that gave rise to its need be improved enough so that long-term stability is enhanced, but in some cases this may be too high a standard. "Tourniquet operations," narrowly conceived humanitarian missions, may sometimes be wiser in the long run. Joshua Muravchik contends that UNITAF's contribution to ending starvation in Somalia was a worthy achievement in and of itself while later attempts at nation building were counterproductive. It would have been better, he argued, if "Washington had avoided being drawn into this Sisyphean task."[3] If for no other reason, Muravchik may be right when one considers the impact of the Somalian experience on shaping the attitudes that led to the present era of retrenchment in peace support. Certainly, in the United States reference to that case has become a mantra for those who would sharply limit American participation in UN-sanctioned or UN-sponsored operations.[4]

To our mind, that is highly unfortunate. If any crisis fit the first of the criteria we laid out above as the criteria for intervention, it was the slaughter in Rwanda. What is needed at the outbreak of any such crisis is a nation willing to take charge, and we believe that the United States, because of its unique capabilities for political leadership and military deployment, has a special responsibility. A factor contributing to American skittishness is an understandable concern for casualties. The prospect for and the occurrence of casualties must never be taken lightly, but, compared with that of other nations such as the United Kingdom or France, the United States' casualty-tolerance index seems especially low. One does not have to accept that the United States should become the world's policeman to argue that its political leaders nonetheless should work harder to prepare its people to act when action is justified. If the result is nothing more than the application of a tourniquet, then so be it. Even a limited operation provides some crisis containment, giving scope to peacemakers and peacebuilders to make things better.

Finally, in the introduction we noted that the concept "coercive inducement" was Kofi Annan's refinement of the "inducement" concept that we had floated earlier. We trust that this volume in turn refines his improvement and provides impetus for others to carry the process further and to apply it as well to the recommended principles and guidelines. Although there may be little prospect that the international community will be much involved in any hazardous operations in the near future, history suggests that Annan was correct when he predicted that the need to undertake both coercive and positive inducement will not go away. The current era of retrenchment provides time to think about how to do both well. This volume is offered in that spirit.

NOTES

In each chapter, every work is referenced in full at its first citation; subsequent citations within that chapter use a shortened reference.

INTRODUCTION

1. Boutros Boutros-Ghali, *Confronting New Challenges: 1995 Report on the Work of the Organization from the Forty-ninth to the Fiftieth Session of the General Assembly* (New York: United Nations, 1995), 223, para. 599.

2. Adam Roberts, "From San Francisco to Sarajevo: The UN and the Use of Force," *Survival* 37, no. 4 (winter 1995–96): 26.

3. Donald C. F. Daniel and Bradd C. Hayes, "Securing Observance of UN Mandates through the Employment of Military Force," *International Peacekeeping* 3, no. 4 (winter 1996): 107–127.

4. Kofi Annan, "Peace Operations and the United Nations: Preparing for the Next Century" (unpublished paper, February 1996), 4–5.

5. The need to develop doctrine and guidelines is widely recognized among those who accept the possibility of a response such as coercive inducement. See, for example, Christopher Lord, *Intermediate Deployments: The Strategy and Doctrine of Peacekeeping-Type Operations*, Occasional Paper no. 25 (Camberley, England: Staff College, Strategic and Combat Studies Institute, 1996), 10–20; Andrew J. Goodpaster, *When Diplomacy Is Not Enough: Managing Multinational Military Interventions*, a report to the Carnegie Commission on Preventing Deadly Conflict (Washington, D.C.: Carnegie Corporation of New York, 1966), chap. 5; and Olara Otunnu, "The Peace and Security Agenda of the United Nations: From a Crossroads into the Next Century," in *Peacemaking and Peacekeeping for the Next Century: Report of the 25th Vienna Seminar*, ed. Ameen Jan, Robert C. Orr, and Timothy A. Wilkins (New York: International Peace Academy, 1995), 71.

1. CONFUSION AND DISCORD IN RECENT UN PEACE SUPPORT OPERATIONS

1. Alan James, *Peacekeeping in International Politics*, Studies in International Security no. 29 (London: Macmillan in association with the International Institute for Strategic Studies, 1990), 77.

2. See Dag Hammarskjöld, *Report of the Secretary-General: Summary Study of the Experience Derived from the Establishment and Operation of the Force*, A/3943, 9 October 1958, reprinted in *Basic Documents on United Nations and Related Peace-Keeping Forces*, ed. C. R. Siekmann (Dordrecht: Martinus Nijhoff, 1989), 53–54, para. 180.

3. See Shashi Tharoor, "Should UN Peacekeeping 'Go Back to Basics'?" *Survival* 37, no. 4 (winter 1995–96): 56.

4. Boutros Boutros-Ghali, *Supplement to an Agenda for Peace: Paper of the Secretary-General on the Occasion of the Fiftieth Anniversary of the United Nations*, A/50/60, S/1995/1, 25 January 1995, para. 21. Hereafter cited as *SAFP*.

5. The United Nations Mission in Haiti (UNMIH), which took over from the Multinational Force on 31 March 1995, also had Chapter VII authority. It is not mentioned above because this development did not occur within the second era.

6. The distinction will be clarified in chapter 2.

7. *SAFP*, para. 80.

8. Brian Urquhart, "Beyond the 'Sheriff's Posse,'" *Survival* 32, no. 3 (May–June 1990): 203.

9. Jarat Chopra, Åge Eknes, and Toralv Nordbø, *Fighting for Hope in Somalia* (Oslo: Norwegian Institute of International Affairs, 1995), 88.

10. Boutros Boutros-Ghali, *Report of the Secretary-General Pursuant to Security Council Resolutions 982 (1995) and 987 (1995)*, S/1995/444, 30 May 1995, para. 60.

11. Ibid., para. 75.

12. Boutros Boutros-Ghali at press conference, UN Headquarters, New York, 6 January 1995; Federal News Service transcript.

13. *SAFP*, "Executive Summary."

14. Though the United Nations lists the Mission in Bosnia and Herzegovina (UNMIBH) among its peace support missions, UNMIBH is not included in ours since it is a civilian police mission with only five military personnel as liaison.

15. See Tharoor, "UN Peacekeeping," 58. See also United Nations, *The Blue Helmets: A Review of United Nations Peace-keeping*, 3d ed. (New York: United Nations, 1996), 7.

16. See *SAFP*, para. 80. U.S. Ambassador to the United Nations Madeleine Albright spoke of a model in which a coalition force acting under UN endorsement responds and stabilizes a crisis area and then turns over responsibility to a UN-controlled force. She made her remarks at the United Nations Association of the USA conference on "The Future of the U.S. Relationship with the UN," New York City, 21 May 1996. Something of an exception in regard to potentially coercive operations being delegated to coalitions of the willing is the Transitional Administration for Eastern Slavonia, Baranja, and Western Sirmium (UNTAES), a UN-controlled operation in which "Member States are authorized, acting nationally or through regional organizations [particularly NATO in its IFOR role], to take all necessary measures, including close air support to defend or help withdraw UNTAES." Such requests are to be "based on UNTAES' request and procedures communicated to the United Nations." UNTAES is an exception that proves the rule in that its coercive credibility is grounded in national and NATO determination to provide coercive support to the mission on request. Citation is from the United Nations, *United Nations Peace-Keeping* (New York: United Nations, August 1996), 55. UN Secretariat officials opposed UNTAES being UN-controlled because of its potentially coercive nature, but were overruled by the United States and other IFOR participants, which, for domestic political reasons, wished to limit their perceived responsibility to maintain stability in the former Yugoslavia.

17. Kofi Annan, "Peace Operations and the United Nations: Preparing for the Next Century" (unpublished paper, February 1996), 4–5.

18. Urquhart, "Beyond the 'Sheriff's Posse,'" 203.

19. This issue is more fully developed in Donald C. F. Daniel, *Issues and Considerations in UN Gray Area and Enforcement Operations*, Research Memorandum 4–94 (Newport, R.I.: Naval War College, Strategic Research Department, 1994). See also Olara Otunnu, "The Peace and Security Agenda of the United Nations: From a Crossroads into the Next Century," in *Peacemaking and Peacekeeping for the Next Century: Report of the 25th Vienna Seminar,* ed. Ameen Jan, Robert C. Orr, and Timothy A. Wilkins (New York: International Peace Academy, 1995), 70–73.

20. Jarat Chopra, "The Space of Peace-Maintenance," *Political Geography* 15, no. 3–4 (1996): 337.

21. See above, p. 13.

22. Edward Hallett Carr, *The Twenty Years' Crisis, 1919–1939* (New York: Harper Torchbooks, 1964), 8.

23. As quoted in Steven R. Ratner, *The New UN Peacekeeping* (New York: St. Martin's, 1995), 44.

24. Tharoor, "UN Peacekeeping," 60.

25. "UN Bosnia Commander Wants More Troops, Fewer Resolutions," *New York Times,* 31 December 1993, A3.

26. See Bo Huldt, "Working Multilaterally: The Old Peacekeepers' Viewpoint," in *Beyond Traditional Peacekeeping,* ed. Donald C. F. Daniel and Bradd C. Hayes (London: Macmillan, 1995), chap. 6.

27. Brian Urquhart, "Who Can Stop Civil Wars?" *New York Times,* 29 December 1991, sec. 4, p. 9.

28. John Gerard Ruggie, "Wandering in the Void: Charting the UN's New Strategic Role," *Foreign Affairs* 72, no. 5 (November–December 1993): 26. The UN Secretariat was still utilizing similar language in 1996: "The United Nations, its Member States and their military establishments have entered uncharted territory. . . . Today's . . . operations defy simple definitions." See United Nations, "Peace-keeping in 1996:

Lessons Learned, Lessons Applied," in *Year in Review 1996, United Nations Peace Missions* (New York: United Nations, December 1996), 3.

29. Tharoor states that it fell "out of fashion after the disasters of Somalia." See Tharoor, "UN Peacekeeping," 56.

30. See [British Army], *Wider Peacekeeping*, Army Field Manual (Wiltshire, England: Headquarters Doctrine and Training, 1994).

31. Charles Dobbie, "A Concept for Post–Cold War Peacekeeping," *Survival* 36, no. 3 (autumn 1994): 142.

32. Ibid., 141–145.

33. Boutros Boutros-Ghali, *An Agenda for Peace: Preventive Diplomacy, Peacemaking and Peace-Keeping* (New York: United Nations, 1992), paras. 44–45. Hereafter cited as *AFP*. It was elliptical for two reasons. One was that he did not in *AFP* speak directly about peace enforcement per se but rather of the use of peace enforcement *units*. Also, he embedded that discussion in a chapter on peacemaking, which he defined as "action to bring hostile parties to agreement, essentially through such peaceful means as those foreseen under Chapter VI." This contributed to confusion because Chapter VI does not contemplate enforcement, which is reserved for Chapter VII.

34. Boutros Boutros-Ghali, "Empowering the United Nations," *Foreign Affairs* 71, no. 5 (winter 1992–93): 93–94.

35. See above, p. 13.

36. See, for example, *SAFP*, 23; and Boutros-Ghali's statement as quoted in John M. Goshko, "Balkan Peacekeeping Exposes Limits of UN, Boutros-Ghali Says," *Washington Post,* 10 October 1995, 21.

37. United Nations, "UN Peace-keeping: Some Questions and Answers" (fact sheet accessed on the UN homepage, September 1996).

38. Shashi Tharoor, "United Nations Peacekeeping in Europe," *Survival* 37, no. 2 (summer 1995): 126–127, 133 n. 4. Similar views surfaced in conversations with personnel in the secretary-general's entourage.

39. Chopra, Eknes, and Nordbø, *Fighting for Hope,* 16.

40. The citation is from James Sutterlin, *The United Nations and the Maintenance of International Security* (Westport, Conn.: Praeger, 1995), 67.

2. A PRACTICABLE MIDDLE OPTION AND ASSOCIATED PRINCIPLES

1. Thomas Schelling, *Arms and Influence* (New Haven: Yale University Press, 1966), 2. See also Alexander George, *Forceful Persuasion: Coercive Diplomacy as an Alternative to War* (Washington, D.C.: United States Institute of Peace Press, 1991).

2. The use of the word "unduly" reflects the Haiti case, in which the Governors Island Agreement called for the reinstatement of Aristide.

3. One of the best treatments of this important distinction is found in [British Army], *Wider Peacekeeping*, Army Field Manual (Wiltshire, England: Headquarters Doctrine and Training, 1994).

4. An excellent treatment of decaying consent is found in Steven R. Ratner, *The New UN Peacekeeping* (New York: St. Martin's, 1995), 37–41.

5. Jarat Chopra, Åge Eknes, and Toralv Nordbø, *Fighting for Hope in Somalia* (Oslo: Norwegian Institute of International Affairs, 1995), 93. See also Adam Roberts, "The Crisis in UN Peacekeeping," *Survival* 36, no. 3 (autumn 1994): 115, in which the following quotation is found:

> Impartiality is no longer interpreted to mean, in every case, impartiality toward the parties. . . . In some cases, the UN may . . . be tougher on one party than another. . . . [That is,] "impartiality" may have come to mean . . . impartiality in carrying out UN Security Council decisions.

6. Shashi Tharoor, "Peace-Keeping: Principles, Problems, and Prospects," Strategic Research Department Report 9–93 (Newport, R.I.: Naval War College, Center for Naval Warfare Studies, 1993), 10–11.

7. It must be stressed that these labels and the ideas grouped beneath them do not conform to what all practitioners or commentators say about the terms or the phenomena attributed to each. To try to do so would be to sleep on a procrustean bed. Comparing arguments and texts in this area of discourse reveals a confusing melange of concepts, views, and idea groupings, with some people using the same words with slightly to radically different meanings and different words with the same or closely related meanings. Also relevant here is an observation made decades ago by the political scientist Harold Lasswell. He would often remind his readers that a declarative statement can indicate what the speaker believes is reality, or what he expects reality to be, or what he wants it to be. It is often the case that speakers do not make clear what perspective guides their statements, and one reason may be that they may have not consciously settled the issue for themselves. See Harold Lasswell and Abraham Kaplan, *Power and Society: A Framework for Political Inquiry* (New Haven: Yale University Press, 1950), 16–28.

8. Dag Hammarskjöld, *Second and Final Report of the Secretary-General on the Plan for an Emergency International United Nations Force Requested in Resolution 998 (ES-1), Adopted by the General Assembly on 4 November 1956*, A/3302/6, November 1956, paras. 10, 12, reprinted in Robert C. R. Siekmann, ed., *Basic Documents on United Nations and Related Peace-Keeping Forces* (Dordrecht: Martinus Nijhoff, 1989), 5.

9. See, for example, Clement Adibe, *Disarmament and Conflict Resolution in a Stateless Society: The UN and Conflict in Somalia* (New York: United Nations; Geneva: United Nations Institute for Disarmament Research [UNIDIR], 1995), 35–36.

10. Dag Hammarskjöld, *First Report of the Secretary-General on the Implementation of Security Council Resolution 143 (1960) of 14 July 1960*, S/4389, 15 November 1960, para. 4, reprinted in Siekmann, *Basic Documents*, 76.

11. Dag Hammarskjöld, *Report of the Secretary-General: Summary Study of the Experience Derived from the Establishment and Operation of the Force*, A/3943, 9 October 1958, para. 156, reprinted in Siekmann, *Basic Documents*, 51.

12. Ibid., paras. 157–158. See also *First Report of the Secretary-General*, S/4389, para. 8, reprinted in Siekmann, *Basic Documents*, 76.

13. See William J. Durch, "Getting Involved: Political-Military Context," in *The Evolution of UN Peacekeeping: Case Studies and Comparative Analysis*, ed. William J. Durch (New York: St. Martin's, 1993), 30–31.

14. See Marrack Goulding, "The Use of Force by the United Nations," *International Peacekeeping* 3, no. 1 (spring 1996): 14; and Shashi Tharoor, "Should UN Peacekeeping 'Go Back to Basics'?" *Survival* 37, no. 4 (winter 1995–96): 56.

15. See Tharoor, "UN Peace-Keeping," 52–53; and U Thant, *Aide-Memoire of the Secretary-General Concerning Some Questions Relating to the Operation of the United Nations Peace-Keeping Force in Cyprus, 10 April 1964*, S/5653, 11 April 1964, para. 15, reprinted in Siekmann, *Basic Documents*, 153.

16. Goulding, "Use of Force," 12.

17. Roger Cohen, "NATO Demands Serbs Withdraw Guns near Sarajevo," *New York Times*, 4 September 1995, 3.

18. Hammarskjöld, *Report of the Secretary-General*, A/3943, paras. 175, 179, reprinted in Siekmann, *Basic Documents*, 53. "The basic element," he stated, was "the prohibition against any *initiative* in the use of armed force." Emphasis in original (para. 179).

19. Thant, *Aide-Memoire*, S/5653, paras. 16–18, reprinted in Siekmann, *Basic Documents*, 153. A UN legal officer stated in an interview on 16 October 1996 that UN rules of engagement were expanding to include the protection of innocent bystanders.

20. See, for example, United Nations, *The Blue Helmets: A Review of United Nations Peace-keeping*, 2d ed. (New York: United Nations, 1990), 7; and the annexes to Jane Boulden, "Rules of Engagement and Force Structure and Composition in UN Operations" (Geneva: UNIDIR, Disarmament and Conflict Resolution Project, draft of 4 July 1995; subsequently published in United Nations Institute for Disarmament Research, *Managing Arms in Peace Processes: The Issues* [New York: United Nations, 1998]).

21. Gustav Hagglund, "Peacekeeping in a Modern War Zone," *Survival* 32, no. 3 (May–June 1990): 239.

22. Kurt Waldheim, *Report of the Secretary-General on the Implementation of Security Council Resolution 340 (1973)*, S/11052/Rev. 1, 27 October 1973, para. 4d, reprinted in Siekmann, *Basic Documents*, 190.

23. Marrack Goulding, "The Evolution of United Nations Peacekeeping," *International Affairs* 69, no. 3 (July 1993): 455. See also Tharoor, "Peace-Keeping," 10–11.

24. Alvaro de Soto, letter to the editor, *Foreign Affairs* 74, no. 1 (January–February 1995): 186.

25. The North Korea and Iraq cases are well accepted, but for reasons that are not entirely clear, the Congo case is usually not mentioned along with them. Yet in February 1961 the Security Council urged the use of "all appropriate measures . . . and the use of force, if necessary," and in November it authorized the secretary-general to "take vigorous action, including the use of a requisite measure of force, if necessary, for the immediate apprehension, . . . [and] deportation of all foreign military and para-military personnel and political advisors . . . and mercenaries." Transcripts of the resolutions are found in Brookings Institution, *United Nations Peacekeeping in the Congo: 1960–1964,* vol. 3, *Appendices* (Washington, D.C.: Brookings Institution, 1966), appendix B–6 and appendix B–12.

26. As noted in Boutros Boutros-Ghali, *Report of the Secretary-General Pursuant to Security Council Resolutions 982 (1995) and 987 (1995),* S/1995/444, 30 May 1995, para. 60, this is the point of view of Boutros-Ghali and many who served with him in the Secretariat. A factor that may be at play here is the division that the UN Charter makes between Chapter VI's consensual resolution of disputes and Chapter VII's authority to undertake enforcement or war. In a report of the results of a conference bringing together peace support practitioners, Trevor Findlay observes:

> One . . . consequence of clearly separating Chapter 6 and . . . 7 operations . . . is that it gives the impression that there are only two stark options facing the UN: peacekeeping . . . and war-fighting. This impression is reinforced by the counsel of several UN force commanders [at the meeting] that anything that goes beyond [consensual] peacekeeping is war.

See Findlay, "The Use of Force in Peace Operations" (paper presented at a conference of the Stockholm International Peace Research Institute, Stockholm, 1995), 3. Findlay's observation applies equally to a meeting of UN officials and practitioners convened by UNIDIR's Project on Disarmament and Conflict Resolution and hosted by the Ministry of Defense of Finland at its Training Center for UN Peacekeepers, Niinisalo, Finland, on 6–8 July 1995. The writer of this chapter helped arrange and cochair the meeting. See also Roberts, "Crisis in UN Peacekeeping," 101–102; and John Mackinlay, "Powerful Peacekeepers," *Survival* 32, no. 3 (May–June 1990): 245, which discusses the mindset of many people closely involved with peacekeeping.

27. One of the best treatments of this issue is by the French General Staff. See, for example, the paper prepared by the Etat-Major des Armées, "Réflexion sur la conception, la préparation, la planification, le commandement et l'emploi des forces dans les operations militaires fondées sur une résolution du Conseil de securité de l'ONU" (paper published in 1995; copy in author's files).

28. This was a strongly held view of many officials and practitioners at the UNIDIR meeting held in Finland in July 1995 and referenced at note 26.

29. See above, p. 19.

30. John Gerard Ruggie, "Wandering in the Void: Charting the UN's New Strategic Role," *Foreign Affairs* 72, no. 5 (November–December 1993): 31.

31. Mackinlay, "Powerful Peacekeepers," 245.

32. The term "new paradigm" is used by Elisabeth Lindenmayer, a UN official who works for Annan and who in conversation and public meetings eloquently makes the case for consideration of an option distinct from both classical peacekeeping and enforcement.

33. See above, p. 4.

34. As noted earlier (see p. 18), Charles Dobbie was instrumental in the formulation of the British "Wider Peacekeeping" doctrine. In four separate off-the-record interviews with individuals in positions of appropriate responsibility in the British military, two of the authors were told that a shortcoming of the doctrine was that it did not explicitly make provisions for a concept such as coercive inducement. One problem in issuing a revision highlighting such a change was that the original document, which very prominently stressed that there was no middle ground, had become too well accepted as it stood, not only in the United Kingdom but also abroad (not the least at UN Headquarters).

35. See Charles Dobbie, "A Concept for Post–Cold War Peacekeeping," *Survival* 36, no. 3 (autumn 1994): 145.

36. This point was especially emphasized to the author of this chapter by one of the critical players in UNITAF headquarters.

37. Clement Adibe, *Disarmament and Conflict Resolution in a Stateless Society: The UN and Conflict in Somalia* (New York: United Nations; Geneva: UNIDIR, 1995), 88.

38. See Boutros-Ghali, *SAFP*, para. 36.

39. Robert Cooper and Mats Berdal, "Outside Intervention in Ethnic Conflicts," *Survival* 35, no. 1 (spring 1993): 137.

40. This assertion is based on numerous interviews and on what many participants have said at meetings on peace support operations.

41. Alexander George has noted how "coercive diplomacy" or "forceful persuasion" is an especially "beguiling" option that can tempt policymakers to bluff. See George, *Forceful Persuasion,* 6.

42. See Tharoor, "Peace-Keeping," 6; Hammarskjöld, *Report of the Secretary-General,* A/3943, para. 167, reprinted in Siekmann, *Basic Documents,* 52; and chapters by Dorinda Dallmeyer, Bo Huldt, and Angela Kane in *Beyond Traditional Peacekeeping,* ed. Donald C. F. Daniel and Bradd C. Hayes (London: Macmillan, 1995).

43. Interview with a UN official, 9 December 1994.

44. An article published in 1997 characterized peace enforcement as "in disrepute." See "Reworking the UN," *Economist,* 15 February 1997, 18.

45. Kofi Annan, "Peace Operations and the United Nations: Preparing for the Next Century" (unpublished paper, February 1996), 1–2.

3. BOSNIA

The author wishes to thank Michael E. Brown, James A. Schear, and Shashi Tharoor for their many useful comments on an earlier draft of this chapter.

1. The other four constituent republics of Yugoslavia were Bosnia and Herzegovina, Macedonia, Montenegro, and Serbia.

2. For details on the causes of the Yugoslav conflict, see Ivo Daalder, "Fear and Loathing in the Former Yugoslavia," in *The International Dimensions of Internal Conflict,* ed. Michael E. Brown (Cambridge, Mass.: MIT Press, 1996), 35–67.

3. The war in Slovenia ended with a cease-fire agreement brokered by the European Community (EC) in which Slovenia agreed to suspend implementation of its independence declaration for three months. Unlike Croatia, Slovenia had a small Serb population. The secession of Slovenia was hence easily agreed to by Slobodan Milosevic, the Serbian president. He withdrew the Yugoslav People's Army from Slovenia a few weeks after the signing of the cease-fire. The end of the Socialist Federal Republic of Yugoslavia was officially confirmed in April 1992 when the new Federal Republic of Yugoslavia (consisting of Montenegro and Serbia) was proclaimed in Belgrade.

4. The JNA had been strongly in favor of a federal and united Yugoslavia. The breakup of Yugoslavia threatened the existence of seventy thousand career officers, 70 percent of whom were Serbs or Montenegrins. See Misha Glenny, *The Fall of Yugoslavia: The Third Balkan War* (London: Penguin, 1992), 134. The defeat of the JNA in Slovenia diminished the influence of Yugo-federalists in the high command. The army then quickly became an instrument of the Serb cause. See Mark Almond, *Europe's Backyard War: The War in the Balkans* (London: Heinemann, 1994), 236; and John Zametica, *The Yugoslav Conflict,* Adelphi Paper no. 270 (London: International Institute for Strategic Studies, 1992), 17–19, 40–45.

5. Milosevic and Tudjman had agreed to the deployment of UN peacekeepers, albeit for different reasons. Croatian forces had been militarily exhausted. Tudjman thought that deployment of UN troops legitimized Croatia's call for independence and he believed that, in time, they might bring Serb-occupied territories back to Croatia. Milosevic, who no longer had any illusions regarding the secession of Croatia, thought that the UN presence might ultimately favor his aim of creating a Greater Serbia. Local Serbs had taken firm control in Slavonia and the Krajina, and occupied close to one-third of Croatian territory. Milosevic thought that UN peacekeepers would help freeze that situation and eventually facilitate the return of those territories back to the rump Yugoslav state.

6. For details, see United Nations, *The United Nations and the Situation in the Former Yugoslavia*, Reference Paper, July 1995, DPI/1312/Rev. 4. Hereafter referred to as *Yugoslavia.*

7. See Glenny, *Fall of Yugoslavia,* 148; Zametica, *Yugoslav Conflict,* 36; and Susan L. Woodward, *Balkan Tragedy: Chaos and Dissolution after the Cold War* (Washington, D.C.: Brookings Institution, 1995), 7.

8. Muslims made up 43 percent, Serbs 32 percent, and Croats 17 percent of the population. In the elections the Muslim Party of Democratic Action (SDA) received 33.8 percent of the votes, the Serbian Democratic Party (SDS) 29.6 percent, and the Croatian Democratic Union (HDZ) 18.3 percent. See Woodward, *Balkan Strategy,* 122.

9. A third of the Bosnian Croat population was concentrated in the western part of Bosnia. This region quickly became a de facto part of Croatia. Croatian flags, laws, and currency ruled the region, and the central Bosnian presidency lost all control. See Woodward, *Balkan Strategy,* 193–194.

10. Croat regions had declared their intention to recognize the central government as long as the republic maintained its independence from the former or any future Yugoslavia. See ibid.

11. The United Nations' reluctance to deploy peacekeepers in Bosnia at the end of 1991 has been criticized as shortsighted and a de facto endorsement of Serb behavior. Henri Wijnaendts, the Dutch ambassador to Paris and deputy to Lord Carrington, the president of the European Community (EC) Conference on Yugoslavia, accused Vance of surrendering to Serb wishes. Although it is probable that Vance did not want to antagonize Milosevic, whose cooperation he needed for the deployment of the UN force in Croatia, it is also true that he knew few countries were willing to contribute troops to a UN operation that might suffer casualties and become entangled in what many considered to be an internal conflict. After all, Europeans had rebuffed a Bosnian request for observers in July 1991. See Henri Wijnaendts, *L'Engrenage: Chroniques Yougoslaves, juillet 1991–août 1992* (Paris: Denoël, 1993), 63, 141.

12. See Woodward, *Balkan Strategy,* 194, 472 n.138. The cease-fire between military representatives of Croatia and representatives of the JNA had been signed on 2 January 1992 in Sarajevo.

13. Serbs were also scattered throughout the country. However, unlike the Muslims, they lived largely in the countryside with some strong concentrations in the north and south of Bosnia. The western part of Bosnia was almost exclusively Croat. Two-thirds of the Bosnian Croat population lived in central and northern Bosnia. The latter tended to be against partition. However, with the intensification of the war, particularly in 1993, they too succumbed to the ethnic logic of the war.

14. In February 1992, Izetbegovic agreed to a Serb proposal for the formation of three national territorial units within Bosnia. However, he reneged on his pledge in March 1992 and denounced the plan, which had been negotiated with the help of the EC, as an ethnic partition plan. The February 1992 agreement might have been one of the last chances to stave off the war.

15. The Bosnian presidency sought EC recognition on 20 December 1991. As a condition for recognition, the EC demanded that a referendum be held. The referen-

dum, organized in late February 1992, was boycotted by the Bosnian Serbs, but Bosnian Muslims and Croats overwhelmingly supported independence.

16. For details see Lewis MacKenzie, *Peacekeeper: The Road to Sarajevo*
(Toronto: HarperCollins, 1994), 212–299.

17. See Almond, *Europe's Backyard War,* 269. By the end of 1992, close to 2 million Bosnians had lost their homes. In March 1993 the UN High Commissioner for
Refugees reported that some 2,280,000 (half the original population) were beneficia-
ries of humanitarian assistance from the UNHCR. In June 1994 these numbers had
risen to 4,259,000 for the whole of the former Yugoslavia, including 2,740,000 for
Bosnia. See United Nations, *Yugoslavia,* 62–63.

18. The 1991 operation in northern Iraq (Operation Provide Comfort) was
inspirational in that regard. In northern Iraq, the Western allies successfully defused a
Kurdish refugee problem in Turkey by creating a humanitarian protection zone (safe
haven), including a flight exclusion zone. See also Woodward, *Balkan Strategy,* 295.

19. See UNSC Res. 757 (1992), 30 May 1992, para. 17; UNSC Res. 758 (1992),
8 June 1992; and UNSC Res. 761 (1992), 29 June 1992.

20. See UNSC Res. 761 (1992), 29 June 1992; and Boutros Boutros-Ghali,
Report of the UN Secretary-General, S/24075, 6 June 1992.

21. See UNSC Res. 776 (1992), 12 September 1992. On 13 August 1992, the
Security Council adopted Resolution 770 (1992), in which the council, acting under
Chapter VII of the UN Charter, called on "states to take nationally or through
regional agencies or arrangements all measures necessary to facilitate, in coordination with the United Nations, the delivery of humanitarian assistance to Sarajevo and
wherever needed in other parts of Bosnia and Herzegovina." Resolution 776 (1992)
authorized UNPROFOR to carry out this task. The "all measures necessary" clause of
Resolution 770 (1992) was believed by some to authorize the use of force. However,
Resolution 776 (1992) did not make reference to Chapter VII, and subsequent
remarks by the UN secretary-general made clear that the drafters of the resolution
had no such intentions. Indeed, the secretary-general stipulated that UNPROFOR
was to follow normal peacekeeping rules of engagement. Military protection forces
would deter or defend against random attacks by rogue elements. In no circumstances were the convoys to fight their way through to their destinations. See Boutros
Boutros-Ghali, *Report of the UN Secretary-General Pursuant to Security Council Resolutions 982 (1995) and 987 (1995),* S/1995/444, 30 May 1995, para. 29.

22. Both eventually rescinded their positions—Owen, when he became the EC
mediator and cochairman of the EC–UN Peace Conference on the former Yugoslavia
in September 1992, and Clinton when he assumed office in January 1993. See David
Owen, *Balkan Odyssey* (New York: Harcourt Brace, 1995), 11–20.

23. When the war broke out in the former Yugoslavia, international intervention was spearheaded by the European Community. In the summer of 1991, and after
many EC-brokered cease-fires had been disregarded by the combatants, France proposed to deploy a Western European Union (WEU) interposition force. Although the

proposal was supported by Germany, Italy, and the Netherlands, the United Kingdom opposed sending such a force. The British view was that there was no peace to keep, and that French appeals for an interposition force reeked of previous suggestions made by France for European autonomy in defense matters. From London's perspective, this raised suspicions that this was an attempt to outflank NATO. The British, whose participation in such a force would have been crucial, managed to shelve the idea in September 1991. See Zametica, *Yugoslav Conflict,* 66; and Joseph Fitchett, "EC's Missteps: Did They Fuel Yugoslav Conflict?" *International Herald Tribune,* 21–22 September 1991.

24. For details, see Ivo Daalder, "The United States and Military Intervention in Internal Conflict," in Brown, ed., *International Dimensions,* 461–488; and Michael R. Gordon, "U.S. Military Chief on Bosnia: Stay Out," *International Herald Tribune,* 29 September 1992.

25. See Owen, *Balkan Odyssey,* 14–20. The British military experience in Northern Ireland made the British wary of intervening in civil conflicts.

26. Lieutenant General Barry McCaffrey, assistant to the chairman of the U.S. Joint Chiefs of Staff, Colin Powell, speculated that around four hundred thousand troops deployed for a year or so would be needed to end the violence in Bosnia. See John Barry, "By Air—or Land?" *Newsweek,* 10 May 1993, 24. See also Brett D. Barkey, "Bosnia: A Question of Intervention," *Strategic Review* 21, no. 4 (fall 1993): 48–59. The successful Croat and Bosnian government offensives of 1995 proved how misguided those assertions had been. See also Ed Vulliamy, "America's Big Strategic Lie: Bosnia—the Secret War," *Guardian,* 20 May 1996.

27. See ibid.

28. See UNSC Res. 781 (1992), 8 October 1992; and 786 (1992), 10 November 1992.

29. See UNSC Res. 816 (1993), 31 March 1993. The Security Council adopted this resolution acting under Chapter VII, thereby notifying all concerned that it had taken this measure as an action to restore international peace and security and that its decision was binding. Moreover, the ban was extended to include all fixed- and rotary-wing aircraft.

30. The Vance-Owen Peace Plan (VOPP) defined Bosnia as a decentralized state made up of ten provinces, each of which would have received substantial autonomy. It also provided for the separation of, on the one hand, Serb and, on the other hand, Croat and Muslim armed forces. Armed forces were to withdraw to designated provinces and eventually be demobilized. Sarajevo was to be demilitarized immediately. Serbs protested that they had to give up too much territory. Moreover, they objected to the fact that "their" provinces were noncontiguous. The Muslims thought that the plan did not provide for sufficient central government authority, and that it sanctioned ethnic cleansing. Even so, Izetbegovic later grudgingly accepted the plan. For details, see Owen, *Balkan Odyssey.*

31. The authors of the VOPP would repeatedly deny the ethnic partition logic of the plan. They argued that the division of Bosnia into ten noncontiguous provinces would prevent any of the three ethnic entities from creating a state within the state. See ibid.

32. That said, the Americans did not seem really committed to the strategy. "Mr. Christopher [when visiting Europe in the spring of 1993] seemed more interested in discussing options than hard selling." See "The Bosnian Stall," *Economist*, 5 February 1994, 23. "If Mr. Christopher had gone to Europe with nothing but the strike part of his strategy, he would have found agreement (no great enthusiasm, but agreement) in Paris and London, notwithstanding the inevitable dangers to troops on the ground." See "Into Bosnia?" *Economist*, 15 May 1993, 25. The Europeans were "shocked to meet a U.S. Secretary of State who humbly accepted their rebuttal and trundled back to tell the President." See Karen Breslau, "The Virtues of Being a Grown-Up in Washington," *Newsweek*, 26 June 1995, 33.

33. See Eliot A. Cohen, "The Mystique of U.S. Air Power," *Foreign Affairs* 73, no. 1 (January–February 1994): 110.

34. U.S. Senator Joseph Biden's outburst against the Europeans on 11 May 1993 is quoted in "Into Bosnia?" 25.

35. See Woodward, *Balkan Strategy,* 312.

36. The resolutions concerned a strengthening of the sanctions regime imposed on Serbia and Montenegro (UNSC Res. 820 [1993], 17 April 1993); the establishment of an International War Crimes Tribunal (UNSC Res. 808 [1993], 23 February 1993 and UNSC Res. 827 [1993], 25 May 1993); the enforcement of the Bosnian no-fly zone (UNSC Res. 816 [1993], 31 March 1993); and the establishment of six safe areas to be protected by UN troops and threats of NATO air strikes (UNSC Res. 819 [1993], 16 April 1993; UNSC Res. 824 [1993], 6 May 1993; UNSC Res. 836 [1993], 4 June 1993; and UNSC Res. 844 [1993], 18 June 1993).

37. The Union of Three Republics plan was first proposed in March 1992 and was reintroduced in June 1993. It called for the Muslim Republic to control a minimum of 33.3 percent of Bosnian territory and the Croat Republic 17.5 percent. The Serb Republic would control the remaining territory. For details, see Owen, *Balkan Odyssey.*

38. The EU Action Plan was a variant of the Union of Three Republics plan and was introduced in December 1993. For details, see ibid.

39. For details on U.S. efforts to repair the Croat-Muslim alliance, see Laura Silber and Allan Little, *Yugoslavia: Death of a Nation* (New York: TV Books, and Penguin USA, 1996), 319–323.

40. Despite the arms embargo on all states of the former Yugoslavia, arms were readily available. However, because of Bosnia's landlocked situation, Croatia controlled the pipeline of arms to Bosnia. Reports in 1996 confirmed that the Clinton administration had given the green light for arms deliveries to Bosnia in April 1994. See William Safire, "Oversight Evader," *New York Times*, 11 April 1996, 25; Walter

Pincus, "Bosnia Arms Fracas Not about Broken Law," *Washington Post,* 22 April 1996, 9; Walter Pincus, "U.S. Details Decision on Bosnia Arms," *Washington Post,* 24 April 1996, 24; and John Pomfret and David Ottaway, "U.S. Allies Fed Pipe-Line of Covert Arms to Bosnia," *Washington Post,* 12 May 1996, 1.

41. Moreover, Croatia was threatened with economic sanctions if it did not stop its ethnic-cleansing practices and withdraw its troops from Bosnia. See the statement by the president of the UN Security Council of 3 February 1994. The 1995 Croat offensives in western Slavonia and the Krajina were planned with the help of U.S. advisers. See Silber and Little, *Death of a Nation,* 345–354.

42. Ironically, the new alliance, while designed to counter the strength of the Bosnian Serbs, provided the Serbs with arguments in support of their attachment to Serbia. If Bosnian Croats and Muslims could be confederated with Croatia, why not the Bosnian Serbs with Serbia?

43. A referendum held on 27 and 28 August 1994 confirmed the vote of the Bosnian Serb Assembly.

44. See UNSC Res. 942 (1994), 23 September 1994. In recognition of Milosevic's closure of the border with Bosnia, the Security Council suspended several sanctions imposed in April 1993. See UNSC Res. 943 (1994), 23 September 1994.

45. Izetbegovic's declaration in September 1994 that his government had suspended, for six months, its demand to have the arms embargo lifted should be seen in this context. See "Bosnia: Only Postponing," *Economist,* 1 October 1994, 65–66.

46. See Owen, *Balkan Odyssey,* 293–294.

47. U.S. secretary of defense William Perry said that the Muslims had lost the war, and insisted that air power alone could not reverse the outcome. See "A Sly Game of Liars Poker," *Newsweek,* 19 December 1994, 37. See also "U.S. and Bosnia: How a Policy Changed," *New York Times,* 4 December 1994, 1, 20.

48. Jimmy Carter had received an invitation from Karadzic several months before his December 1994 trip.

49. See Mladen Klemencic and Clive Schofield, "Calm after the Storm? Croatia's Strategic Outlook," *RUSI Journal* (February 1996): 38–39.

50. See Boutros-Ghali, *Report of the UN Secretary-General,* S/1995/444, 30 May 1995, para. 7.

51. See Bruce W. Nelan, "Bosnia: Not So Rapid Response," *Time,* 19 June 1995, 30.

52. The force was made up of British, French, and Dutch soldiers. Since the force would inhibit the free movement of Bosnian military forces, the Bosnian Federation placed severe restrictions on the movements of the RRF. Hence, it took the RRF a long time to get to the field. It arrived on Mount Ignam, outside Sarajevo, on 23 July. For details, see D. V. Nicholls, "Bosnia: UN and NATO," *RUSI Journal* (February 1996): 31–36.

53. Zepa fell soon thereafter. NATO's threat was extended to cover Bihac, Tuzla, and Sarajevo on 1 August 1995. For the texts of the press statements by NATO secretary-general Willy Claes, see *NATO Review* 43, no. 5 (September 1995): 7.

54. At the same time the Croat-Bosnian ground campaign contributed to making the NATO air campaign a success.

55. For some time "Bosniac" had become the politically correct term to denote Muslims and all other non-Croat or non-Serb citizens of Bosnia.

56. See UNSC Res. 1031 (1995), 15 December 1995, which authorized the establishment of IFOR.

57. See UNSC Res. 1035 (1995), 21 December 1995.

58. In July 1996 Clinton called on Holbrooke to convince Milosevic that Karadzic had to relinquish all power and disappear from public life. While Holbrooke was successful in having Karadzic removed as head of the SDS, he fell short of having him sent to the International Criminal Tribunal in The Hague.

59. The municipal elections were first postponed to November, and then postponed twice more. They were finally held in September 1997. Elections for the National Assembly of the Republika Srpska were held two months later. Elections for the presidency, the presidents of the Entities, the National Assemblies, and Cantonal Government were held on 12 and 13 September 1998. Simultaneously, elections were held in ten municipalities where no elections took place in 1997.

60. See, for example, the remarks made by U.S. secretary of defense William Perry, quoted by Thomas L. Friedman, "Exit Strategy," *New York Times*, 24 April 1996, A21.

61. See NATO Press Communiqué M-NAC-2 (96) 166, 10 December 1996; and UNSC Res. 1088 (1996), 12 December 1996, adopted under Chapter VII of the UN Charter.

62. This chapter does not address the NATO and WEU enforcement operation at sea—Operation Sharp Guard—nor does it address the NATO and WEU enforcement operations on the River Danube. Indeed, unlike the no-fly zone, Operation Sharp Guard and the WEU Danube mission were not integral parts of the UN operation in Yugoslavia. In November 1992, NATO and WEU forces started enforcement operations in support of the UN arms embargo against all states of the former Yugoslavia (UNSC Res. 713 [1991]) and the economic sanctions against Serbia (UNSC Res. 757 [1992]; 820 [1993]). See UNSC Res. 787 (1992), 16 November 1992. This operation came under combined NATO-WEU command in June 1993. Between 22 November 1992 and 26 April 1996 more than 71,335 ships had been challenged; 5,623 were boarded and inspected at sea; 1,471 were diverted and inspected in port. Six ships were caught attempting to break the embargo between April 1993 and April 1996. Operation Sharp Guard proceeded without major mishaps. See NATO, "NATO's Role in Peacekeeping in the Former Yugoslavia" (NATO Basic Factsheet, no. 4, February 1996), 1; and NATO-WEU Operation Sharp Guard @ gopher://marvin.stc.nato.int:70/00/yugo/nw2604.96. The WEU Danube mission was established in June 1993. It never resorted to the use of force. For details, see Colonel Vincenzo Basso (head of the Danube mission from July 1995 to September 1996), "The WEU Danube Mission," and Colonel Angelo Cardile (head of the Danube mission from February 1994 to July 1995), "An Analysis on the Organization and Progress of the Joint Operation

Carried Out on the Danube by Police and Customs Forces of WEU Countries," both in Copenhagen Round Table on UN Sanctions, *The Report of the Copenhagen Round Table on UN Sanctions: The Case of the Former Yugoslavia, Copenhagen 24–25 June 1996 and Annexes* (Brussels: SAMCOMM, European Commission, 1996), 198–202, 224–235.

63. See UNSC Res. 816 (1993), 31 March 1993.

64. See Boutros-Ghali, *Report of the UN Secretary-General*, S/1995/444, para. 31.

65. See Paul Claesson and Trevor Findlay, "Appendix 1B: Case Studies on Peace-keeping: UNOSOM II, UNTAC, and UNPROFOR," in *SIPRI Yearbook 1994*, 77.

66. The NATO air strikes of 21 November 1994, which hit the Ubdina airstrip in Croatia in response to the attack by Krajina Serb aircraft on Bihac, were authorized in support of the defense of Bihac as a UN safe area. They were not carried out as an enforcement action of the no-fly zone. See UNSC Res. 958 (1994), 19 November 1994.

67. See Silber and Little, *Death of a Nation*, 352.

68. See UNSC Res. 819 (1993), 16 April 1993; UNSC Res. 824 (1993), 6 May 1993; UNSC Res. 836 (1993), 4 June 1993; and UNSC Res. 844 (1993), 18 June 1993.

69. See Boutros Boutros-Ghali, *Report of the UN Secretary-General*, S/1994/555, 9 May 1994, para. 2.

70. Ibid., para. 3

71. See Bruce D. Berkowitz, "Rules of Engagement for UN Peacekeeping Forces in Bosnia," *Orbis* (fall 1994): 635–646. It includes the text of the rules of engagement issued by General Jean Cot, commander of the UN Forces in the Former Yugoslavia, as issued on 24 March 1992 and revised on 19 July 1993. Many analysts have pointed to the restrictive nature of the UN rules of engagement to explain the failure of UNPROFOR. However, it is often forgotten that rules of engagement are only a translation in military terms of policy objectives as defined by Security Council members. Moreover, the concept of self-defense is not static and can be stretched. As General Cot has put it, "the contingents who do not want to take risks are those who most criticize the rules of engagement, and those who do not make full use of the rules in the context of self-defence." See "Practitioners' Questionnaire on Weapons Control, Disarmament, and Demobilization during Peacekeeping Operations," in Barbara Ekwall-Vebelhart and Andrei Raevsky, *Managing Arms in Peace Processes: Croatia and Bosnia-Herzegovina* (New York: United Nations; Geneva: United Nations Institute for Disarmament Research, 1996), 298.

72. Moreover, it took more than one year to deploy the 7,950 peacekeepers.

73. See decisions of 2 and 9 August 1993; NATO Press Release (93) 52, August 1993; and the Declaration of NATO's summit meeting in January 1994, Press Communiqué M-1 (94) 3, 11 January 1994, paras. 23–25.

74. As it turned out, the first real threat to use force came from the North Atlantic Council, not the United Nations.

75. See NATO Press Release (94) 103, 28 October 1994.

76. See Boutros-Ghali, *Report of the UN Secretary-General*, S/1995/444, para. 48.

77. For the decisive role of the French and how they brought the British on board, see Eliane Sciolino and Douglas Jehl, "As U.S. Sought a Bosnia Policy, the French Offered a Good Idea," *New York Times*, 14 February 1994.

78. See NATO Press Release (94) 15, 9 February 1994. Locations of the weapon collection sites were not specified and were subject to negotiation. The heavy-weapon exclusion zone excluded Pale.

79. See "Counting Down," *Newsweek*, 28 February 1994, 7.

80. Ibid.

81. These were troops he had earlier refused to send to Bosnia. See Silber and Little, *Death of a Nation*, 317.

82. For more details, see ibid., 309–318.

83. Owen, *Balkan Odyssey*, 268.

84. See "Bosnia: A Text Book Written in Blood," *Economist*, 26 February 1994, 22; and Misha Glenny, "Bosnian Quicksand," *New York Times*, 18 February 1994.

85. This occurred despite the agreement between NATO and the United Nations that stipulated that the secretary-general would have control over air strikes.

86. A UN Security Council meeting open to all parties concerned was called by Russia. That said, the meeting held on 14–15 February 1994 carefully steered away from adopting a resolution or a statement concerning the situation in Sarajevo and NATO's ultimatum.

87. Even so, Madeleine Albright, U.S. ambassador to the United Nations, and Anthony Lake, the U.S. national security adviser, were not completely silenced. The "lift and strike" strategy, while dropped in 1993 at the strong insistence of the Europeans, who feared that a lifting of the arms embargo would greatly endanger their troops on the ground, would continue to pop up and sour relations between the United States and Western Europe.

88. See "Shooting the Messenger," *Newsweek*, 18 April 1994, 34.

89. Ibid.

90. Ibid. See also "Darkness at Dawn," *Economist*, 16 April 1994, 53.

91. One died later.

92. See Silber and Little, *Death of a Nation*, 329.

93. Ibid. See also "Tightening the Noose," *Newsweek*, 25 April 1994, 23.

94. See Fred Kaplan, "Russia in a Reversal Backs NATO's Threat to Bomb Bosnia Serbs," *Boston Globe*, 24 April 1994; and Celestine Bohlen, "Russian General Opposes Air Strikes on Serbs," *New York Times*, 26 April 1994.

95. See NATO Press Releases (94) 31, 22 April 1994; and (94) 32, 22 April 1994. The secretary-general had requested that NATO establish heavy-weapon exclusion zones around all safe areas.

96. See Boutros Boutros-Ghali, *Report of the UN Secretary-General*, S/1994/600, 19 May 1994. The Ukrainian troops were later reinforced by British troops.

Ultimately, some 432 UN personnel were deployed in Gorazde. French troops that were slated to go to Gorazde received orders from Paris not to proceed. See Silber and Little, *Death of a Nation,* 333.

97. See Boutros-Ghali, *Report of the UN Secretary-General,* S/1994/600.

98. Initial estimates mentioned 700 dead and 1,900 wounded. See "Testing the West's Resolve," *Newsweek,* 2 May 1994, 50. However, UN sources put the number of dead at 300 to 400. It also believed that satellite intelligence had overstated the damage inflicted on Gorazde.

99. For details, see Owen, *Balkan Odyssey,* 255–292. The core group of the Contact Group consisted of the United States, France, and the United Kingdom. Russia played a role when the Western allies were divided. Its position was close to the French and British positions. Germany played a relatively marginal role. For details on Germany's position in the Yugoslav conflict, see Hanns W. Maull, "Germany in the Yugoslav Crisis," *Survival* 37, no. 4 (winter 1995–96): 99–130.

100. See UNSC Res. 958 (1994), 19 November 1994.

101. Moreover, as one peacekeeper has observed, the air strike on the Ubdina airfield took place several days after the request for a strike came from UNPROFOR. By then the Serbs were fully aware that an air strike was coming, and they could take measures to minimize the effects of the strike. See "Practitioners' Questionnaire," 291.

102. The hostages were released on 13 December 1994.

103. See Michael Gordon et al., "U.S. and Bosnia: How a Policy Changed," *New York Times,* 4 December 1994.

104. Ibid. This was a very serious charge. Although it was denied by U.S. officials at the time, it later proved to be accurate. See also note 39.

105. Ibid.

106. According to David Owen, General Smith received the precise coordinates of all Serb heavy weapon emplacements—most of which were fixed and in unpopulated areas—from the Bosnian government, which called for air strikes. See Owen, *Balkan Odyssey,* 321.

107. They also feared the wider consequences of bombing targets near Pale. They believed it would induce Croatia to go into the offensive.

108. See Owen, *Balkan Odyssey,* 321–323; and Boutros-Ghali, *Report of the UN Secretary-General,* S/1995/444, 30.

109. The change in the French position may have been related to the change in the French presidency. On 17 May 1995, Jacques Chirac took over from François Mitterand. During the presidential campaign, Chirac had gone on record in favor of a strong military response against all parties violating Security Council resolutions. In the absence of such a response, he favored a withdrawal of UN troops.

110. Rupert Smith wanted to continue the air strikes. He was rebuked on 30 May and was henceforth denied the authority to request air strikes without the prior approval of Janvier. See "Slachting Srebrenica gevolg van bewuste keuze," *NRC Handelsblad*, 29 May 1996, 6.

111. The last hostages were released at the end of June.

112. See Boutros-Ghali, *Report of the UN Secretary-General*, S/1995/444, para. 77.

113. See UNSC Res. 998 (1995), 16 June 1995. The RRF consisted of troops from France, the United Kingdom, and the Netherlands. One of the main tasks of the RRF, which was primarily deployed around Sarajevo, consisted of keeping open a supply route for UN convoys to the city across Mount Igman. When these convoys were kept from reaching the city, the RRF would use military force. Its actions managed to keep the road open for UN convoys.

114. Some commentators have argued that Chirac was gaining the moral high ground by his tough statements and that Clinton took this as a personal and political challenge. See Michael Brenner, *The United States Policy in Yugoslavia*, Ridgeway Papers, no. 6 (Pittsburgh: Matthew B. Ridgeway Center for International Security Studies, 1995), 20–21; and Bob Woodward, *The Choice* (New York: Simon and Schuster, 1996), 253–270.

115. Srebrenica was a traumatic experience for the Dutch. Had the Dutch battalion welcomed the Serb killers and stood by while Muslim men were slaughtered? Or were they the victims of a policy, made by others, who had decided to let the safe areas go? The Dutch requested air support on several occasions when the attack on the safe area started. These requests were denied repeatedly. On the evening of 10 July, four planes appeared in the sky of Srebrenica and destroyed two tanks and a small ammunition dump. Immediately afterwards, the Serbs threatened to kill thirty Dutch peacekeepers who had been taken hostage. The Dutch minister of defense, Joris Voorhoeve, requested cancellation of further air attacks. General Bernard Janvier, the UNPROFOR commander, and Akashi, the representative of the UN secretary-general, had already decided that further air strikes would serve no purpose. The Dutch battalion fled to neighboring Potocari with some 20,000 terrified people in its wake. While Mladic held the Dutch battalion at gunpoint, the refugees were separated, some were shipped off, others were slaughtered. In Srebrenica, Mladic's troops murdered and raped the remaining men, women, and children. Subsequent investigations by the Dutch government and by the UN secretary-general absolved the Dutch peacekeepers of any blame, but within the Netherlands the debate regarding the behavior of the Dutch peacekeepers is far from closed. They are blamed for failing to protect the Muslim population and accused of having had an anti-Muslim bias. For the moralistic Dutch, the nation that made Anne Frank a national symbol, the awakening has been rude. See Frank Westerman, "De aanval die niet kwam," *NRC Handelsblad*, 14 October 1995; Frank Westerman, "Spookrijders in Srebrenica," *NRC Handelsblad*, 11 November 1995; and Stephen Engelberg and Tim Weiner, "Srebrenica: The Days of Slaughter," *New York Times*, 29 October 1995. See also Frank Westerman and Bart Rijs, *Srebrenica: Het zwartste scenario* (Amsterdam, Antwerp: Uitgeverij Atlas, 1997); David Rohde, *Endgame: The Betrayal and Fall of Srebrenica, Europe's Worst Massacre* *since World War II* (New York: Farrar, Strauss and Giroux, 1997); and Jan Willem Honig and Norbert Both, *Srebrenica: Record of a War Crime* (London: Penguin, 1996).

116. Faced with the imminent fall of Zepa, UN peacekeepers were rounded up, and Bosnian government forces threatened to kill seventy-nine Ukrainian soldiers if the United Nations did not come to their rescue. Zepa was a much smaller enclave with an estimated total population of 6,700, compared to 40,000 for Srebrenica. It was spared the slaughter that took place in Srebrenica.

117. As they had tried in Zepa. The UN disengagement from the safe areas was to proceed quietly. The Dutch battalion had been scheduled to rotate out of Srebrenica, without any replacement waiting. A similar plan existed for their British counterparts in Gorazde. See Silber and Little, *Death of a Nation*, 360.

118. See North Atlantic Council decisions of 25 July and 1 August 1995 and the NATO/UN memorandum of agreement on air operations signed 10 August 1995. See also "Focus on NATO," *NATO Review* 43, no. 5 (September 1995): 7; and NATO Press Release (95) 23, 10 August 1995.

119. The exact nature of the attack was left unspecified.

120. That said, news reports in 1996 suggested that Chirac had concluded a secret deal with Milosevic in June 1995 and had been directly responsible for the fall of Srebrenica. In exchange for the liberation of the 300 peacekeepers held hostage, many of whom were French, Mladic would have been permitted to take Srebrenica without fear of air strikes. The hostages were freed in June 1995, but the French Ministry of Foreign Affairs denied the existence of a secret deal. See "Slachting Srebrenica," *NRC Handelsblad*, 6–7. See also "Srebrenica: La France en accusation," *Libération*, 31 May 1996.

121. See Woodward, *Choice*, 253.

122. The atrocities committed by the Croat forces and the plight of the Krajina Serb refugees were raised briefly by France and the United Kingdom, but the geopolitical outcome of the Croat offensive provided an opportunity to stop the war that could not go unexploited. The United States, which had been so vocal about the plight of the Muslims, was silent when it came to condemning Croat behavior.

123. See Silber and Little, *Death of a Nation*, 362.

124. For the text of the Joint Statement and the Agreed Basic Principles, see UN Document S/1995/780, 8 September 1995. After the signing of the agreement, the Russians protested the continuation of air strikes.

125. See "Silence of the Guns," *Time*, 25 September 1995, 40.

126. During this time, Mladic was not present in Bosnia. He underwent hospital treatment in Belgrade and thus could not be blamed for these Serb defeats on the battlefield.

127. See, for example, "Make War, Make Peace," *Newsweek*, 11 September 1995, 38; and NATO, "NATO's Role in the Implementation of the Bosnian Peace Agreement" (NATO Basic Factsheet, no. 11, January 1996), 1.

128. See "Louder Than Words," *Time*, 11 September 1995, 57.

129. In an ironic twist of fate, the fact that Karadzic and Mladic were indicted in July 1995 by the International Criminal Tribunal for Yugoslavia played into Milosevic's hand by making those two virtual prisoners in their own country.

130. Woodward, *Choice*, 253–270.

131. Congress planned to consider an override vote in the second week of September 1995. The administration was, hence, under considerable pressure to act forcefully. See Brenner, *United States Policy in Yugoslavia*, 21; and Woodward, *Choice*, 253–270.

132. The overall force was composed of troops from thirty-three countries. The other main troop-contributing countries were France (about 10,000 troops), the United Kingdom (about 13,000), and Russia (about 1,800).

133. See Admiral Leighton W. Smith, Jr., "The Pillars of Peace in Bosnia," *NATO Review* 44, no. 4 (July 1996): 11, 13.

134. See United Nations, *IFOR Report to the UN Security Council*, S/1996/696, 27 August 1996; and United Nations, *IFOR Report to the UN Security Council*, S/1996/783, 25 September 1996. See also "Bosnian Serbs Threaten to Attack U.S. Troops," *New York Times*, 8 July 1996; Daniel Williams, "Peacekeepers Placed on Alert after Threat," *Washington Post*, 13 August 1996; Daniel Williams, "Serbs End Standoff over Arms, Permitting Inspection by Nato," *Washington Post*, 14 August 1996; and Ian Fisher, "Bosnian Serbs End Standoff by Allowing Inspection," *New York Times*, 13 August 1996.

135. See United Nations, *IFOR Report to the UN Security Council*, S/1996/600, 29 July 1996; United Nations, *IFOR Report*, S/1996/696; and John Pomfret, "Mujaheddin Remaining in Bosnia," *Washington Post*, 8 July 1996.

136. United Nations, *Report of the High Representative to the UN Security Council*, S/1996/814, 1 October 1996, para. 83.

137. SFOR settled down at the operational number of 31,000 troops. Of the 31,000, some 26,000 were deployed in Bosnia, with 5,000 troops outside Bosnia capable of providing tactical reinforcement.

138. See UNSC Res. 1088 (1996), 12 December 1996.

139. For the texts, see United Nations, UN Security Council Document, S/1996/1025, 10 December 1996.

140. Even air support was risky since those under attack would not always appreciate the differences among those strikes.

4. Somalia

1. Historical background was gathered from a number of sources, including John L. Hirsch and Robert B. Oakley, *Somalia and Operation Restore Hope* (Washington, D.C.: United States Institute of Peace Press, 1995); Mohamed Sahnoun, *Somalia: The Missed Opportunities* (Washington, D.C.: United States Institute of Peace Press,

1994); Jeffrey I. Sands, *The United States and the United Nations in Somalia: A Retrospective Overview* (Alexandria, Va.: Center for Naval Analyses, 1997); United Nations, *The United Nations and Somalia 1992–1996* (New York: United Nations, 1996), hereafter referred to as *Somalia;* Maryann K. Cusimano, *Operation Restore Hope: The Bush Administration's Decision to Intervene in Somalia* (Washington, D.C.: Institute for the Study of Diplomacy Publications, School of Foreign Service, Georgetown University, 1995); Jarat Chopra, Åge Eknes, and Toralv Nordbø, *Fighting for Hope in Somalia* (Oslo: Norwegian Institute of International Affairs, 1995); and Walter S. Clarke, *SSI Special Report on Somalia* (Carlisle Barracks, Pa.: Strategic Studies Institute, U.S. Army War College, 1992).

2. In October 1981 the Somali Salvation Front merged with another rebel group and formed the Somali Salvation Democratic Front.

3. Mahdi's expanded group was eventually known as the Group of 12.

4. The evacuation mission was known as Operation Eastern Exit and was undertaken primarily by U.S. Navy and Marine Corps forces diverted from Operation Desert Shield in the Persian Gulf. For more details, see Adam B. Siegel, *Eastern Exit: The Noncombatant Evacuation Operation (NEO) from Mogadishu, Somalia, in January 1991,* CRM 91-211 (Alexandria, Va.: Center for Naval Analyses, 1991). Barre eventually fled to Kenya and finally to Nigeria, where he died on 2 January 1995.

5. Keith B. Richburg, "Somali Aid May Spur New Violence: Armed Clans Battle to Steal, and to Guard, Food," *Washington Post,* 26 August 1992, A14.

6. Hirsch and Oakley, *Somalia and Operation Restore Hope,* 16.

7. Ibid., 21–22.

8. Sahnoun, *Missed Opportunities,* 39.

9. Boutros Boutros-Ghali, *Report of the Secretary-General on the Situation in Somalia, Proposing the Expansion of UNOSOM and the Creation of Four Operational Zones,* S/24343, 22 July 1992.

10. Smith Hempstone, "Dispatch from a Place Near Hell," *Washington Post,* 23 August 1992, A13.

11. Senators Paul Simon and Nancy Kassenbaum had traveled to Somalia in early July and upon their return introduced a resolution calling for the deployment of UN forces with or without the consent of Somali factions. The resolution passed both the Senate and House within a week. (Senate Congressional Resolution 132, adopted 10 August 1992).

12. Jane Perlez, "U.S. Says Airlift Fails Somali Needy," *New York Times,* 31 July 1992, A9.

13. At its peak the United States was flying fourteen C-130s to three Kenyan and seven Somali cities, which accounted for 80 percent of the total missions. The Canadians flew three C-130s, the Belgians one, and the Germans two C-160s. For more details, see Jay E. Hines, Jason D. Mims, and Hans S. Pawlisch, *USCENTCOM in*

Somalia: Operations Provide Relief and Restore Hope (Tampa, Fla.: USCENTCOM, November 1994).

14. Another 719 persons were authorized by the Security Council on 8 September, bringing the total UNOSOM I authorization to 4,219.

15. Hirsch and Oakley, *Somalia and Operation Restore Hope,* 40.

16. Ibid., 25.

17. Once UNITAF deployed, the ICRC did come to rely on UNITAF protection after it was subject to repeated payroll robberies. Ibid., 25, 69.

18. Ibid., 55.

19. Ibid., 56–57.

20. Kenneth Allard, *Somalia Operations: Lessons Learned* (Washington, D.C.: National Defense University Press, 1995), 36.

21. *JTF for Somalia Relief Operation Ground Forces Rules of Engagement,* quoted in Jonathan T. Dworken, *Rules of Engagement (ROE) for Humanitarian Intervention and Low-Intensity Conflict: Lessons from Restore Hope* (Alexandria, Va.: Center for Naval Analyses, 1993), 10.

22. Ibid., 37.

23. Ibid., 60.

24. Participating nations included Australia, Belgium, Botswana, Canada, Egypt, France, India, Italy, Kuwait, Morocco, New Zealand, Nigeria, Pakistan, Saudi Arabia, Sweden, Tunisia, Turkey, the United Arab Emirates, the United States, and Zimbabwe.

25. Aideed presumably attacked the Nigerians because he believed them to be the weakest contingent and because Nigeria had granted Siad Barre asylum.

26. Hirsch and Oakley, *Somalia and Operation Restore Hope,* 79. Assessing that the demonstrations had little popular support, UNITAF allowed them to burn themselves out without having to mount any counteroffensive.

27. Allard, *Somalia Operations,* 37–38.

28. Ibid., 40.

29. Ibid., 43.

30. It makes compliance easier because all sides know that compliance can be enforced.

31. United Nations, *Somalia,* 41.

32. Walter Clarke, "Failed Visions and Uncertain Mandates in Somalia," in Walter Clarke and Jeffrey Herbst, eds., *Learning From Somalia* (Boulder, Colo.: Westview, 1997), 15.

33. Chopra, Eknes, and Nordbø, *Fighting for Hope,* 31.

34. The term "mission shrink" is borrowed from Richard Connaughton, *Military Support and Protection for Humanitarian Assistance: Rwanda, April–December 1994,* The Occasional, no. 18 (Camberley, England: Strategic and Combat Studies Institute, 1996), 61.

35. Chopra, Eknes, and Nordbø, *Fighting for Hope*, 43.

36. United Nations, *Somalia*, 4.

37. Guinean ambassador Lansana Kouyate had been picked to succeed Kittani but instead became Howe's deputy.

38. The agreement was signed on 27 March, the day after Resolution 814 was passed. See United Nations, *Somalia*, 264–266.

39. Hirsch and Oakley, *Somalia and Operation Restore Hope*, 99.

40. Ibid., 105–106.

41. Ibid., 104.

42. Chopra, Eknes, and Nordbø, *Fighting for Hope*, 44.

43. Ibid., 34. How much or how little one thinks UNITAF accomplished is very subjective. As noted, fom December to mid-February, UNITAF collected 1.27 million rounds of light ammunition along with 2,255 small arms. It also confiscated 636 heavy weapons. However, compared with the enormous amount of weapons available in Somalia, this was a drop in the bucket.

44. Howe recognized that his unique position facilitated close liaison in the field, but he asserts that the overall Somalia policy was crafted through close consultation between Washington and New York. See Jonathan T. Howe, "Relations between the United States and United Nations in Dealing with Somalia," in Clarke and Herbst, *Learning from Somalia*, 183.

45. Ibid., 188–189.

46. Hirsch and Oakley. *Somalia and Operation Restore Hope*, 114.

47. Ibid., 116.

48. Walter Clarke argues that marginalizing all the warlords, not just Aideed, was the proper strategy to follow. Unfortunately, by the time UNOSOM II assumed its responsibilities, it was too late to pursue such a strategy. See Clarke, "Failed Visions and Uncertain Mandates in Somalia," 319.

49. Hirsch and Oakley, *Somalia and Operation Restore Hope*, 116.

50. In a letter to former President Jimmy Carter, Aideed wrote that he and his SNA followers were under attack in an unjust war. Ibid., 126.

51. Comments from a discussion with Admiral Howe in Stockholm during a meeting organized by the Stockholm International Peace Research Institute and the Australian Department for Foreign Affairs and Trade, 10–11 April 1995.

52. "According to published reports, the commander of the Italian contingent went so far as to open separate negotiations with the fugitive warlord Mohammed Aideed—apparently with the full approval of his home government. With American backing, the United Nations requested this officer's relief from command for insubordination. The Italian government refused and life went on—a useful demonstration of both the fundamental existence of parallel lines of authority and the fundamental difficulties of commanding a coalition force under combat conditions." Allard, *Somalia Operations*, 56–57.

53. Hirsch and Oakley, *Somalia and Operation Restore Hope*, 122.

54. The additional forces included AC-130 gunships, a light infantry battalion, an armored battalion task force, and two Marine Expeditionary Units.

55. France and Belgium withdrew in December 1993, Turkey in February 1994, with Germany and Italy departing in March 1994 along with the United States.

56. The actual number was 29,732 soldiers. Participating nations included Australia (staff only), Bangladesh, Belgium, Canada (staff only), Egypt, France, Germany, Greece, India, Ireland, Italy, South Korea, Kuwait, Malaysia, Morocco, Nepal, New Zealand (staff only), Nigeria, Norway (headquarters support only), Pakistan, Romania, Saudi Arabia, Sweden, Tunisia, Turkey, the United Arab Emirates, the United States, and Zimbabwe. Of those, the largest troop contributors were India, Pakistan, the United States, and Italy.

57. Boutros Boutros-Ghali, *Further Report of the Secretary-General Submitted in Pursuance of Resolution 886 (1993), Reviewing the Options for the Future Mandate of UNOSOM II*, S/1994/12, 6 January 1994.

58. Ibid.

59. Ibid.

60. *Measure for Measure*, act 2, scene 2.

61. Hirsch and Oakley, *Somalia and Operation Restore Hope*, 162.

62. Ibid., 157.

63. Sahnoun, *Missed Opportunities*, xiii.

64. In both cases, several thousand troops were moved long distances in a matter of days.

65. Clarke, "Failed Visions and Uncertain Mandates in Somalia," 8.

66. United Nations, *Somalia*, 5.

67. Howe, "Relations between the United States and United Nations in Dealing with Somalia," 189.

68. Sahnoun, *Missed Opportunities*, 16.

69. Clarke, "Failed Visions and Uncertain Mandates in Somalia," 11.

70. Ibid., 4.

71. Hirsch and Oakley, *Somalia and Operation Restore Hope*, 166.

72. Ibid., 21.

73. Clarke, "Failed Visions and Uncertain Mandates in Somalia," 13.

74. Chopra, Eknes, and Nordbø, *Fighting for Hope*, 49.

75. Allard, *Somalia Operations*, 21.

76. Clarke, "Failed Visions and Uncertain Mandates in Somalia," 9.

77. Anthony Zinni, keynote address delivered 26 October 1995 in Washington, D.C., at the Center for Naval Analyses conference entitled "Military Support to Complex Humanitarian Emergencies: From Practice to Policy."

78. Chopra, Eknes, and Nordbø, *Fighting for Hope*, 52.

79. Stanley Meisler, "Kofi Annan: The Soft-Spoken Economist Who Runs UN Peacekeeping Forces," *Los Angeles Times*, 21 June 1994.

5. RWANDA

1. Background material was drawn from Central Intelligence Agency, *The World Factbook 1995* (Washington, D.C.: Central Intelligence Agency, 1995), 356–358; Alex de Waal and Rakiya Omaar, "The Genocide in Rwanda and the International Response," *Current History* (April 1995): 156–161; R. A. Dallaire and B. Poulin, "UNAMIR: Mission to Rwanda," *Joint Force Quarterly* (spring 1995): 66–71; Richard M. Connaughton, *Military Support and Protection for Humanitarian Assistance: Rwanda, April–December 1994*, The Occasional, no. 18 (Camberley, England: Strategic and Combat Studies Institute, 1996); United Nations, *The United Nations and the Situation in Rwanda* (New York: United Nations, 1995), hereafter referred to as *UN in Rwanda*; United Nations, *The United Nations and Rwanda 1993–1996* (New York: United Nations, 1996), hereafter referred to as *Rwanda*; and Jaana Karhilo, "Case Study on Peacekeeping: Rwanda," appendix 2C, in *SIPRI Yearbook 1995* (Oxford: Stockholm International Peace Research Institute, 1995), 100–116.

2. Rwanda also has a small Twa (pygmoid) group that represents 1 percent of the population. These are CIA figures following the massacre of Tutsis, others have placed the proportion of Tutsis as high as 15 percent.

3. For an excellent background discussion, see Gérard Prunier, *The Rwanda Crisis* (New York: Columbia University Press, 1995).

4. Ibid., 40.

5. See "Tutsi v Hutu," *Economist*, 26 August 1994, 34.

6. Helen Fein, with Orlando Brugnola and Louise Spirer, eds., *The Prevention of Genocide: Rwanda and Yugoslavia Reconsidered* (New York: Institute for the Study of Genocide, John Jay College of Criminal Justice, 1994). A document that came to be known as the Bahutu Manifesto argued that the suppression of "racial" identity on official papers "would create a risk of preventing the statistical law from establishing the reality of the facts." Prunier, *Rwanda Crisis*, 46. In other words, the Hutus were afraid that, since the Tutsis were generally better educated, the Tutsis would end up with most of the good jobs unless affirmative action laws were enacted guaranteeing the Hutu majority their fair share. If "racial" identity was removed from official papers, enforcement of such laws would have been difficult.

7. Ibid., 44.

8. Ibid., 53.

9. Rwanda received its independence after having been the Belgium-administered UN trusteeship of Rwanda-Urundi.

10. An estimated two hundred thousand Rwandan Tutsis fled during this period. Larry Minear and Philippe Guillot, *Soldiers to the Rescue: Humanitarian Lessons from Rwanda* (Paris: Organization for Economic Cooperation and Development, 1996), 55.

11. The president of Burundi, Cyprien Ntaryamira, was also killed in this incident.

12. Prunier, *Rwanda Crisis,* 84.

13. Once the conflict became intransigent, Belgium, because of legislative restrictions, cut off military aid to Rwanda; however, France persisted in supplying aid.

14. Shortly after taking command, Kagame promoted himself to major general.

15. The French had unquestionably supported Habyarimana against the RPF by supplying his forces with both training and arms, and thus he felt compelled to accommodate French desires.

16. The RPF eventually increased in size to approximately 25,000 by April 1994.

17. The main parties emerging in Rwanda were Habyarimana's Mouvement Révolutionnaire National pour la Développement (MRND); Mouvement Démocratique Républicain (MDR); Parti Démocrate Chrétien (PDC); Parti Social Démocrate (PSD); Parti Libéral (PL); and Coalition pour la Défense de la République (CDR). CDR was not included in the government.

18. United Nations, *Rwanda,* 19. Observers came from Bangladesh, Botswana, Brazil, Hungary, the Netherlands, Senegal, Slovakia, and Zimbabwe.

19. The agreement was brokered by the Organization of African Unity and the government of Tanzania. Dallaire and Poulin, "UNAMIR," 66. UNOMUR continued to function under UNAMIR's control until September 1994 when it was administratively integrated into UNAMIR.

20. United Nations, *Rwanda,* 22–23.

21. These personnel were to be drawn from both the FAR and the RPF, which at the time had a combined total of nearly 50,000 troops under arms. The military integration agreement provided for a 60:40 makeup of the army (in favor of the FAR) and a 50:50 split in the officer corps. Disarmament and job creation were critical for the 31,000 personnel who would not be selected for national service.

22. Prunier, *Rwanda Crisis,* 133.

23. The United Nations established 22 March 1994 as the date all phase-one tasks were completed, primarily because of delays in establishing the transitional government. See United Nations, *Rwanda,* 118.

24. An interesting twist to the situation was added when, on 1 January 1994, Rwanda became a nonpermanent member of the Security Council for a two-year term.

25. Karhilo, "Case Study on Peacekeeping," 101. On 10 January 1994 a senior figure in the Interahamwe militia sought political asylum from Belgian colonel Luc

Marchal, because he did not want to carry out orders from Hutu leadership to draw up plans on how to exterminate the Tutsis. See Connaughton, *Military Support*, 20. The next day UNAMIR informed UN Headquarters that the Interahamwe was formulating a plot to kill large numbers of Tutsis in Kigali using stockpiled weapons. New York directed UNAMIR to inform Habyarimana of these plans and request him to ensure that these activities were discontinued.

26. United Nations, *Rwanda*, 32. "They [UN Headquarters] refused," said Colonel Luc Marchal, "because UNAMIR was deployed under a Chapter VI mandate, traditional peacekeeping. New York argued that a cordon and search was an offensive operation for which permission would not be granted." See Connaughton, *Military Support*, 21.

27. Ibid., 22.

28. L. Hilsum, "Rwanda Tribal Rampage Feared after Two Politicians Are Killed," *Guardian*, 23 February 1994.

29. Nations contributing troops included Austria (15), Bangladesh (942), Belgium (440), Botswana (9), Brazil (13), Canada (2), the Congo (26), Egypt (10), Fiji (1), Ghana (843), Hungary (4), Malawi (5), Mali (10), the Netherlands (9), Poland (5), Romania (5), Russia (15), Senegal (35), Slovakia (5), Togo (15), Tunisia (61), Uruguay (25), and Zimbabwe (29).

30. J. Bone, "Presidents' Deaths Raise UN Fears of Tribal Violence," *Times*, 7 April 1994.

31. There were widespread reports that white men were witnessed climbing into a vehicle and speeding off the hill from which the missiles were fired. But nothing has ever been proven.

32. See African Rights, *Rwanda: Who Is Killing; Who Is Dying; What Is to Be Done—A Discussion Paper* (London: African Rights, May 1994*); Human Rights Watch/Africa, Genocide in Rwanda April–May 1994* (New York: Human Rights Watch/Africa, May 1994; and Amnesty International, *Rwanda: Mass Murder by Government Supporters and Troops in April and May 1994* (London: Amnesty International, May 1994).

33. The advance party arrived at the Kigali airport without providing any warning to Dallaire.

34. The reasons why generally gentle, loving people turned so quickly hateful and murderous are not completely clear. However, Gérard Prunier posits it was because the Rwandese have a long history of blind obedience to government orders; most people were illiterate and believed what they heard on the radio; the killings were carried out as part of an organized community program (*umuganda* or "community work") and euphemistically called "bush clearing"; and the Tutsis had been dehumanized from years of propaganda. See Prunier, *Rwanda Crisis*, 141–142.

35. Donatella Lorch, "Rwanda Rebels: Army of Exiles Fights for a Home," *New York Times*, 9 June 1994, A10.

36. "The Bleeding in Rwanda," *Economist*, 16 April 1994, 45.

37. Ibid.

38. "Justice for Some," *Economist*, 6 January 1996, 33.

39. "Émigrés Return to Fight in Rwanda's Backlands," *New York Times*, 17 May 1994, A8.

40. Eventually, the United Nations admitted that "allegations by representatives of the interim Government and the Rwandese Armed Forces and the Gendarmerie that RPF bore equal culpability for the killings were not corroborated by other sources." See United Nations, *UN in Rwanda*, 11–12.

41. M. Leitenberg, "Rwanda, 1994: International Incompetence Produces Genocide," *Peacekeeping and International Relations* 23, no. 6 (November–December 1994): 6.

42. See Connaughton, *Military Support*, 28; and Minear and Guillot, *Soldiers to the Rescue*, 77–78.

43. Dallaire and Poulin, "UNAMIR," 69.

44. As noted earlier, ten Belgian peacekeepers were killed by the Presidential Guard while attempting to protect the prime minister. The commander of the Belgian contingent was later acquitted at court-martial for placing his troops in extremis.

45. Dallaire and Poulin, "UNAMIR," 69.

46. One of the African members was the Rwandan envoy who remained on the Security Council throughout the crisis. He voted for the agreement because "it expressed support for the Arusha Agreement and called for a cease-fire." See Karhilo, "Case Study on Peacekeeping," 106 n. 30.

47. On the day the secretary-general sent his letter to the Security Council, "UNHCR reported the outpouring of 250,000 Rwandan refugees into Tanzania within a period of 24 hours, the largest and fastest such exodus hither-to witnessed by the world body." Ibid., 106.

48. Boutros Boutros-Ghali, "Letter of the Secretary-General to the Security Council," S/1994/518, 29 April 1994.

49. *African Research Bulletin* 31, no. 5 (April 1994): 11424 C, quoted in Karhilo, "Case Study on Peacekeeping," 106 n. 33.

50. United Nations, *Rwanda*, 47.

51. Dallaire and Poulin, "UNAMIR," 70.

52. See Donald C. F. Daniel, *U.S. Perspectives on Peacekeeping: Putting PDD-25 in Context*, Strategic Research Report 3–94 (Newport, R.I.: Center for Naval Warfare Studies, June 1994).

53. Paul Lewis, "U.S. Forces U.N. to Put Off Plan to Send 5,500 Troops to Rwanda," *New York Times*, 17 May 1994, A1.

54. Stephen Kinzer, "European Leaders Reluctant to Send Troops to Rwanda," *New York Times*, 25 May 1994, A1. The United Nations approached over fifty potential contributing countries.

55. The countries pledging forces were the Congo, Ethiopia, Ghana, Malawi, Mali, Nigeria, Senegal, Zambia, and Zimbabwe.

56. Boutros Boutros-Ghali, *Report of the Secretary-General on the Situation in Rwanda*, S/1994/640, 31 May 1994, 12.

57. De Waal and Omaar, "Genocide in Rwanda," 158.

58. Dallaire later noted that "the mandate provided for creating secure areas to protect refugees and displaced persons, supporting and securing the distribution of relief supplies, and imposing an arms embargo against Rwanda. It also called for an immediate cease-fire and end to violence." See Dallaire and Poulin, "UNAMIR," 70.

59. Paul Lewis, "U.N. Chief Seeks an African Peace Force for Rwanda," *New York Times*, 3 May 1994, A3. The secretary-general claimed that the UN special mission to Rwanda had "gained assurances from both sides that they would cooperate with the United Nations effort to implement UNAMIR II's expanded mandate." But he also admitted that the situation remained "uncertain and insecure." See United Nations, *Rwanda*, 49. Under such conditions, consent of the parties could hardly be assumed.

60. Barbara Crossette, "When This Rwandan Speaks, the Big Guys Listen," *New York Times*, 27 December 1995, A4.

61. See John Darnton, "U.N. Faces Refugee Crisis That Never Ends," *New York Times*, 8 August 1994, A6.

62. Shawn H. McCormick, "The Lessons of Intervention in Africa," *Current History* (April 1995): 164.

63. Prunier, *Rwanda Crisis*, 282–290.

64. Boutros Boutros-Ghali, "Letter Dated 19 June 1994 From the Secretary-General Addressed to the President of the Security Council," S/1994/728, 20 June 1996. The formal notification of the French arrived in a letter the following day from the French permanent representative. See United Nations, *Rwanda*, 54.

65. The resolution was passed, although there was an unusually high number of abstentions—five (Brazil, China, New Zealand, Nigeria, and Pakistan).

66. The African troops came from Chad, Congo, Guinea, Guinea-Bissau, Nigeria, and Senegal.

67. United Nations, *UN in Rwanda*, 14.

68. Raymond Bonner, "Rwandan Enemies Struggle to Define French Role," *New York Times*, 27 June 1994, A1.

69. Ibid., A9.

70. BBC Summary of World Broadcasts, 28 June 1994, "Head of French Operation Says He Will Use Force to End Massacres If Necessary," from French TF-1 television interview in French, 26 June 1994 (Lexis/Nexis on-line database).

71. Minear and Guillot, *Soldiers to the Rescue*, 104.

72. Ibid., 103–104.

73. Raymond Bonner, "French Establish a Base in Rwanda to Block Rebels," *New York Times*, 5 July 1994, A1.

74. Karhilo, "Case Study on Peacekeeping," 109.

75. Connaughton, *Military Support*, 50.

76. Guy Dinmore, "Rwandan Rebels Set Up Government," *Washington Times*, 20 July 1994, 1.

77. Connaughton, *Military Support*, 51.

78. BBC Summary of World Broadcasts, 27 July 1994, "Bizimungu Criticizes UN; Meets Zairian President Mobutu in Mauritius," from France Inter radio in French, 26 July 1994 (Lexis/Nexis).

79. Connaughton, *Military Support*, 49.

80. Ibid.

81. BBC Summary of World Broadcasts, 28 July 1994, "Head of Operation Turquoise Interviewed on French Clashes with Hutu Militias," from TF-1 TV in French, 26 July 1994 (Lexis/Nexis).

82. "President Mobutu of Zaire confirmed [on 26 July 1994] that the territory of Zaire would never be used by Rwandans or by anyone else for the purpose of destabilizing Rwanda, that former RGA [Rwandan Government Army] military personnel in Zaire would be disarmed and confined to barracks and that radio transmissions containing incitements to ethnic hatred would be stopped immediately." United Nations, *Rwanda*, 57.

83. Minear and Guillot, *Soldiers to the Rescue*, 60.

84. Andrew Purvis, "Collusion with Killers," *Time*, 7 November 1994, 52.

85. "Fleeing Rwanda, Again," *Economist*, 20 August 1994, 33.

86. Raymond Bonner, "As French Leave Rwanda, Critics Reverse Position," *New York Times*, 23 August 1994, A6.

87. As quoted in ibid.

88. Robert B. Oakley, "A Slow Response on Rwanda," *Washington Post*, 27 July 1994, A27.

89. Bonner, "As French Leave Rwanda," A6.

90. Ibid.

91. The force actually peaked at 2,600 on 9 August.

92. Minear and Guillot, *Soldiers to the Rescue*, 113.

93. Quoted in ibid., 112.

94. Bill Gertz, "NATO Chief: GI Effort a 'Success' in Rwanda," *Washington Times*, 30 August 1994, 1.

95. Connaughton, *Military Support*, 61.

96. "DoD Strategy for Sub-Saharan Africa," *Defense 95*, no. 6, 45.

97. Connaughton, *Military Support*, 53.

98. These raids were conducted "in pursuance of its mandate to protect displaced persons." United Nations, *UN in Rwanda*, 33.

99. Karhilo, "Case Study on Peacekeeping," 113.

100. Dallaire and Poulin, "UNAMIR," 68–69.

101. Karhilo, "Case Study on Peacekeeping," 114.

102. The most notable, and in the end fatal, exception was the CDR, which was not a party to the Arusha agreement.

103. Connaughton, *Military Support*, 69.

104. Minear and Guillot, *Soldiers to the Rescue*, 108.

105. Ibid.

106. Kathi Austin, "Rwanda Readies for Another Bloodbath," *Providence Journal*, 25 November 1994, A19.

107. Connaughton, *Military Support*, 70.

108. Dallaire and Poulin, "UNAMIR," 68.

109. *Economist*, 20 August 1994, 14.

110. These operations would presumably have been mounted using UNAMIR's Chapter VII authority, which had been granted for enforcing an arms embargo.

111. Connaughton, *Military Support*, 66.

112. James Schear, "Beyond Traditional Peacekeeping: The Case of Cambodia," in *Beyond Traditional Peacekeeping*, ed. Donald C. F. Daniel and Bradd C. Hayes (London: Macmillan, 1995), 257.

113. Connaughton, *Military Support*, 69.

114. United Nations, *UN in Rwanda*, 23.

6. HAITI

The author wishes to thank Michael E. Brown for his many useful comments on an earlier draft of this chapter.

1. See UNSC Res. 940 (1994), 31 July 1994.

2. The United States recognized Haiti only in 1862, once the fact that Haiti was a republic created by a slave revolt was no longer an issue with respect to U.S. recognition. By this time, Abraham Lincoln had proclaimed freedom for all slaves in the Union. Ironically, in view of later developments, "Lincoln and others saw Haiti as a place that might absorb blacks induced to leave the United States. (Liberia was recognized in the same year, in part for the same reason.)" See Noam Chomsky, "The Tragedy of Haiti," in *The Haiti Files: Decoding the Crisis*, ed. James Ridgeway (Washington, D.C.: Essential Books; Azul Editions, 1994), 8. See also Sidney W. Mintz, "Can Haiti Change?" *Foreign Affairs* 74, no. 1 (January–February 1995): 73–86.

3. Political violence was particularly problematic. From 1843 until the American occupation in 1915, only one of Haiti's twenty-two presidents served out his term of office. The majority had to flee the country. See Elizabeth Abbott, *Haiti: The Duvaliers and Their Legacy* (New York: McGraw-Hill, 1988), 25; see also Chomsky, "Tragedy of Haiti," 8–13; and Ernest H. Preeg, *The Haitian Dilemma: A Case Study in Demographics, Development, and U.S. Foreign Policy* (Washington, D.C.: Center for Strategic and International Studies, 1996), 13.

4. According to the Monroe Doctrine, foreign influence in the Western Hemisphere, including the Caribbean, was unwelcome as far as the United States was concerned. See Gaddis Smith, "Haiti: From Intervention to Intervasion," *Current History* 59, no. 589 (February 1995): 55. Germany had expressed an interest in a naval base in the Caribbean before the outbreak of World War I. In 1910, Germany controlled 80 percent of Haiti's international trade and all its major utilities, including its one railroad. Like many other small countries in the Caribbean, Haiti was financially overextended. A German intervention in the event of a default on its debts was a real possibility. The other European power that had considerable financial stakes in Haiti was France. In 1838 Haiti had accepted to pay France substantial reparations in exchange for recognition. See Anthony P. Maingot, "Haiti: The Political Rot Within," *Current History* 59, no. 589 (February 1995) 59; and Chomsky, "Tragedy of Haiti," 7.

5. Papa Doc took over as president on 22 September 1957, following elections that were widely viewed as rigged. On 25 May 1964 Duvalier was declared "President-for-Life," a title that, on his death in April 1971, passed to his son, Jean-Claude.

6. The *tonton macoutes* were organized more formally in the early 1960s as the Volunteers for National Security.

7. That said, many migrated to the United States. Contrary to the migration flows of the late 1970s and the 1990s, these migrants were relatively affluent. They arrived by plane, instead of on rickety boats. Moreover, their number was relatively small, around 3,500 per year during the 1960s. See Preeg, *Haitian Dilemma,* 56.

8. Many of these enterprises produced essential commodities such as flour, sugar, oils, and cement. On the extent of the economic plunder by Duvalier and subsequent regimes, see Maingot, "Haiti," 59–64.

9. The Alliance for Progress was a $20 billion economic assistance program launched by President Kennedy in the early 1960s. It was designed to prevent the emergence of Communist—Castro-type—regimes in Latin America.

10. Foreign assistance increased from $9 million in 1970 to $106 million in 1980. The U.S. share rose from $2 million to $27 million. In the 1970s the assembly industry rose by more than 20 percent per year. The manufacturing sector increased at an annual rate of 7 percent. See Preeg, *Haitian Dilemma,* 17–18.

11. The backlash started a little before Carter's unsuccessful bid for a second term in 1980. It was triggered by declining U.S. attention to human rights abuses in Haiti (in 1979–80, the Carter administration was totally preoccupied with the problem of the American hostages in Iran) and the marriage of Jean-Claude to Michèle Bennett in 1980. Bennett brought the kleptocracy of the Duvaliers to new levels. Staggering amounts of state money were embezzled during her "reign." See Abbott, *Duvaliers and Their Legacy,* 244–265; and Maingot, "Haiti," 60–62.

12. See Preeg, *Haitian Dilemma,* 57.

13. Ibid., 59.

14. See Abbott, *Duvaliers and Their Legacy,* 291–292.

15. See Maingot, "Haiti," 61–63.

16. For the broader picture in Central and South America, see Marc W. Chernik, "Peacemaking and Violence in Latin America," in *The International Dimensions of Internal Conflict,* ed. Michael E. Brown (Cambridge, Mass.: MIT Press, 1996), 267–307.

17. See UNGA Res. 45/2, 10 October 1990.

18. See Donald E. Schulz and Gabriel Marcella, *Reconciling the Irreconcilable: The Troubled Outlook for U.S. Policy toward Haiti* (Carlisle Barracks, Pa.: U.S. Army War College, Strategic Studies Institute, 10 March 1994), 7–12; Anthony P. Maingot, "Haiti and Aristide: The Legacy of History," *Current History* 91, no. 562 (February 1992): 65–69; and United Nations, *Les Nations Unies et Haiti 1990–1996,* Série Livres bleus (New York: United Nations, 1996), 16–17, hereafter referred to as *Haiti.*

19. In an effort to win international support for their coup, the military appointed Bazin prime minister of a "government of consensus" in June 1992. Bazin's government fell in June 1993. See Kim Ives, "The Coup and U.S. Foreign Policy: The Unmaking of a President," in Ridgeway, *Haiti Files,* 87–103.

20. This principle of *"non-refoulement"* is embodied in Article 33 of the Convention Relating to the Status of Refugees (1951). Text reproduced in United Nations, *The United Nations and Human Rights 1945–1995* (New York: United Nations, 1995), 177. The United States ratified the convention in 1967. See also Preeg, *Haitian Dilemma,* 60; and Human Rights Watch/Americas-National Coalition for Haitian Refugees-Jesuit Refugee Service, USA, "No Port in a Storm," in Ridgeway, *Haiti Files,* 191–198.

21. Quoted in J. F. O. McAllister, "Lives on Hold," *Time,* 1 February 1993, 50. See also Preeg, *Haitian Dilemma,* 61–62.

22. See Yves Daudet, "L'ONU et l'OEA en Haiti et le Droit International," *Annuaire Français de Droit International* 38 (1992): 106.

23. See OASGA Res. 1080 (XXI-0/91), 5 June 1991.

24. See UNGA Res. 46/7, 11 October 1991.

25. A resolution of the UN General Assembly requested the UN secretary-general "to take necessary measures in order to assist, in cooperation with the OAS, in the solution of the Haitian crisis." See UNGA Res. 47/20 A, 24 November 1992. Following this resolution, the UN secretary-general appointed Dante Caputo, former foreign minister of Argentina, as his special envoy for Haiti. To maximize the efforts of the United Nations and the OAS, the OAS secretary general also appointed Caputo as his special envoy for Haiti. For details on UN-OAS cooperation, see Daudet, "L'ONU," 89–111. For details on UN action in Haiti see United Nations, *Haiti,* 18.

26. See Daudet, "L'ONU," 92–93.

27. Some of Aristide's allies disagreed with his effort to get the United Nations involved in the crisis. For many of Aristide's supporters, the United Nations was not much different from the OAS in that it was believed to be an instrument completely controlled by the United States. The United States was widely thought to be opposed to Aristide and the enemy of the Haitian poor. See Ives, "The Coup," 87–103.

28. See UNGA Res. 47/20 B, 20 April 1993. The dialogue was to focus on three main issues: Aristide's return; the appointment of a prime minister to head a government of national accord; and the question of amnesty for members and supporters of the military junta.

29. See UNSC Res. 841 (1993), 16 June 1993.

30. See UNSC Res. 867 (1993), 23 September 1993.

31. See UNSC Res. 861 (1993), 27 August 1993.

32. On 3 October 1993, eighteen American soldiers had been killed and seventy-five wounded while attempting to capture Somali warlord Mohammed Aideed. Television footage showing dead U.S. soldiers being dragged through the streets of Mogadishu led to intense congressional pressure to withdraw U.S. forces from Somalia. Three days later, Clinton announced that all U.S. troops would be withdrawn from the country within six months. See chapter 4 on Somalia.

33. In December 1995, Emmanuel Constant, leader of the infamous *Front pour l'Avancement et le Progrès Haitien* (FRAPH)—a paramilitary organization with close ties to the military—revealed that he had organized the demonstration. He said that he had forewarned his contact in the CIA of the demonstration, and had assured him that no American lives would be in danger. He also declared that he had transmitted false medical documents that portrayed Aristide as mentally unstable. These documents were presented to the U.S. Senate by the CIA after the October incident. They bolstered the position of those who believed that the U.S. should not interfere in Haitian affairs, and those who were opposed to the idea of a U.S. military intervention. Press reports also revealed that Constant, together with other junta members, had been on the CIA payroll from 1992 to 1994. At the time Constant went public with his story, he was detained in a prison in Maryland on immigration charges and bitter about the CIA's lack of support. Although the CIA has admitted having Constant on its payroll until mid-1994, its exact role in the Haiti crisis remains murky. In June 1996, Constant struck a deal with U.S. officials and was released into the custody of his mother, who lives in Brooklyn, New York. See Allan Nairn, "He's Our S.O.B.," *Nation*, 31 October 1994, 481–482; Hugh Crosskill, "Presidents in Poverty," *World Today* 52, no. 2 (February 1996): 37–39; Andrew Reding, "Exorcising Haiti's Ghosts," *World Policy Journal* (spring 1996): 15–26; Sylvie Kaufmann, "L'étrange jeu de la CIA dans l'affaire haitienne," *Le Monde*, 11 December 1995; Larry Rohter, "Cables Show U.S. Deception on Haitian Violence," *New York Times*, 6 February 1996, 8; and Tim Weiner, "A '93 Report by the CIA Tied Haiti Agent to Slaying," *New York Times*, 13 October 1996, 9.

34. Some have argued that the Governors Island Agreement was flawed from the beginning. The military, it is said, signed the agreement in bad faith and Aristide had signed only after being pressured by the United Nations and the United States. One of the major flaws of the agreement was the provision to lift the embargo on Haiti and resume economic aid to Haiti before Aristide's return. Moreover, there was no provision in the agreement to purge the military. That the agreement had no enforcement mechanism, beyond the threat of renewed sanctions, is also frequently cited as a flaw. However, if the parties had signed the agreement in good faith, no enforcement mechanism would have been necessary. It is precisely because the international community was not willing to impose the agreement on the parties that no enforcement mechanism was provided for. For a critical examination of the agreement, see Schulz and Marcella, *Reconciling the Irreconcilable,* 23–25; and Roland I. Perusse, *Haitian Democracy Restored: 1991–1995* (Lanham, Md.: University Press of America, 1995), 51–53.

35. A small number of human rights observers remained in Haiti until July 1994. At that time, they were declared persona non grata and given forty-eight hours to leave the country.

36. See note 33.

37. See UNSC Res. 873 (1993), 13 October 1993. See also UNSC Res. 875 (1993), 16 October 1993, which authorized member states to enforce the embargo. Henceforth, they could stop and inspect ships traveling toward Haiti and verify their destinations and cargoes.

38. In December 1993, the U.S. Coast Guard picked up 645 Haitians at sea, but an unknown number perished at sea. See "Haitian Refugees: Drowning," *Economist,* 19 March 1994, 54.

39. On 23 March 1994, a one-page advertisement denouncing Clinton's policy was published in the *New York Times* and signed by a wide range of prominent Democrats. On 12 April 1994, Randall Robinson, a well-known black U.S. human rights activist, started a hunger strike in protest of the U.S. repatriation policy. On 19 April 1994, five Democratic senators introduced legislation that, if passed, would have imposed a comprehensive package of sanctions on Haiti and its military. Finally, on 22 April, six members of the U.S. House of Representatives protested Clinton's Haitian policy in front of the White House and were arrested on charges of civil disobedience. For details, see Perusse, *Haitian Democracy,* 170.

40. See ibid., 86. UNHCR's assistance consisted of designing procedures to determine the status of asylum seekers from Haiti and monitoring the situation of those who returned.

41. See UNSC Res. 917 (1994), 6 May 1994. The United States had already frozen the assets of forty-one Haitians involved in the coup. In May 1994, an additional 523 Haitian military officers were added to the list, and all visas for travel to the United States held by Haitian military officers were revoked. See Perusse, *Haitian Democracy,* 67.

42. In addition, the United States banned all commercial flights to Haiti as well as all financial transfers to and from Haiti.

43. See Marguerite Michaels, "Haiti: Incident at Baie du Mèsle," *Time*, 11 July 1994, 36; and Kevin Fedarko, "Haiti: Policy at Sea," *Time*, 18 July 1994, 23.

44. Quoted in Michaels, "Haiti Incident," 37.

45. See "America's Least Wanted," *Economist*, 16 July 1994, 23–24; and Fedarko, "Haiti: Policy at Sea," *Time*, 20–24.

46. See "Mixing the Signals," *Time*, 16 May 1994, 41.

47. See Margaret Daly Hayes and Gary F. Wheatley, eds., *Interagency and Political-Military Dimensions of Peace Operations: Haiti—A Case Study* (Washington, D.C.: Institute for National Strategic Studies, National Defense University, 1996), 13, 20, 30.

48. Jonassaint replaced Supreme Court Justice Joseph Nerette, who had been sworn in as provisional president of Haiti on 8 October 1991.

49. See UNSC Res. 940 (1994), 31 July 1994.

50. See Boutros Boutros-Ghali, *Report of the UN Secretary-General*, S/1994/828, 15 July 1994.

51. As had been the case in Bosnia. See chapter 3 on Bosnia.

52. At which time, one may note, Operation Restore Democracy became Operation Uphold Democracy.

53. See Hayes and Wheatley, *Dimensions of Peace Operations*, 44.

54. See Boutros-Ghali, *Report of the UN Secretary-General*, S/1994/828.

55. Hayes and Wheatley, *Dimensions of Peace Operations*, 48. See also "Caught in the Middle," *Newsweek*, 10 October 1994, 36–39; and Kevin Fedarko, "Haiti: Walking a Thin Line," *Time*, 10 October 1994, 42–48.

56. Quoted in Bruce W. Nelan, "The Road to Haiti," *Time*, 3 October 1994, 34.

57. See P. Martin, ed., "Practitioner's Questionnaire on: Weapons Control, Disarmament, and Demobilization during Peacekeeping Operations: Analysis Report: Haiti," in Sarah Meek and Mendiburu Marcos, *Managing Arms in Peace Processes: Haiti* (New York: United Nations; Geneva: UNIDIR, 1996).

58. See Fedarko, "Haiti: Walking a Thin Line," 44; and the second *Report of the Multinational Force in Haiti to the UN Security Council*, S/1994/1148, 10 October 1994.

59. Cédras and Biamby left for Panama on 11 October aboard a U.S. plane. François, the metropolitan police chief, had fled to the Dominican Republic on 4 October 1994.

60. The MNF was composed mainly of U.S. troops. The non-U.S. components included 295 troops from a Caribbean Community (CARICOM) battalion who joined during the third week of operation; 1,050 troops from Bangladesh and 134 troops from Guatemala who joined between 19 and 21 October 1994; and 860 Nepalese troops who joined in February 1995. See the second, third, and eleventh

Report of the Multinational Force in Haiti to the UN Security Council, S/1994/1148, 10 October 1994; S/1994/1208, 24 October 1994; and S/1995/149, 21 February 1995.

61. In addition, 602 police monitors were deployed. See the third *Report of the Multinational Force,* S/1994/1208, para. 5.

62. For troop and police deployments, see the relevant issues of *Report of the Multinational Force to the UN Security Council.* From September 1994 through March 1995 the MNF submitted thirteen reports to the Security Council, as had been requested by the council. Even so, the information in these reports was very sketchy.

63. The creation of a new Haitian police force was supposed to have been carried out by UNMIH in phase two of the Haitian operation, but the disintegration of the Haitian security establishment led to a change in that plan.

64. The new Haitian police academy was opened on 3 February 1995. The first 361 new policemen graduated in June 1995. Each time a new class of policemen graduated, an equal number of IPSF officers were demobilized. See Boutros Boutros-Ghali, *Report of the UN Secretary-General,* S/1995/614, 24 July 1995, paras. 28, 31.

65. In 1994 and 1995, the Presidential Guard, the Ministerial Security Unit, the Court Security Unit, the Seaport Security Unit, and the Airport Security Unit were created. See ibid., para. 27.

66. In 1996 the Haitian government sought to neutralize resentments against such efforts by considering reparation for those Haitians victimized by the military. See Boutros Boutros-Ghali, *Report of the UN Secretary-General,* S/1996/813/Add. 1, 12 November 1996, para. 4.

67. The last soldiers were demobilized in July 1995.

68. See Boutros Boutros-Ghali, *Report of the UN Secretary-General,* S/1996/813, 1 October 1996, para. 6.

69. See Boutros-Ghali, *Report of the UN Secretary-General,* S/1996/813, para. 6; and S/1996/813/Add. 1, 12 November 1996, para. 2.

70. Many documents were seized at the FRAPH headquarters, which the Haitian government tried to recover in 1995 and 1996. However, because of links between the CIA and members of the military junta and FRAPH, including Constant, the United States was slow to return these documents. See note 33.

71. Shortly after his pledge, Constant left for the United States.

72. See Boutros-Ghali, *Report of the UN Secretary-General,* S/1995/46, 17 January 1995, paras. 25–29; S/1996/416, 5 June 1996, para. 7; S/1996/813, paras. 8–12; and S/1996/813/ Add. 1, paras. 2–4.

73. See Boutros-Ghali, *Report of the UN Secretary-General,* S/1995/46, para. 11.

74. See Donald Schulz, *Whither Haiti?* (Carlisle Barracks, Pa.: Strategic Studies Institute, U.S. Army War College, April 1996), 47 n. 41.

75. Prices were doubled, in January 1995; however, the program did not pick up. Only the poor turned in weapons and the quality of these weapons was terrible.

Some of them were so old that they were shipped to museums in the United States. See Meek and Marcos, *Managing Arms*; and Martin, "Practitioner's Questionnaire."

76. The MNF seized and confiscated some 16,719 weapons. See the thirteenth and final *Report of the Multinational Force in Haiti to the UN Security Council*, S/1995/221, 20 March 1995, para. 9. It is not clear how many of these weapons were seized from the Haitian military and how many were confiscated from civilians stopped at roadblocks and carrying them in public. UNMIH did not have the authority to disarm the military or paramilitary forces.

77. See Larry Rohter, "Aristide Urges UN to Disarm Thugs in Haiti," *New York Times*, 29 March 1995.

78. See Schulz, *Whither Haiti?* 74; Kathie Klarreich, "Haiti's Hidden Arms Are Worry as Cash for Guns Swap Starts," *Christian Science Monitor*, 29 September 1994, 1; Laurent Belsie, "U.S. Forces Walk a Fine Line to Disarm Haiti," *Christian Science Monitor*, 5 October 1994, 1; and "Haiti: Not Quite Normal," *Economist*, 27 July 1996, 38.

79. See Boutros-Ghali, *Report of the UN Secretary-General*, S/1995/46, para. 79.

80. See Perusse, *Haitian Democracy*, 109.

81. See UNSC Res. 940 (1994), 31 July 1994; Res. 975 (1995), 30 January 1995; UNSC Res. 1007 (1995), 31 July 1995; and UNSC Res. 1048 (1996), 29 February 1996. In practice, UNMIH carried out a variety of tasks ranging from escorting humanitarian relief convoys to carrying out law-and-order assignments. It assumed prison guard duties, conducted harbor patrols, and maintained a presence in police stations. See Boutros-Ghali, *Report by the UN Secretary-General*, S/1995/614; and S/1995/922, 6 November 1995.

82. See Boutros-Ghali, *Report of the UN Secretary-General*, S/1995/46, para. 88.

83. See ibid.; and UNSC Res. 940 (1994), 31 July 1994.

84. See Boutros Boutros-Ghali, *Report of the UN Secretary-General*, S/1995/305, 13 April 1995, paras. 15–16.

85. See ibid., paras. 64–65.

86. Such concerns were expressed by the UN secretary-general and by some Haitians. See Boutros-Ghali, *Report of the UN Secretary-General*, S/1995/305, para. 15.

87. See Boutros-Ghali, *Report of the UN Secretary-General*, S/1995/922, paras. 12–16. The fact that judicial and penal systems in Haiti had to be built from scratch and lacked trained personnel and equipment was debilitating in this regard.

88. See United Nations Association of the United States of America, *A Report on the Fourth Annual Peacekeeping Mission, May 19–23, 1995: Republic of Haiti–UN Mission in Haiti* (New York, UNA-USA, 1995), 8–9.

89. See Larry Rohter, "Tensions Build Again in Haiti, Imperiling Peace," *New York Times*, 30 November 1995.

90. The economic question was not resolved and it remained up to Préval to deal with that issue.

91. See the request by Préval, UN Security Council Document, S/1996/99, 9 February 1996; and UNSC Res. 1048 (1996), 29 February 1996.

92. See Boutros Boutros-Ghali, *Report of the UN Secretary-General,* S/1996/112, February 1996.

93. The Russians also voiced opposition to the extension of UNMIH because of the financial implications, but they did not threaten a veto.

94. Already in October 1993 the Chinese had blocked the Security Council from issuing a statement that would have insisted on Aristide's return. At the time the Chinese had been piqued by Aristide's support for the demand by Taiwan to be admitted as a member of the United Nations. See Perusse, *Haitian Democracy,* 62. More generally, China used this occasion to warn not only the Haitians but also all other UN members, including the United States, that Taiwan remained an extremely sensitive issue for China. In 1995, China had been extremely upset when the United States had granted a visa to the Taiwanese president, Lee Teng-hui.

95. In March 1996, the Canadian brigadier general J. R. P. Daigle was appointed military commander of UNMIH.

96. It may be recalled that in December 1995 the United States had committed 20,000 U.S. troops to Bosnia.

97. Canada has traditionally been a very active supporter of UN peacekeeping operations. That said, Canada had its own domestic political reasons to be generous in Haiti's case. The ruling government party wanted to win a parliamentary seat in Montreal, a city that is home to sixty thousand Haitians. More generally, in the October 1995 referendum French-Canadian separatists were only narrowly defeated. Hence, any occasion was good for the Canadian government to demonstrate "to Quebec the positive role of a united Canada in a francophone foreign-policy setting." See Robert Maguire et al., *Haiti Held Hostage: International Responses to the Quest for Nationhood 1986 to 1996,* Watson Occasional Paper, no. 23 (Providence, R.I.: Thomas J. Watson Institute for International Studies; Tokyo: United Nations University, 1996), 113–114.

98. See UNSC Res. 1063 (1996), 28 June 1996; and UNSC Res. 1086 (1996), 5 December 1996, authorizing UNSMIH to operate until 30 November 1996 and 31 May 1997, or 31 July 1997 if the secretary-general so recommended in a report submitted to the council by 31 March 1997. Resolution 1086 (1996) stipulated that this would be the final extension of UNSMIH. See also the requests by the Haitian president: S/1996/431, 31 May 1996; and S/1996/956, 18 November 1996; and Boutros-Ghali, *Report of the UN Secretary-General,* S/1996/416; S/1996/813; and S/1996/813/Add. 1.

99. Of the 1,200 troops, 700 were financed on a voluntary basis by Canada and the United States.

100. See "U.S. Troops Go to Haiti to Ward Off Violence," *Boston Globe*, 3 August 1996, 9; and Larry Rohter, "An Extended Stay in Haiti," *New York Times*, 17 September 1996.

101. The increase of violence in the summer of 1996 was widely believed to be the work of former FAdH and FRAPH members intended to test the resolve of the Haitian National Police and that of the international community. See Boutros-Ghali, *Report of the UN Secretary-General*, S/1996/813.

102. See United Nations Association of the United States of America, *Report*, 80.

103. On post-UNMIH difficulties, see Schulz, *Whither Haiti?* 74.

104. See Boutros Boutros-Ghali, *The 50th Anniversary Report on the Work of the Organization* (New York, United Nations, 1996), para. 803; and Boutros-Ghali, *Report of the UN Secretary-General*, S/1996/813, para. 43.

105. In 1994, it had been estimated that Haiti needed 7,000 police officers. However, because of financial constraints, the Haitian government had been obliged to reduce the police force to 5,000 men. See Boutros-Ghali, *Report of the UN Secretary-General*, S/1995/922, para. 17. In 1996 the force was increased to 6,000. However, because of the economic situation, members of the police force were regularly paid with a one- to two-month delay. This in turn led to absenteeism and poor performance. On U.S. involvement in the protection of Préval, see Steve Fainaru, "In Haiti, U.S. Protects Political Investments: Agents Take Over Presidential Security after Execution of Two Préval Rivals," *Boston Globe*, 16 October 1996, 1, A8–9.

106. See UNSC Res. 1123 (1997) of 30 July 1997, which established UNTMIH. See also the *Report of the UN Secretary-General on UNSMIH*, S/1997/564, 19 July 1997, and on *UNTMIH*, S/1997/832, 31 October 1997.

107. Twenty police officers were deployed in various command and support functions. The total mission comprised 290 police officers. See UNSC Res. 1141 (1997) of 28 November 1997, which established MIPONUH. See also the *Report of the UN Secretary-General on UNTMIH*, S/1997/832/Add.1, 20 November 1997.

108. Together these three countries account for three-quarters of the total Caribbean island population. See Preeg, *Haitian Dilemma*, 28, 100.

7. OPERATIONAL GUIDELINES

1. See Bradd C. Hayes and Jeffrey I. Sands, *Doing Windows: Non-Traditional Military Responses to Complex Emergencies*, Decision Support Department Research Report, 97–1 (Newport, R.I.: Naval War College, Center for Naval Warfare Studies, 1997).

2. Impartiality was not a significant issue with the MNF. The MNF was there to reinstall one faction in power at the expense of another. Nevertheless, making clear what it expected and what it intended to do reinforced its enforcement role.

3. It is even more understandable when a mandate on its face does seem biased. The "safe areas" injunction is exemplary, for it did not restrict Bosnian government military operations within or from the six areas. In effect, they constituted sanctuaries where the Bosnian military counted on being free from Bosnian Serb attack if the Serbs abided by the mandate.

4. Gideon Rose, "The Exit Strategy Delusion," *Foreign Affairs* 77, no. 1 (January–February 1998): 66.

8. FINAL THOUGHTS

1. This was an oft-used term, for example, at a workshop on "The Use of Force in Peace Operations," organized by the Stockholm International Peace Research Institute and the Australian Department for Foreign Affairs and Trade, held in Stockholm on 10–11 April 1995.

2. We have drawn on suggestions made in a study by Ernst B. Haas, "Beware the Slippery Slope: Notes toward the Definition of Justifiable Intervention," in *Emerging Norms of Justified Intervention,* ed. Laura W. Reed and Carl Kaysen (Cambridge, Mass.: Committee on International Security Studies, American Academy of Arts and Sciences, 1993), 81.

3. Joshua Muravchik, "Using Force as a Tourniquet," *New York Times Magazine,* 15 December 1996, 58.

4. See, for example, Jesse Helms, "Saving the U.N.," *Foreign Affairs* 75, no. 5 (September–October 1996): 27. Limiting U.S. participation in UN operations was also an oft-used theme of the Dole presidential campaign of 1996.

BIBLIOGRAPHY

Abbott, Elizabeth. *Haiti: The Duvaliers and Their Legacy.* New York: McGraw-Hill, 1988.

Adibe, Clement. *Disarmament and Conflict Resolution in a Stateless Society: The UN and Conflict in Somalia.* New York: United Nations; Geneva: United Nations Institute for Disarmament Research, 1995.

African Rights. *Rwanda: Who Is Killing; Who Is Dying; What Is to Be Done—A Discussion Paper.* London: African Rights, May 1994.

Allard, Kenneth. *Somalia Operations: Lessons Learned.* Washington, D.C.: National Defense University Press, 1995.

Almond, Mark. *Europe's Backyard War: The War in the Balkans.* London: Heinemann, 1994.

Amnesty International. *Rwanda: Mass Murder by Government Supporters and Troops in April and May 1994.* London: Amnesty International, May 1994.

Annan, Kofi. "Peace Operations and the United Nations: Preparing for the Next Century." Unpublished paper, February 1996.

Barkey, Brett D. "Bosnia: A Question of Intervention." *Strategic Review* 21, no. 4 (fall 1993): 48–59.

Basso, Vincenzo. "The WEU Danube Mission." In *The Report of the Copenhagen Round Table on UN Sanctions: The Case of the Former Yugoslavia, Copenhagen 24–25 June 1996 and Annexes,* 260–272. Brussels: European Commission, 1996.

Berkowitz, Bruce D. "Rules of Engagement for UN Peacekeeping Forces in Bosnia." *Orbis* (fall 1994): 635–646.

Boulden, Jane. "Rules of Engagement and Force Structure and Composition in UN Operations." In United Nations Institute for Disarmament Research, *Managing Arms in Peace Processes: The Issues.* New York: United Nations, 1998.

Boutros-Ghali, Boutros. *An Agenda for Peace: Preventive Diplomacy, Peacemaking and Peace-Keeping.* New York: United Nations, 1992.

———. Comments at press conference, UN Headquarters, New York, 6 January 1995. Federal News Service transcript.

———. *Confronting New Challenges: 1995 Report on the Work of the Organization from the Forty-ninth to the Fiftieth Session of the General Assembly.* New York: United Nations, 1995.

————. "Empowering the United Nations." *Foreign Affairs* 71, no. 5 (winter 1992–93): 89–102.

————. *The 50th Anniversary Report on the Work of the Organization.* New York: United Nations, 1996.

————. *Further Report of the Secretary-General Submitted in Pursuance of Resolution 886 (1993), Reviewing the Options for the Future Mandate of UNOSOM II,* S/1994/12, 6 January 1994.

————. "Letter Dated 19 June 1994 from the Secretary-General Addressed to the President of the Security Council," S/1994/728, 20 June 1994.

————. "Letter of the Secretary-General to the Security Council," S/1994/518, 29 April 1994.

————. *Report of the Secretary-General,* S/24075, 6 June 1992.

————. *Report of the Secretary-General,* S/1994/555, 9 May 1994.

————. *Report of the Secretary-General,* S/1994/600, 19 May 1994.

————. *Report of the Secretary-General,* S/1994/828, 15 July 1994.

————. *Report of the Secretary-General,* S/1994/1389, 1 December 1994.

————. *Report of the Secretary-General,* S/1995/46, 17 January 1995.

————. *Report of the Secretary-General,* S/1995/305, 13 April 1995.

————. *Report of the Secretary-General,* S/1995/614, 24 July 1995.

————. *Report of the Secretary-General,* S/1995/922, 6 November 1995.

————. *Report of the Secretary-General,* S/1996/112, February 1996.

————. *Report of the Secretary-General,* S/1996/416, 5 June 1996.

————. *Report of the Secretary-General,* S/1996/813, 1 October 1996.

————. *Report of the Secretary-General,* S/1996/813/Addendum 1, 12 November 1996.

————. *Report of the Secretary-General on the Situation in Rwanda,* S/1994/640, 31 May 1994.

————. *Report of the Secretary-General on the Situation in Somalia, Proposing the Expansion of UNOSOM and the Creation of Four Operational Zones,* S/24343, 22 July 1992.

————. *Report of the Secretary-General Pursuant to Security Council Resolutions 982 (1995) and 987 (1995),* S/1995/444, 30 May 1995.

————. *Supplement to an Agenda for Peace: Paper of the Secretary-General on the Occasion of the Fiftieth Anniversary of the United Nations,* A/50/60, S/1995/1, 25 January 1995.

Brenner, Michael. *The United States Policy in Yugoslavia.* Ridgeway Papers, no. 6. Pittsburgh: Matthew B. Ridgeway Center for International Security Studies, 1995.

[British Army]. *Wider Peacekeeping.* Army Field Manual. Wiltshire, England: Headquarters Doctrine and Training, 1994.

Brookings Institution. *United Nations Peacekeeping in the Congo: 1960–1964*. Vol 3: *Appendices*. Washington, D.C.: Brookings Institution, 1966.

Cardile, Angelo. "An Analysis on the Organization and Progress of the Joint Operation Carried out on the Danube by Police and Customs Forces of WEU Countries." In *The Report of the Copenhagen Round Table on UN Sanctions: The Case of the Former Yugoslavia, Copenhagen 24–25 June 1996 and Annexes,* 224–235. Brussels: European Commission, 1996.

Carr, Edward Hallett. *The Twenty Years' Crisis, 1919–1939*. New York: Harper Torchbooks, 1964.

Central Intelligence Agency. *The World Factbook 1995*. Washington, D.C.: Central Intelligence Agency, 1995.

Chernik, Marc W. "Peacemaking and Violence in Latin America." In *The International Dimensions of Internal Conflict*, edited by Michael E. Brown, 267–307. Cambridge, Mass.: MIT Press, 1996.

Chomsky, Noam. "The Tragedy of Haiti." In *The Haiti Files: Decoding the Crisis*, edited by James Ridgeway. Washington, D.C.: Essential Books; Azul Editions, 1994.

Chopra, Jarat. "The Space of Peace-Maintenance." *Political Geography* 15, no. 3–4 (1996): 335–358.

Chopra, Jarat, Åge Eknes, and Toralv Nordbø. *Fighting for Hope in Somalia*. Oslo: Norwegian Institute of International Affairs, 1995.

Claesson, Paul, and Trevor Findlay. "Appendix 1B: Case Studies on Peacekeeping: UNOSOM II, UNTAC, and UNPROFOR." In *SIPRI Yearbook 1994*. Oxford: Oxford University Press, 1994.

Clarke, Walter S. *SSI Special Report on Somalia*. Carlisle Barracks, Pa.: Strategic Studies Institute, U.S. Army War College, 1992.

Clarke, Walter, and Jeffrey Herbst, ed. *Learning from Somalia: The Lessons of Armed Humanitarian Intervention*. Boulder, Colo.: Westview, 1997.

Cohen, Eliot A. "The Mystique of U.S. Air Power." *Foreign Affairs* 73, no. 1 (January–February 1994): 109–124.

Connaughton, Richard M. *Military Support and Protection for Humanitarian Assistance: Rwanda, April–December 1994*. The Occasional, no. 18. Camberley, England: Strategic and Combat Studies Institute, 1996.

Cooper, Robert, and Mats Berdal. "Outside Intervention in Ethnic Conflicts." *Survival* 35, no. 1 (spring 1993): 118–142.

Copenhagen Round Table on UN Sanctions. *The Report of the Copenhagen Round Table on UN Sanctions: The Case of the Former Yugoslavia, Copenhagen 24–25 June 1996 and Annexes*. Brussels: European Commission, 1996.

Crosskill, Hugh. "Presidents in Poverty." *World Today* 52, no. 2 (February 1996): 37–39.

Cusimano, Maryann K. *Operation Restore Hope: The Bush Administration's Decision to Intervene in Somalia.* Washington, D.C.: Institute for the Study of Diplomacy Publications, School of Foreign Service, Georgetown University, 1995.

Daalder, Ivo. "Fear and Loathing in the Former Yugoslavia" In *The International Dimensions of Internal Conflict,* edited by Michael E. Brown, 35–67. Cambridge, Mass.: MIT Press, 1996.

———. "The United States and Military Intervention in Internal Conflict." In *The International Dimensions of Internal Conflict,* edited by Michael E. Brown, 461–488. Cambridge, Mass.: MIT Press, 1996.

Dallaire, R. A., and B. Poulin. "UNAMIR: Mission to Rwanda." *Joint Force Quarterly* (spring 1995): 66–71.

Dallmeyer, Dorinda. "National Perspectives on International Intervention: From the Outside Looking In." In *Beyond Traditional Peacekeeping,* edited by Donald C. F. Daniel and Bradd C. Hayes, 20–39. New York: Macmillan; St. Martin's, 1995.

Daniel, Donald C. F. *Issues and Considerations in UN Gray Area and Enforcement Operations.* Research Memorandum 4–94. Newport, R.I.: U.S. Naval War College, Strategic Research Department, 1994.

———. *U.S. Perspectives on Peacekeeping: Putting PDD-25 in Context.* Strategic Research Report 3–94. Newport, R.I.: Center for Naval Warfare Studies, June 1994.

Daniel, Donald C. F., and Bradd C. Hayes, ed. *Beyond Traditional Peacekeeping.* London: Macmillan, 1995.

———. "Securing Observance of UN Mandates through the Employment of Military Force." *International Peacekeeping* 3, no. 4 (winter 1996): 105–125.

Daudet, Yves. "L'ONU et l'OEA en Haiti et le Droit International." *Annuaire Français de Droit International* 38 (1992): 89–101.

De Soto, Alvaro. Letter to the Editor. *Foreign Affairs* 74, no. 1 (January–February 1995): 185–187.

De Waal, Alex, and Rakiya Omaar. "The Genocide in Rwanda and the International Response." *Current History* (April 1995): 156–161.

Dobbie, Charles. "A Concept for Post–Cold War Peacekeeping." *Survival* 36, no. 3 (autumn 1994): 121–148.

Durch, William J. "Getting Involved: Political-Military Context." In *The Evolution of UN Peacekeeping: Case Studies and Comparative Analysis,* edited by William J. Durch. New York: St. Martin's, 1993.

Dworken, Jonathan T. *Rules of Engagement (ROE) for Humanitarian Intervention and Low-Intensity Conflict: Lessons from Restore Hope.* Alexandria, Va.: Center for Naval Analyses, 1993.

Ekwall-Vebelhart, Barbara, and Andrei Raevsky. *Managing Arms in Peace Processes: Croatia and Bosnia-Herzegovina.* New York: United Nations; Geneva: United Nations Institute for Disarmament Research, 1996.

Fein, Helen, ed. "An Interview with Alison L. Des Forges." In *The Prevention of Genocide: Rwanda and Yugoslavia Reconsidered.* Working Paper of the Institute for the Study of Genocide, 1994.

Fein, Helen, with Orlando Brugnola and Louise Spirer, eds. *The Prevention of Genocide: Rwanda and Yugoslavia Reconsidered.* New York: Institute for the Study of Genocide, John Jay College of Criminal Justice, 1994.

Findlay, Trevor. "The Use of Force in Peace Operations." A report from the workshop organized by the Stockholm International Peace Research Institute and the Australian Department for Foreign Affairs and Trade, Stockholm, 11 October 1995.

George, Alexander. *Forceful Persuasion: Coercive Diplomacy as an Alternative to War.* Washington, D.C.: United States Institute of Peace, 1991.

Glenny, Misha. *The Fall of Yugoslavia: The Third Balkan War.* London: Penguin, 1992.

Goodpaster, Andrew J. *When Diplomacy Is Not Enough: Managing Multinational Military Interventions.* A Report to the Carnegie Commission on Preventing Deadly Conflict. Washington, D.C.: Carnegie Corporation of New York, 1966.

Goulding, Marrack. "The Use of Force by the United Nations." *International Peacekeeping* no. 1 (spring 1996): 118.

———. "The Evolution of United Nations Peacekeeping." *International* Affairs 69, no. 3 (July 1993): 461–464.

Haas, Ernst B. "Beware the Slippery Slope: Notes toward the Definition of Justifiable Intervention." In *Emerging Norms of Justified Intervention,* edited by Laura W. Reed and Carl Kaysen, 63–87. Cambridge, Mass.: Committee on International Security Studies, American Academy of Arts and Sciences, 1993.

Hagglund, Gustav. "Peacekeeping in a Modern War Zone." *Survival* 32, no. 3 (May–June 1990): 233–240.

Hammarskjöld, Dag. *Report of the Secretary-General: Summary Study of the Experience Derived from the Establishment and Operation of the Force,* A/3943, 9 October 1958. Reprinted in Robert C. R. Siekmann, ed., *Basic Documents on United Nations and Related Peace-Keeping Forces.* Dordrecht: Martinus Nijhoff, 1989.

———. *First Report of the Secretary-General on the Implementation of Security Council Resolution 143 (1960) of 14 July 1960,* S/4389, 15 November 1960. Reprinted in Robert C. R. Siekmann, ed. *Basic Documents on United Nations and Related Peace-Keeping Forces.* Dordrecht: Martinus Nijhoff, 1989.

———. *Second and Final Report of the Secretary-General on the Plan for an Emergency International United Nations Force Requested in Resolution 998 (ES-1), Adopted by the General Assembly on 4 November 1956,* A/3302/6, November 1956. Reprinted in Robert C. R. Siekmann, ed. *Basic Documents on United Nations and Related Peace-Keeping Forces.* Dordrecht: Martinus Nijhoff, 1989.

Hayes, Bradd C., and Jeffrey I. Sands. *Doing Windows: Non-Traditional Military Responses to Complex Emergencies.* Decision Support Department Research Report 97–1. Newport, R.I.: Center for Naval Warfare Studies, 1997.

Hayes, Margaret Daly, and Gary F. Wheatley, eds. *Interagency and Political-Military Dimensions of Peace Operations: Haiti—A Case Study.* Washington, D.C.: National Defense University, Institute for National Security Studies, 1996.

Helms, Jesse. "Saving the U.N." *Foreign Affairs* 75, no. 5 (September–October 1996): 2–7.

Hines, Jay E., Jason D. Mims, and Hans S. Pawlisch. *USCENTCOM in Somalia: Operations Provide Relief and Restore Hope.* Tampa, Fla.: USCENTCOM, November 1994.

Hirsch, John L., and Robert B. Oakley. *Somalia and Operation Restore Hope.* Washington, D.C.: United States Institute of Peace Press, 1995.

Honig, Jan Willem, and Norbert Both. *Srebrenica: Record of a War Crime.* London: Penguin, 1996.

Huldt, Bo. "Working Multilaterally: The Old Peacekeepers' Viewpoint." In *Beyond Traditional Peacekeeping,* edited by Donald C. F. Daniel and Bradd C. Hayes, 101–119. London: Macmillan, 1995.

Human Rights Watch/Africa. *Genocide in Rwanda April–May 1994.* New York: Human Rights Watch/Africa, May 1994.

Human Rights Watch/Americas–National Coalition for Haitian Refugees–Jesuit Refugee Service, USA. "No Port in a Storm." In *The Haiti Files: Decoding the Crisis,* edited by James Ridgeway. Washington, D.C.: Essential Books; Azul Editions, 1994.

Ives, Kim. "The Coup and U.S. Foreign Policy: The Unmaking of a President." In *The Haiti Files: Decoding the Crisis,* edited by James Ridgeway. Washington, D.C.: Essential Books; Azul Editions, 1994.

James, Alan. *Peacekeeping in International Politics.* Studies in International Security, no. 29. London: Macmillan in association with the International Institute for Strategic Studies, 1990.

Karhilo, Jaana. "Case Study on Peacekeeping: Rwanda." Appendix 2C in *SIPRI Yearbook 1995.* Oxford: Stockholm International Peace Research Institute, 1995.

Klemencic, Mladen, and Clive Schofield. "Calm after the Storm? Croatia's Strategic Outlook." *RUSI Journal* (February 1996): 37–44.

Lasswell, Harold, and Abraham Kaplan. *Power and Society: A Framework for Political Inquiry.* New Haven: Yale University Press, 1950.

Leitenberg, Milton. "Rwanda, 1994: International Incompetence Produces Genocide." *Peacekeeping and International Relations* 23, no. 6 (November–December 1994): 6–10.

Lord, Christopher. *Intermediate Deployments: The Strategy and Doctrine of Peacekeeping-Type Operations.* Occasional Paper no. 25. Camberley, England: Staff College, Strategic and Combat Studies Institute, 1996.

MacKenzie, Lewis. *Peacekeeper: The Road to Sarajevo.* Toronto: HarperCollins, 1994.

Mackinlay, John. "Powerful Peacekeepers." *Survival* 32, no. 3 (May–June 1990): 241–250.

Maguire, Robert, et al. *Haiti Held Hostage: International Responses to the Quest for Nationhood 1986 to 1996.* Watson Occasional Paper, no. 23. Providence, R.I.:

Thomas J. Watson Institute for International Studies; Tokyo: United Nations University, 1996.

Maingot, Anthony P. "Haiti and Aristide: The Legacy of History." *Current History* 91, no. 562 (February 1992): 65–69.

———. "Haiti: The Political Rot Within." *Current History* 59, no. 589 (February 1995): 59–64.

Martin, P. "Practitioner's Questionnaire on: Weapons Control, Disarmament, and Demobilization during Peacekeeping Operations: Analysis Report: Haiti." In Sarah Meek and Mendiburo Marcos, *Managing Arms in Peace Processes: Haiti*, 51–99. New York: United Nations; Geneva: United Nations Institute for Disarmament Research, 1997.

Maull, Hanns W. "Germany in the Yugoslav Crisis." *Survival* 37, no. 4 (winter 1995–96): 99–130.

McCormick, Shawn H. "The Lessons of Intervention in Africa." *Current History* (April 1995): 162–166.

Meek, Sarah, and Mendiburu Marcos. *Managing Arms in Peace Processes: Haiti.* New York: United Nations; Geneva: United Nations Institute for Disarmament Research, 1997.

Minear, Larry, and Philippe Guillot. *Soldiers to the Rescue: Humanitarian Lessons from Rwanda.* Paris: Organization for Economic Cooperation and Development, 1996.

Mintz, Sidney W. "Can Haiti Change?" *Foreign Affairs* 74, no. 1 (January–February 1995): 73–86.

NATO. *NATO's Role in Peacekeeping in the Former Yugoslavia.* NATO Basic Factsheet, no. 4, February 1996.

———. *NATO's Role in the Implementation of the Bosnia Peace Agreement.* NATO Basic Factsheet, no. 11, January 1996.

Nicholls, D. V. "Bosnia: UN and NATO." *RUSI Journal* (February 1996): 31–36.

Otunnu, Olara. "The Peace and Security Agenda of the United Nations: From a Crossroads into the Next Century." In *Peacemaking and Peacekeeping for the Next Century: Report of the 25th Vienna Seminar,* edited by Ameen Jan, Robert C. Orr, and Timothy A. Wilkins. New York: International Peace Academy, 1995.

Owen, David. *Balkan Odyssey.* New York: Harcourt Brace, 1995.

Perusse, Roland I. *Haitian Democracy Restored: 1991–1995.* Lanham, Md.: University Press of America, 1995.

Preeg, Ernest, H. *The Haitian Dilemma: A Case Study in Demographics, Development, and U.S. Foreign Policy.* Washington, D.C.: The Center for Strategic and International Studies, 1996.

Prunier, Gérard. *The Rwanda Crisis.* New York: Columbia University Press, 1995.

Ratner, Steven R. *The New UN Peacekeeping.* New York: St. Martin's, 1995.

Reding, Andrew. "Exorcising Haiti's Ghosts." *World Policy Journal* (spring 1996): 15–26.

Reed, Laura W., and Carl Kaysen, eds. *Emerging Norms of Justified Intervention.* Cambridge, Mass.: American Academy of Arts and Sciences, 1993.

Ridgeway, James, ed. *The Haiti Files: Decoding the Crisis.* Washington, D.C.: Essential Books; Azul Editions, 1994.

Roberts, Adam. "The Crisis in UN Peacekeeping." *Survival* 36, no. 3 (autumn 1994): 93–120.

———. "From San Francisco to Sarajevo: The UN and the Use of Force." *Survival* 37, no. 4 (winter 1995–96): 7–28.

Rohde, David. *Endgame: The Betrayal and Fall of Srebrenica, Europe's Worst Massacre since World War II.* New York: Farrar, Strauss and Giroux, 1997.

Rose, Gideon. "The Exit Strategy Delusion." *Foreign Affairs* 77, no. 1 (January–February 1998): 56–67.

Ruggie, John Gerard. "Wandering in the Void: Charting the UN's New Strategic Role." *Foreign Affairs* 72, no. 5 (November–December 1993): 26–31.

Sahnoun, Mohamed. *Somalia: The Missed Opportunities.* Washington, D.C.: United States Institute of Peace, 1994.

Sands, Jeffrey I. *The United States and the United Nations in Somalia: A Retrospective Overview.* Alexandria, Va.: Center for Naval Analyses, 1997.

Schear, James. "Beyond Traditional Peacekeeping: The Case of Cambodia." In *Beyond Traditional Peacekeeping,* edited by Donald C. F. Daniel and Bradd C. Hayes, 248–266. London: Macmillan, 1995.

Schelling, Thomas. *Arms and Influence.* New Haven: Yale University Press, 1966.

Schulz, Donald E. *Whither Haiti?* Carlisle Barracks, Pa.: U.S. Army War College, Strategic Studies Institute, April 1996.

Schulz, Donald E., and Gabriel Marcella. *Reconciling the Irreconcilable: The Troubled Outlook for U.S. Policy toward Haiti.* Carlisle Barracks, Pa.: U.S. Army War College, Strategic Studies Institute, March 1994.

Siegel, Adam B. *Eastern Exit: The Noncombatant Evacuation Operation (NEO) from Mogadishu, Somalia, in January 1991,* CRM 91-211. Alexandria, Va.: Center for Naval Analyses, 1991.

Siekmann, Robert C. R., ed. *Basic Documents on United Nations and Related Peace-Keeping Forces.* 2d ed. Dordrecht: Martinus Nijhoff, 1989.

Silber, Laura, and Allan Little. *Yugoslavia: Death of a Nation.* New York: TV Books, Inc.; Penguin USA, 1996.

SIPRI. *SIPRI Yearbook 1995.* Oxford: Stockholm International Peace Research Institute, 1995.

Smith, Gaddis. "Haiti: From Intervention to Intervasion." *Current History* 59, no. 589 (February 1995): 54–58.

Smith, Leighton W., Jr. "The Pillars of Peace in Bosnia." *NATO Review* 44, no. 4 (July 1996): 11–16.

Sutterlin, James. *The United Nations and the Maintenance of International Security.* Westport, Conn.: Praeger, 1995.

Thant, U. *Aide-Memoire of the Secretary-General concerning Some Questions Relating to the Operation of the United Nations Peace-Keeping Force in Cyprus, 10 April 1964,* S/5653, 11 April 1964. Reprinted in *Basic Documents on United Nations and Related Peace-Keeping Forces,* edited by Robert C. R. Siekmann. Dordrecht: Martinus Nijhoff, 1989.

Tharoor, Shashi. *Peace-Keeping: Principles, Problems, and Prospects.* Strategic Research Department Report 9–93. Newport, R.I.: Naval War College, Center for Naval Warfare Studies, 1993.

———. "Should UN Peacekeeping 'Go Back to Basics'?" *Survival* 37, no. 4 (winter 1995–96): 52–64.

———. "United Nations Peacekeeping in Europe." *Survival* 37, no. 2 (summer 1995): 121–134.

Note: For bibliographic details of materials issued by UN secretary-generals, see the respective individuals (Boutros-Ghali, Hammarskjöld, etc.)

United Nations. *The Blue Helmets: A Review of United Nations Peace-keeping.* 2d ed. New York: United Nations, 1990.

———. *The Blue Helmets: A Review of United Nations Peace-keeping.* 3d ed. New York: United Nations, 1996.

———. *IFOR Report to the UN Security Council,* S/1996/600, 29 July 1996.

———. *IFOR Report to the UN Security Council,* 9th report, S/1996/696, 27 August 1996.

———. *IFOR Report to the UN Security Council,* 10th report, S/1996/783, 25 September 1996.

———. *Les Nations Unies et Haiti 1990–1996.* Série Livres bleus. New York: United Nations, 1996.

———. "Peace-keeping in 1996: Lessons Learned, Lessons Applied." In *Year in Review 1996, United Nations Peace Missions.* New York: United Nations, December, 1996.

———. *Report of the High Representative to the UN Security Council,* S/1996/814, 1 October 1996.

———. *Report of the Multinational Force in Haiti to the UN Security Council,* S/1994/1148, 10 October 1994.

———. *Report of the Multinational Force in Haiti to the UN Security Council,* S/1994/1208, 24 October 1994.

———. *Report of the Multinational Force in Haiti to the UN Security Council,* S/1995/149, 21 February 1995.

———. *Report of the Multinational Force in Haiti to the UN Security Council,* S/1995/221, 20 March 1995.

————. "Statement by the President of the Security Council," S/PRST/1997/34, 19 June 1997.

————. "UN Peace-keeping: Some Questions and Answers." New York: United Nations, September 1996. Fact sheet accessed on the UN Homepage.

————. *The United Nations and Human Rights, 1945–1995.* New York: United Nations, 1995.

————. *The United Nations and Rwanda, 1993–1996.* New York: United Nations, 1996.

————. *The United Nations and Somalia, 1992–1996.* New York: United Nations, 1996.

————. *The United Nations and the Situation in Rwanda.* New York: United Nations, April 1995.

————. *The United Nations and the Situation in the Former Yugoslavia.* New York: United Nations, July 1995.

————. *United Nations Peace-Keeping.* New York: United Nations, August 1996.

United Nations Association of the United States of America. *A Report on the Fourth Annual Peacekeeping Mission, May 19–23, 1995: Republic of Haiti—UN Mission in Haiti.* New York: United Nations Association of the United States of America, 1995.

Urquhart, Brian. "Beyond the 'Sheriff's Posse.'" *Survival* 32, no. 3 (May–June 1990): 196–205.

Waldheim, Kurt. *Report of the Secretary-General on the Implementation of Security Council Resolution 340 (1973),* S/11052/Rev. 1, 27 October 1973. Reprinted in Robert C. R. Siekmann, ed., *Basic Documents on United Nations and Related Peace-Keeping Forces.* Dordrecht: Martinus Nijhoff, 1989.

Westerman, Frank, and Bart Rijs. *Sbrenica: Het Zwartste Scenario.* Amsterdam, Antwerp: Uitgeverij Atlas, 1997.

Wijnaendts, Henri. *L'Engrenage: Chroniques Yougoslaves, juillet 1991–août 1992.* Paris: Denoël, 1993.

Woodward, Bob. *The Choice.* New York: Simon and Schuster, 1996.

Woodward, Susan L. *Balkan Tragedy: Chaos and Dissolution after the Cold War.* Washington, D.C.: Brookings Institution, 1995.

Zametica, John. *The Yugoslav Conflict.* Adelphi Paper no. 270. London: International Institute for Strategic Studies, summer 1992.

INDEX

Note: Page numbers in italics refer to charts or illustrations; page numbers in parentheses indicate the context for a reference that is not specifically named on the page.

United States *(cont.)*
    and Somalia
        see also Unified Task Force;
            United Nations Operation
            in Somalia
    and the Soviet Union, 80
    Support Group (Haiti), 164
    tolerance of casualties and, 108, 162,
        180, 184, 191–192, 227 n. 32
    see also Congress; Senate
UNMIBH. *See* United Nations Mission
    in Bosnia and Herzegovina
UNMIH. *See* United Nations Mission
    in Haiti
UNOMUR. *See* United Nations Ob-
    server Mission Uganda-Rwanda
UNOSOM (UNOSOM I). *See* United
    Nations Operation in Somalia
    (first)
UNOSOM II. *See* United Nations
    Operation in Somalia (second)
UNPAs. *See* United Nations Protected
    Areas
UNPROFOR. *See* United Nations Pro-
    tection Force (UNPROFOR)
    (Bosnia); United Nations Pro-
    tection Force (UNPROFOR)
    (Croatia)
UNSMIH. *See* United Nations Support
    Mission in Haiti
UNTAES. *See* Transitional Adminis-
    tration for Eastern Slavonia,
    Baranja, and Western Sirmium
urgency, and UN responsiveness, 15,
    175–176, 217 n. 64
Urquhart, Brian, 12, 17
Uruguay, troops from, in Rwanda, 220
    n. 29
USAID, Office of Foreign Disaster
    Assistance (OFDA), 93–94
USCENTCOM. *See* United States,
    Central Command
USC. *See* United Somali Congress

USLO. *See* United States, Liaison
    Office
USS *Harlan County,* fiasco of, 154–
    155, 178, 227 n. 33
U.S.S.R. *See* Russia
Uwilingiyamana, Agathe, 121

Vance, Cyrus, 42, 44, 202 n. 11
Vance–Owen Peace Plan (VOPP), 47,
    48, 204 n. 30, 205 n. 31
Venezuela, and Haiti, 156
Vietnam War, effect of, on U.S. mili-
    tary doctrine, 46
Voorhoeve, Joris, 211 n. 115
VOPP. *See* Vance–Owen Peace Plan

war
    civil, 46, 81–86, 114, 122, 132
    coercive inducement and, 22
    laws of, 41
    peacekeeping as, 26, 102, 189
weapons, for peacekeeping, 29
    see also disarmament; heavy-
        weapons exclusion zone
Western European Union (WEU)
    Danube mission, 207 n. 62
    and intervention in Yugoslavia, 203
        n. 23
West Irian, United Nations Temporary
    Executive Authority/Security
    Force in, 9
WEU. *See* Western European Union
Wijnaendts, Henri, 202 n. 11
will, political, and international peace-
    keeping
    in Bosnia, 178, 183–184
    in Haiti, 147, 164, 167, 178
    in Rwanda, 128, 140, 141, 143–144,
        145
    in Somalia, 183–184
World Bank, and Rwanda, 115

Yeltsin, Boris, 60, 61

Donald C. F. Daniel is the Milton E. Miles Professor of International Relations and Director of the Strategic Research Department of the Center for Naval Warfare Studies at the Naval War College, Newport, Rhode Island. He was previously Professor of National Security Affairs at the Naval Postgraduate School in Monterey, California; a Ford Foundation Fellow at the Brookings Institution in Washington, D.C.; a Research Associate at the International Institute for Strategic Studies in London; and a researcher-in-residence at the United Nations Institute for Disarmament Research in Geneva. He has received research grants from several entities, including the United States Institute of Peace. His previous books include *Beyond Traditional Peacekeeping* (coeditor with Bradd C. Hayes). Daniel received his Ph.D. in political science from Georgetown University, and is a former lieutenant commander in the U.S. Navy.

Bradd C. Hayes, a former Federal Executive Fellow at the RAND Corporation, is a research professor in the Decision Support Department of the Center for Naval Warfare Studies, Naval War College, Newport, Rhode Island. His previous publications include *Beyond Traditional Peacekeeping* (coeditor with Donald C. F. Daniel), and several articles for books, journals, and magazines, among them "Securing Observance of UN Mandates through the Employment of Military Forces" (in *The UN, Peace, and Force*, ed. Michael Pugh) and "Non-Traditional Military Responses to End Wars" (with Jeffrey Sands, in *Millenium: Journal of International Studies*).

Chantal de Jonge Oudraat is an Associate at the Carnegie Endowment for International Peace. Prior to that she was a Research Affiliate at Harvard University's Belfer Center for Science and International Affairs. From 1981 until 1994 she was Senior Research Associate at the United Nations Institute for Disarmament Research in Geneva. She is currently writing a book, "The United Nations and Divided Nations: The Use and Misuse of Economic Sanctions and Military Force in Internal Conflicts."

United States Institute of Peace

The United States Institute of Peace is an independent, nonpartisan federal institution created by Congress to promote research, education, and training on the peaceful resolution of international conflicts. Established in 1984, the Institute meets its congressional mandate through an array of programs, including research grants, fellowships, professional training programs, conferences and workshops, library services, publications, and other educational activities. The Institute's Board of Directors is appointed by the President of the United States and confirmed by the Senate.

Chairman of the Board: Chester A. Crocker
Vice Chairman: Max M. Kampelman
President: Richard H. Solomon
Executive Vice President: Harriet Hentges

BOARD OF DIRECTORS

Chester A. Crocker (Chairman), Research Professor of Diplomacy, School of Foreign Service, Georgetown University

Max M. Kampelman, Esq. (Vice Chairman), Fried, Frank, Harris, Shriver and Jacobson, Washington, D.C.

Dennis L. Bark, Senior Fellow, Hoover Institution on War, Revolution and Peace, Stanford University

Theodore M. Hesburgh, President Emeritus, University of Notre Dame

Seymour Martin Lipset, Hazel Professor of Public Policy, George Mason University

W. Scott Thompson, Professor of International Politics, Fletcher School of Law and Diplomacy, Tufts University

Allen Weinstein, President, Center for Democracy, Washington, D.C.

Harriet Zimmerman, Vice President, American Israel Public Affairs Committee, Washington, D.C.

Members ex officio

Richard A. Chilcoat, Lieutenant General, U.S. Army; President, National Defense University

Ralph Earle II, Deputy Director, U.S. Arms Control and Disarmament Agency

Phyllis Oakley, Assistant Secretary of State for Intelligence and Research

Walter B. Slocombe, Under Secretary of Defense for Policy

Richard H. Solomon, President, United States Institute of Peace (nonvoting)

Coercive Inducement and the
Containment of International Crises

This book is set in Minion; the display type is Univers. Hasten Design Studio designed the book's cover, and Joan Engelhardt and Day Dosch designed the interior. Pages were made up by Helene Y. Redmond. Graphics were prepared by Ken Allen. David Sweet and Wesley Palmer copyedited the text, which was proofread by M. Kate St. Clair. Frances Bowles prepared the index. The book's editor was Nigel Quinney.